TEXAS TURF

Texas Turf
Horse Racing in 19th Century Texas
ANNE J. BAILEY

State House
Press

Schreiner University • Kerrville, TX
325-660-1752 • www.mcwhiney.org

Cataloging-in-Publication Data

Names: Bailey, Anne J. 1944- author.
Title: Texas turf: horse racing in 19th century Texas / Anne J. Bailey.
Description: First edition. | Kerrville, TX: State House Press, 2025. | Includes Illustrations, notes, select bibliography, and index
Identifiers: ISBN 9781649670267 (soft cover); ISBN 9781649670281 (e-book)
Subjects: LCSH: Horse racing– Texas – History. | Horse racing – United States - History. | Horse racing – History – 19th century. |
Classification: LCC E605 (print) | DCC 973
2025943322 CIP

First edition 2025

Book design by Allen Griffith of Eye 4 Design

Distributed by Texas A&M University Press Consortium
800-826-8911
www.tamupress.com

Dedicated to
Lyndal Jones Wilkerson
1937–2022
and my daughters
Shawn Bailey and Shana Bostic

Contents

List of Illustrations

COVER PAINTING: *"Race Day at Haley's" by George Hallmark. Courtesy of the Layland Museum, Cleburne, Texas.*

Preface

Americans today enjoy sports, both college and professional, throughout the year, and are willing to pay high ticket prices to see their favorite teams play. There is a sport for everyone, and devoted fans proudly follow their favorite athletes, who have become the superstars of the modern world. This love of sports mushroomed in the twentieth century as baseball, basketball, boxing, football, and many others grew in popularity. Such was not the case in the nineteenth century. While Americans followed a variety of sporting activities, none drew the notice of the public nor could claim the attendance of fans as much as horse racing. In the early part of the century, Thoroughbred racing separated itself from any competitors in terms of public appeal. In 1823, an estimated 60,000 spectators watched Sir Henry, the entry from the South, lose to northern-owned American Eclipse at New York's Union Course. This was the first of several North-South challenges that drew huge crowds. In a race for regional supremacy at the Metairie racecourse in New Orleans in 1854 some 20,000 spectators saw the famed Lexington best the field of horses to win.

The growing popularity of the sport extended to all social classes, although it was the more affluent that promoted Thoroughbred racing. It was in the nineteenth century that the Thoroughbred, that sleek, refined animal descended from British imports that traced back to foundation sires from the Middle East, reached its highest development. Today this breed is known to Americans through the running of the Kentucky Derby in Louisville, the Preakness Stakes in Baltimore, and the Belmont Stakes just east of New York City—the current Triple Crown of Thoroughbred racing. In the nineteenth century the use of the term "Thoroughbred" could be misleading, since it suggests centralized pedigreed stock. That did not come into official existence until the end of the century.

It was also the century that the quarter mile running horse, a distinctly American-bred short distance runner often descended from stock the Spanish brought to America centuries before, began to establish itself as a separate breed. The designation "quarter horse" was also a term used loosely, long before there was a registered breed with that name. While the improvement of the Thoroughbred fell to men of wealth, the advancement of the short distance sprinter, or quarter horse, was the realm of the common man. Still, the improvement of horseflesh, whether the Thoroughbred or quarter horse, was sought by all.

There is no better place to see horsemen devoted to these two breeds as separate and distinct than in the state of Texas. First a possession of the Spanish, then under the Mexican flag before gaining independence to become a Republic, Texas joined the United States in 1845. Texas was unique, as it already had tens of thousands of wild horses on the western plains, descendants of animals brought by Spanish Conquistadors. When bred to those horses arriving with the settlers, these feral horses often produced a cross unique to the western states, particularly Texas.

Before the Civil War, racing transcended sectional differences. Both Northerners and Southerners could name the winners on the turf at the better-known Thoroughbred racetracks. The South had a strong hold on the breeding and racing of Thoroughbreds as seen in Kentucky and Tennessee. Before the war, slaves tended the bloodstock of wealthy Southerners and often served as jockeys. After the war, with the slaves freed, fortunes diminished, and many Thoroughbred bloodlines lost, Southerners had to restructure and rethink their breeding establishments. Where Thoroughbreds dominated in the first half of the nineteenth century, the second half saw the quarter running horse slowly become the more popular breed in the Lone Star State.

The Civil War divided the century. Texas, less affected by the war and distant from the devastation seen at breeding farms in Kentucky, Tennessee, Alabama, and Virginia, continued much as it had before the conflict. At the same time, the Thoroughbred industry expanded in the North where the breed became official with the incorporation of The Jockey Club in New York City in the 1890s, a centralized organization for all bloodstock eligible for registration. The quarter running horse of the common man also grew in popularity, especially in Texas, but at a slower pace. The Lone Star State would become the birthplace of the American Quarter Horse Association (AQHA) in Fort Worth, but not until the 1940s, even though its roots could be seen in Texas well more than a century before.

This book looks at the two types of racing popular in Texas from the arrival of American settlers to the beginning of the twentieth century—Thoroughbreds and quarter running horses. Texas already had horse racing, of course, both Mexicans and Native Americans raced their steeds ever since they acquired them in colonial times. But the new immigrants formalized racing to fit the mold practiced at the established tracks found in New York and other states to the east, and they made improving the stock a primary concern.

The nineteenth century was truly a golden age of racing when it was the main entertainment for those seeking a break from their daily routine. The early twentieth century seemed the logical place to end this study, because it was in 1903 when gambling on horse racing became illegal across Texas and eventually much of the nation. It would not be long before automobiles and tractors replaced the horse as transportation and on the farm. Other sports like baseball and boxing began to attract large crowds. The general population no longer talked about popular bloodlines over the dinner table as racing reluctantly relinquished its dominance as the most popular American sport to men like Jack Dempsey and Babe Ruth. Still, before the nineteenth century wound down, it was the jockeys who became America's first superstars, and a fan could follow the exploits of the best known in newspapers from coast to coast. For lovers of the sport the change was both dramatic and rapid, as fewer people owned horses and laws prohibiting gambling at racetracks drove away many spectators. While racing eventually recovered, as seen most prominently at the Triple Crown for Thoroughbreds in the spring, it would never again hold the nation's attention as it had in the nineteenth century.

This is also the story of the men and their horses. Those men, those horses, made Texas different from any other state. One obvious theme is that Texas is a rare blend of southern and western—southern culture mixed with a western frontier environment that marked the state as one of a kind. The horses varied from elegant and expensive Thoroughbreds to the rugged cow ponies usually associated with the ranches that began to appear in western counties in the decades after the Civil War. Breeders of bloodstock frequently called the latter scrubs, animals of inferior breeding and conformation. Only a handful of Texans raised sleek Thoroughbreds, and even those men who did often bred them to local horses, so that many Texas foals ended up being a cross. Since centralized Thoroughbred registration did not formally begin until the 1890s there was a lot of leeway in pedigrees, especially in a frontier society. This book is really two stories—that of Thoroughbred racing at organized tracks run by jockey clubs, but also the rise of the short distance horse of mixed heritage that raced on any track available. In these pages can be found the foundation sires of the modern quarter horse—Steel Dust, Shiloh, and Old Billy, among others, but even many of these horses often claimed Thoroughbred blood in their ancestry. There were, of course, thousands of horses that fell into neither category, horses that would never have a registry but would do much of the work on the farms and ranches from day-to-day and would become race horses at local tracks on weekends.

Most of the stories in this volume come from memoirs, letters, diaries, newspapers, nineteenth century magazines and books, as well as oral histories passed down in families. Some of the stories, particularly those of Steel Dust, Shiloh, and Old Billy, have little in print to prove their accuracy. But those three horses, like some of the other foundation sires in the AQHA, had plenty of folktales detailing their existence as well as descriptions of the sturdy, stocky build of the early "bulldog" type. One of the most prominent historians of the quarter horse, Robert M. Denhardt, while a professor at the Agricultural and Mechanical College of Texas (now Texas A&M University), traveled across the Southwest in the late 1930s tracking down horses whose greatest fame came from running on short distance tracks, and whose greatest use was seen on cattle ranches or in rodeo arenas. He heard hand-me-down tales that formed a pattern of a common origin. Adding these accounts to verifiable facts gives us a probable, if not totally accurate, idea of when and where modern quarter horses in Texas began. Distinguishing a good story from verifiable fact is difficult, as much of what we know has been embellished through the years. As so often is the case, some stories are eventually accepted as truth making it hard for a historian to divorce anecdote from reality. Unlike the history of the Thoroughbred, which has a well-documented background with its origins in England and the Arabian, Barb, and Turkoman of foreign lands, the history of the quarter running horse is harder to compile, and often depends on time-honored myths and legends.[1]

This is also a trip through Texas history, although that was not my intention. In these pages Texas goes from a Spanish possession to a Mexican one to an independent Republic, and finally the state we have today. This transition provides the backdrop for my story but is not a significant factor in the development of racing. Other books, other authors, have covered the history of Texas in detail so I tried to avoid that in this work. Horse racing is its own story, and I chose to tell it by decades, as the sport evolved, and not historical periods. Much of the information I uncovered in my research comes from rare sources, some of it difficult if not almost impossible to read, so any errors are my own.

The reader will come to recognize certain individuals who transcend the century, meaning they raised and raced horses before and after the Civil War. Some of those include Thomas F. McKinney, who is known as the father of Texas Thoroughbreds; George A. Feris, who thought Texas Thoroughbreds could be improved by crossing with Arabians, and he made trips to the Middle East to find the right animals; "Mid" Perry, the owner of legendary Steel Dust, and his partner Jones Greene; Jack Batchler, owner of the famed quarter horse Shiloh; Bill (or Billy) Fleming owner of the celebrated quarter horse Old Billy; Tom and Charley Haley, father and son, who raised running horses, both Thoroughbreds and quarter running horses, including a foundation sire of quarter horses, Rondo; and finally turfman Jim Brown, who went from running quarter horses in Texas to Thoroughbreds on the East Coast and Midwest, but who never lost his love of short distance sprinters nor did he abandon his Texas roots. Of all these men, Jim Brown captures the story of Texas horse racing, both the good and the bad, with a true Texas flamboyance. These men, and others, make the story of Texas turfmen unique and truly Texan. Once asked why he was still in the business at the advanced age of eighty-seven, award winning trainer and former jockey Max Hirsch, a Fredericksburg native, said because being in this sport "keeps you young." There was "always another colt, another filly, to train . . . you always look to tomorrow. There are always more races to run, and you live in the hope of winning your share of them."[2]

I owe a debt of thanks to all those people who helped me with my research and those who encouraged me to publish this book through the years. First to the late Dr. Don Worcester, who directed my master's thesis on horse racing in antebellum Texas and invited me to contribute a chapter on Steel Dust to a book he edited, *Western Horse Tales*, published in 1994. Also, the late Dr. Grady McWhiney who taught me how to write when I finished my doctoral dissertation under him at Texas Christian University. My special thanks goes to the late Dr. Malcolm McLean whom I met when I was an undergraduate at the University of Texas at Arlington. He and his wife Margaret urged me to complete this project, and his excellent research on racing in the Republic of Texas was invaluable. In addition, the archivists at the Texas State Archives and the Dolph Briscoe Center for American History at the University of Texas, Austin, were ready to lend a hand as were those who assisted me in smaller archives throughout the state. Stephanie Montero and Katie Hanes at the

Layland Museum in Cleburne, Texas, generously offered their support. Finally, I cannot forget those special people who helped me in a variety of ways. I have many friends who suggested sources, read various chapters, or just gave me encouragement: Audrey Black, Marla Boswell, Dr. Don Frazier, Susan Frazier, Judy Granger, Martha Hartzog, Terry and Ann King, Dr. Anastatia Sims, Judy Stricklin, Kirk Sweitzer, and Dr. Deborah Vess. I also appreciate the hard work of my copy editor, Carly Kahl. I could not have written this without the help and support of my family: my late sister Lyndal Wilkerson and her three children, Michelle, Gregg, and William Morse, and my three granddaughters, Karly and Alyssa Bostic and Kaitie Bench. Finally, my daughters Shawn Bailey and Shana Bostic have always been my main supporters. There are many other people, too many to name, who deserve my thanks also. When I began my original research for this project in the 1970s, many people shared their stories of long-ago races handed down from generation to generation, offered family information, and took me to the sites of long-gone racetracks. Without their help I could never have completed this picture of racing in nineteenth century Texas.

Dr. Anne J. Bailey
Cleburne, Texas, 2025

TEXAS TURF

1 The Early Years

"Texas is going to be one of the greatest racing countries in the world," wrote a visitor from Natchez, Mississippi, in 1838. A year later a traveler from Louisiana added, "The spirit of racing is already current there. Indeed this . . . amounts to almost a positive mania." Horse racing provided what new settlers wanted and needed, a pastime that made them forget living on the frontier could be harsh. Gambling on an entry was a way to make, or lose, money while enjoying the thrill of competition; drinking whiskey was a way to socialize with friends and neighbors; and owning a race horse was a way to display personal wealth. It was a popular national sport. Even the women could enjoy the occasion and wear their finest dresses, a rare treat in a frontier society, for on the social side there were often parties sponsored by jockey clubs to celebrate race week. The Houston fall races in 1838 concluded with a ball given by the local club. It was a "large assembly of elegant ladies and high bred gentlemen; the festivities of the night were unmarred by any adverse incident," wrote Dr. Ashbel Smith. Moreover, he added, racing was "evidence of the progress of civilization or as some regard it of its vices in this remote land."[1]

The settlers from the United States who migrated to Texas in the early nineteenth century brought with them a love for the turf. The background of Texas racing traces to the first European settlers to arrive on the East Coast. English horses reached the American colonies with the first immigrants. These mounts provided animals suitable for both work and play, although

Native Americans already had horses that were "remarkably handsome" and a "beautiful breed." A visitor to the colonies in the 1770s noted that the Chickasaw had been "very careful in preserving a fine breed of Spanish horses they have long possessed, unmixed with any other." Colonists soon bartered for them and bred them to the animals brought from England.[2]

In the mid-seventeenth century the English Civil War had an unexpected impact on racing in the colonies. With the execution of King Charles I in 1649, many of his supporters sought refuge in Virginia, a haven for them across the Atlantic Ocean. They gave racing an aristocratic quality. In 1674, for example, a tailor in York County arranged a race for his mare, wagering £2,000 of tobacco. The court determined that "it being contrary to Law for a Labourer to make a race, being a sport only for Gentlemen," the tailor was fined £100 of tobacco. Racing was a hobby for the gentry, just as it was in England. By the eighteenth century, upper-class racing enthusiasts called themselves "turfmen," a term that denoted not only money, but the title of gentlemen "marked with the right to rule."[3]

Racing flourished in the South early on. John Ferdinand Dalziel Smyth, writing in the 1780s, noted that there were races at Williamsburg, Virginia, twice a year, every spring and fall, and outside the town was a course suitable for two-, three-, or four-mile heats. The races generally lasted for a week. There were also matches and sweepstakes. Besides those meets at Williamsburg, there were races held annually in almost every town, and "frequent matches, on which large sums of money depend; the inhabitants, almost to a man, being quite devoted to the diversion of horse-racing." Moreover, the quality of the local animals impressed Smyth. He noted the "gentlemen of Virginia" spared "no pains, trouble, or expence [*sic*] in importing the best stock, and improving the excellence of the breed by proper and judicious crossing." Indeed, he added, "nothing can be more elegant and beautiful than the horses bred here, either for the turf, the field, the road, or the coach."[4]

Many early races were for long distances. Most of them held three- and four-mile heats, and involved not only speed but the endurance of the horses that ran. Three-mile heats could be run in from five to six minutes, while four-mile heats lasting from seven to eight minutes proved common. For example, in 1803 Snapdragon, a six-year-old carrying 120 pounds, won four-mile heats on the Newmarket Course at Petersburg, Virginia, in 8:00, 7:57, and 8:04 minutes. Obviously, conditioning was as important as speed in long distance heats, and times were carefully kept and recorded. During the Civil War when Pvt. James Jackson of Alabama was shot through the lungs after an early battle in Virginia, he traded his watch to a Northern soldier for a full canteen of water, telling his Union captor that if he ever raced a horse to use the stopwatch for timing. It had been specially designed to meet the standards for split-second precision. Jackson, who survived his wound, was the son of Irish-born James Jackson of Forks of Cypress in Alabama, one of the first breeders and importers of Thoroughbreds from England. It is likely his son's watch met the elder Jackson's exacting requirements for racing.[5]

Quarter mile racing was different—those sprints lasted barely a blink of an eye. Short distance matches began in colonial times, long before the introduction of course racing and Thoroughbreds. In the early days settlers were busy removing Indians, building houses and, in Virginia, growing tobacco. The wealth that came with tobacco eventually allowed affluent Virginians to import purebred horses from England and build racecourses worthy of the name. But quarter racing was simply matches between two entries open to anyone; a field of horses did not compete as would be the case in course racing. A race-path or race-way was simply a straight strip of ground often measuring fifteen to twenty feet wide and going for a quarter mile to 500 or 600 yards. A quarter running horse was expected to start quickly and attain top speed in just a couple of strides. Any settlement or town could clear a level space to accommodate such a track. In counties with small populations the track could be found near any popular tavern. They often attracted large crowds from miles around as the entertainment was a social event as much as a test of the entries' speed. Spectators, both rich and poor, lined up along both sides of the track, and in more populated areas one could find vendors selling food, whiskey, and almost anything else that could be pawned off on visitors. Gambling flourished. Betting became such a problem that in 1792 the Virginia Assembly passed a law prohibiting wagers of more than seven dollars at "any horse race, cock fighting, or any other sport or pastime."[6]

Match races between two competitors, where the government could not monitor gambling, remained popular on the frontier even after course racing increased in Virginia. Quarter distance racing progressed gradually from Tidewater Virginia to the southern part of the colony and North Carolina until it found new theaters in the lands beyond the Appalachian Mountains, especially Kentucky and Tennessee. Quarter mile races were not only tests of speed, but also of the shrewdness and wit on the part of the jockeys, and even more important, the race starters. A race could be won or lost with the ability to gain the advantage of a quick start. The tap of a drum, the blast of a trumpet, the firing of a pistol, or simply yelling "go" was the signal to start, and the two contenders often ran neck and neck to the finish line. One authority noted in 1944 that "the quarter-horse accompanied the explorer and the pioneer throughout the length and breadth of America as it was settled and developed, and today quarter-racing is still maintained in the West and Southwest, particularly the great cattle-raising regions. The type has been preserved and is being bred and fostered, especially in Texas at the King Ranch."[7]

Long before the quarter horse became a recognized breed in Fort Worth in 1940, the Virginia elite separated themselves from the common man by turning to distance racing as seen in England. Wealthy planters had slaves who did the day-to-day training, feeding, grooming, and upkeep of their imported stock. Slaves often served as jockeys, too. As there were few major cities, population and lifestyle were both rural, and the universal centers of assemblage were the courthouse, churches, and racetracks. The last two were situated in locations most accessible to the scattered population. A traveler observed "that on Sundays the blood horses tied about the houses of worship made them look like precincts of a race meeting; that between sermons their owners talked horse, not theology; and that when divine services for the day had finally dragged out their interminable length, an adjournment would be taken to settle differences of opinion at the near-by course," which finally became so close to the church that eventually both Virginia and Maryland prohibited tracks within a specified distance of religious structures.[8]

Formal course racing grew slowly, partially because it was exclusively for those with the time and money to enjoy the luxury. Democracy in the modern sense did not exist, wealthy landowners controlled colonial governments, and the average man could not vote. Racing became one way to separate the social classes. The wealthy gathered at carefully prepared racecourses, where they eventually organized exclusive jockey clubs, discussed the merits of the entries and placed their bets. A man might be accompanied to the races by a richly dressed lady in an expensive coach and attended to by her black maid. As large plantation owners imported expensive horses from England, the pedigree of a horse took on more importance—the more impressive the bloodline, the more impressive the owner. An English tutor in Virginia wrote of visiting a large plantation home in the early 1770s where "In the Dining-Room, besides many other fine Pieces, are twenty four of the most celebrated among the English Race-Horses, Drawn masterly, & set in elegant gilt Frames." He also recalled a dinner with a well-known Virginia breeder where the conversation turned into "Loud disputes concerning the Excellence of each others Colts—Concerning their Father, Mothers (for so they call the Dams) Brothers, Sisters, Uncles, Aunts, Nephews, Nieces, & Cousins to the fourth Degree!" Bloodlines mattered. "In Texas," wrote a nineteenth century author, "the history of the horse is equally as important as that of its owner." A popular saying was "A man is no better than his horse." Talk of pedigrees could cement friendships and alliances, and often progressed beyond the racecourse to the political arena where deals might be made that went all the way to the seat of government.[9]

Far from the Tidewater region, the inhabitants of southern Virginia, along with their neighbors in North Carolina, enjoyed less formal racing. They preferred dashes between two horses that were a test of speed, not stamina, as required in racing over longer distances. In referring to the animals used for this sport, J. F. D. Smyth wrote in the 1780s that there were no horses in England or in the world that could run as fast. The colonists "are much attached to *quarter-racing*, which is always a match between two horses, to run one quarter of a mile straight out" and "they have a breed that performs it with astounding velocity, beating every other, for that distance, with great ease," he noted. "I am confident that there is not a horse in England, nor perhaps in the whole world, that can excel them in rapid speed," and they also "make excellent saddle horses for the road." Quarter mile races were the first form of amusement devised by the locals. A race between well-known horses always attracted a large crowd of enthusiastic spectators, and anyone with a fast horse could participate. Into the mix came unscrupulous horsemen who would use any means to win, including entering the name of an unknown horse, but after all the bets had been placed, producing a well-known winner. The variety of means a dishonest man might resort to in order to win often resulted in lawsuits that paint a picture of the drama, trickery, and double-dealing that provided lore for the early quarter mile matches in the South.[10]

On the other hand, course racing was for gentlemen who would write specific rules to cover the most obvious infractions. Those same gentlemen wanted to win, but they wanted to win because their horse had the breeding to do so. Therefore, on the East Coast, Virginia planters imported the best breeding stock they could obtain. The earliest of the known imports was Bulle Rock; he reached Virginia in 1730. The first verifiable distance race probably occurred in that colony in the late 1730s. Planters were especially eager to acquire purebred English horses, which were a cross between an English mare and an imported stallion of Arabian, Barb, or Turkoman breeding. But the growing discord with the mother country prior to the American Revolution temporarily interrupted the importing of bloodstock. One historian of racing pointed out that between 1760 and 1770 no less than 115 "bred" horses and mares arrived from England, some sixty-seven stallions and forty-eight mares. Of those arriving before the war, however, two were especially significant to Texas—Janus, imported in the early 1750s by Mordecai Booth, and Fearnought, arriving around a decade later.[11]

Janus, foaled in 1746, was by Old Janus, a son of the Godolphin Arabian. The Godolphin Arabian was foaled in the Middle East and brought to England in 1730. Both Janus and Fearnought were his grandsons. Successful as a four-miler, Janus sired both distance runners and sprinters of the highest quality. Most of the time he stood in southern Virginia and North Carolina, both hotbeds of quarter mile racing. Janus was a chestnut with a speckled rump, a narrow blaze, and one white hind foot. He stood only a fraction over fourteen hands high. (In 1540, Henry VIII prohibited the breeding of mares smaller than fourteen hands and in 1686 the Virginia House of Burgesses forbade owners of stallions under fourteen hands to allow them to run at large as a means of "improving the breed of horses.") Even though the stallion Janus barely made

Babraham, foaled in 1738 and imported in 1775, was by the Godolphin Arabian and shows the fine-boned Thoroughbred in its early years. Fairfax Harrison, *Early American Turf Stock, 1730–1830* (1934–1935).

the minimum height required, he marked the stock of the southern states for years. Janus was small, and more compact and heavily muscled than other English imports. Although he died in 1780 at age thirty-four, his descendants were said to have great muscle, and for decades even a remote cross to him was valued in racers, especially quarter running horses.[12]

One of the first stallions advertised in a Texas newspaper was Bellair by an offspring of Janus. Owen H. Stout, who settled on the coast in Matagorda County, may have brought him from Kentucky, a center of the racing world in the Old South. The stallion stood part of the fall season in 1830 at breeder and racing enthusiast Andrew Roberts's place on Oyster Creek in Fort Bend County. The other half of the season he could be found at the sugar plantation of Josiah Hughes Bell in Brazoria County. An advertisement described Bellair as a beautiful chestnut, fifteen and a half hands high, and "of a fine form and action. His sire was a Genus [Janus], his dam a Diomede [imported Diomed], and is, without doubt, the best horse in the Colony." Despite the incorrect spellings, the stud's owner must have known that both Janus and Diomed were names that anyone familiar with bloodstock would recognize. Bellair stood for $6, or $12 if the mare's owner wanted to ensure a foal. Cattle would be accepted in payment.[13]

A second stud frequently seen in early Texas pedigrees was Fearnought. A bay stallion foaled in 1755, Fearnought's sire was Regulus, considered by some as the best son of the Godolphin Arabian. Breeders sought his colts for their size as well as speed. At a time when most horses were small, Fearnought stood fifteen hands three inches. As a result, patriots during the American Revolution coveted his offspring, and many were killed or captured by the British. Although there were few surviving studs to carry on his line after the war, Fearnought enhanced the dam's side of many pedigrees. The Fearnought line was consistently crossed with the blood of Janus, resulting in a combination that became more influential than any other in improving bloodstock. One authority, A. J. Davie (1758–1850), wrote that Fearnought's colts were "the largest and handsomest on the continent, while their success on the turf left them almost without competitors." A horse whose dam traced to Fearnought raced at the Houston City Jockey Club in April 1839. Another was Lycurgus; he stood at stud near Clarksville, Texas, in 1843. An advertisement claimed that "'dare devil of a horse,' Fear Naught [*sic*], courses [through] his veins." He "is not one of your mustangs, or five *bushels of corn horses*—he is the descendant of the kings and queens of horses. In his horseship, Lycurgus is equal to those high toned and lofty aristocratic *South Carolina and Virginia gentlemen who boast their lordly lineage.*"[14]

While the Revolutionary War temporarily interrupted racing in the colonies, the sport continued on the frontier. Many men, despite their patriotism, moved their families west. One of these was David Smith who fought at the Battle of King's Mountain as a North Carolina volunteer. He did not re-enlist in the summer of 1781, and by May 1782 David and William Smith arrived in the small town of Natchez on the Mississippi River with a large party of Americans. They became Spanish citizens after signing an oath of allegiance to "His Spanish Majesty." David Smith built a home near Natchez that he named "The Hermitage," and a few years later Andrew Jackson, a young lawyer, bought a large tract of land nearby. Jackson erected a log house, and set apart a site for a racetrack, although there is no evidence he completed one.[15]

Natchez residents already enjoyed the pleasures of horse racing when the Smith brothers arrived. A quarter mile track ran from the Mississippi River to the foot of the hill near the town. In the spring of 1783 there was a match race there between the horse of John Burnet and one belonging to Russell Jones. Smith joined a pool of five men, each betting $250 on the Burnet horse, which they lost to Jones's father-in-law, William DeWitt, when the Jones horse came in first. The following year one of the five losers, Arthur Cobb, challenged the DeWitt-Jones group to another race—the same men, and the same amount of money as the year before. This time they won. DeWitt refused to pay and tried to leave the district without a passport. But local authorities apprehended him and, on appeal from the Smith group, ordered him to sell his five slaves to pay the debt. Catherine DeWitt, his wife, filed a lawsuit, insisting that the slaves belonged to her and her children. She produced deeds of gift to prove her claim, dated before the family left North Carolina. But, as it was later shown, the wily DeWitt only prepared the deeds of gift just prior to the first race. Testimony of witnesses whom DeWitt asked to sign the predated documents proved the gifts were false as was the marriage contract of Catherine and William DeWitt. Not only did DeWitt have to sell his slaves to pay his gambling loss at the track, but he was also ordered to pay his many other creditors, a list that included David Smith.[16]

David Smith would indirectly have an influence on Texas horse racing. Although a large number of Americans lived in the Natchez District, Smith left in 1790 on the advice of his friend, Andrew Jackson, after an incident in which a Spaniard was killed. Moving north, Smith eventually settled in an area that would become Christian County, Kentucky. There a son was born on January 2, 1796, Benjamin Fort Smith, who would fight in the Texas Revolution. David's daughter Sarah gave birth to Benjamin Franklin Terry in Kentucky in February 1821. He would command Terry's Texas Rangers (Eighth Texas Cavalry Regiment) in the Civil War. More important to racing in Texas, in May 1812 twin boys were born to David and Obedience Smith—Elias William Shelby Smith and David Andrew Jackson Smith. Known as Shelby and Jack, the two would play a key role in early Texas horse racing. Shelby Smith brought to the Texas Republic some of the finest horses of that era. His string could be found running all across South Texas.[17]

When David Smith moved to Kentucky and Andrew Jackson to Tennessee these areas were just attracting the attention of colonizers. They would later become two of the most important states in the history of Thoroughbred racing. In 1775 the Transylvania Company, organized to colonize the area that now comprises parts of Tennessee and Kentucky, employed Daniel Boone to build a road that settlers could follow into the region. The expedition founded a settlement near present-day Lexington, and eventually organized a short-lived government. Among its first nine bills was one proposed by Boone to preserve the breed of horses.[18]

The new Kentuckians brought with them across the mountains a modified version of the Virginia cavalier tradition and way of life. Many came from the great horse breeding and racing region, and they appreciated good bloodlines. The area that would become known as the Bluegrass region of Kentucky was particularly suitable for the raising of horses. A visitor in 1802 noted that "the horses are generally fed with Indian corn. Its nutritive quality is esteemed double to that of oats; notwithstanding sometimes they are mixed together. In this state horses are not limited as to food. In most of the plantations the manger is filled with corn, they eat of it when they please, leave the stable to go to grass, and return at pleasure to feed on Indian wheat." Kentucky horses were in great demand, and a fine saddle horse cost about $130 to $140. When shipped to Charleston, South Carolina, the price rose by 25 to 30 percent. British artist Benjamin Marshall (1768–1835) summed up the love a man felt for his horse when he observed, "I discover many a man who will pay me fifty guineas for painting his horse who thinks ten guineas too much to pay for painting his wife."[19]

Records show that there were well-bred horses in Kentucky as soon as settlers arrived. Distance racing required bloodstock, and in February 1788 Pilgarlick, a son of Janus, was advertised in Mercer County. By March, another of Janus' sons, Darius, was standing in Nelson County. In April, the "powerful high-blooded horse" Red Bird was brought to Kentucky. Red Bird was by Fearnought and out of a mare by Janus. By 1789, The Godolphin, also known as Dolphin, "a beautiful bay" standing fifteen hands high, was advertised as being able to "beat any horse in the District the four mile heats." Dolphin was a grandson of the renowned Fearnought.[20]

The number of horses continued to grow in Kentucky as did an interest in racing. By 1789, the Fayette County tax rolls counted 9,607 horses, but only fifty-six stallions. Mogul, of pure English ancestry, won the four-mile heat at Lexington in 1795, three years after Kentucky became a state. By this time, the annual three-day race meet at the Lexington Course was already an established event. The Lexington Jockey Club, organized in 1797, built a track after city fathers banned racing on Main Street. That same year one of the first known English imports arrived in Kentucky. Blaze, foaled in 1786, reached Virginia in 1793, and from there crossed the mountains to Kentucky. He was not the only foreign stallion in Kentucky, for Montezuma, "a full bred Spanish stud from Mexico," was advertised in 1797 as "superior to any of his kind that has ever appeared in this country." From this it is assumed that fine Spanish stock, then held equal to the English, was also present in the Bluegrass region.[21]

Kentucky had already earned a reputation for having fine horses. In the last decade of the eighteenth century the army sought Kentucky horses for its soldiers making the following specifications: "about 15 hands, generally dark-colored, 5 to 8 years old, well broke, to both trot and gallop, perfectly sound and healthy, also 'high-spirited and handsome.'" Shortly after this announcement the quartermaster general passed through Lexington with 172 horses that earned praise as mounts of the "highest perfection."[22]

After Virginia and Kentucky, the state of Tennessee played the most important role in early racing in the United States. A dominant figure in the Tennessee racing world was Andrew Jackson. In the late 1780s Jackson crossed the Blue Ridge Mountains and traveled down the Mississippi River to Natchez. A few years later he sold his place near Natchez and resettled in Tennessee, partly because of his romance with Rachel Donelson Robards, whom he married in 1791. The Donelsons moved to Tennessee long before it became a state, bringing with them blooded horses. Grey Medley, believed by many to have been the earliest purebred stallion in Tennessee, was kept at the farm of Jackson's brother-in-law, William Donelson, located ten miles from Nashville. Although Tennessee settlers introduced purebred horses at an early date, their pedigrees have not been preserved. Their names, however, suggest the favorite Virginia strains of Fearnought and Janus.[23]

With a love of horses and a tradition of racing brought with them from the East Coast, racing prospered and expanded. Tennessee soon became a center of racing west of the mountains. Jackson owned an interest in Clover Bottom, the racecourse outside of Nashville. At Gallatin, around twenty miles northeast of

Nashville, another course was established and for many years the important turf events of Tennessee were decided at one of these locations or at the track in Nashville. In the Republic of Texas, former American President Andrew Jackson was made an honorary member of the Velasco Jockey Club in 1838 in recognition of his patronage of racing throughout the United States.[24]

Jockey clubs were for the very wealthy, or men with local prestige who could afford the dues, and members were usually elected by ballot. Three black balls typically prevented an applicant from joining. The rules of the preeminent track in the antebellum South, the Metairie Jockey Club in New Orleans, which opened in the late 1830s, served as the example most Texas organizations copied, although in some cases in a much-abbreviated version. Indeed, some Texas clubs simply adopted the rules of Metairie, and did not print their own rule books. One rule generally enforced was that "No gentleman shall be admitted in the members' or ladies' stand" without a badge proving membership. At Metairie, by 1860, the dues were $50 a year. Out-of-state guests could visit the restricted stands only with a paid-up member (maximum of two visitors) for $10. A badge was issued stating the name of the wearer, the name of the sponsor, and the word "Invitation." To curb disreputable men from coming to the track, any person expelled from a jockey club or ruled off any course was not allowed on the premises. There was also a section that covered betting. The 1860 version of the Metairie club rules listed 224 members out of a city of more than 100,000, only emphasizing the exclusiveness of organized racing across the South, including Texas, and explaining why average Texans ended up racing on informal (scrub) tracks.[25]

A true horseman recognized the importance of knowing the bloodlines popular among breeders. Diomed was one of these horses that turfmen knew well. A bright chestnut standing fifteen hands three inches tall, Diomed's early fame rested on his victory in the first Epsom Derby in England in 1780. In 1798, at twenty-one, an age when most stallions were retired, Col. John Hoomes of Bowling Green, Kentucky, bought the stallion for $250 and shipped him to Virginia. At his death at the age of thirty-one it was said that "there was as much mourning over his demise as there was at the death of George Washington." Breeders recognized his name immediately, and horses advertised in Texas often traced back to Diomed.[26]

Diomed has been called one of the greatest sires of money winners ever brought to America, but a son, Sir Archy (also seen as Sir Archie), foaled in 1805, had more influence on racing stock in the United States, as well as Texas, than any other horse of his day. He imparted his speed to distance runners and latter-day quarter horses alike. A bay, a little over sixteen hands high, Sir Archy lost his first three starts, which occurred following a severe bout of distemper, but one of the spectators saw promise and bought him on the spot for $1,500. After recovering and a series of wins, he sold for $5,000. He was eventually retired to stud and left his mark on horses throughout the United States, and from there his bloodline came to Texas.[27]

Owning a horse that traced to Sir Archy (1805–1833) was a mark of distinction. As one of the best known race horses of his time, Texans looked for horses with his bloodline. Generally known as Sir Archy, his name is often seen as Sir Archie. Henry William Hebert, *Frank Forrester's Horse and Horsemanship of the United States*, New York, 1857.

Breeders of Thoroughbreds could identify for anyone interested the descendants of Sir Archy as easily as remembering their children's names. Unfortunately, the lack of adequate records makes it impossible to give an accurate account of the winners sired by Sir Archy since race results were not regularly published before 1830. But for many seasons his descendants caught the eye of America. When families from the United States first began settling in Texas in the 1820s, Sir Archy's progeny were at the height of their popularity. Copperbottom (also seen as Copper Bottom), a son of Sir Archy, was brought to Texas by Sam Houston. Shipped to Galveston in 1839, his colts could be seen racing along the sandy shores of the island in the 1840s, and many later quarter horses traced to him.[28]

Broadside in 1817 announcing the services of Sir Archy, also seen as Sir Archie. William H. P. Robertson, *The History of Thoroughbred Racing in America*, 1964.

One other sire put his stamp on Texas stock to a degree that rivaled even that of the great Diomed-Sir Archy line. Kentucky Whip, also known as Blackburn's Whip or Cook's Whip, was foaled in 1805. Kentucky Whip was described as a mahogany bay fifteen and a half hands tall. Except for a defect in the withers, he was considered perfect in form. His dam traced to Janus and his sire was Whip, imported from England. Before leaving England, Whip stood for three guineas more than Diomed when both were in their prime. Whip never lost a race of several heats, and his son, Kentucky Whip, could run any distance from one to four miles with ease. In addition, Kentucky Whip won the purple ribbon for the best stallion at the Bourbon, Kentucky, Agricultural Society Fair in 1822. Many early Texas race horses traced to Whip through their dams. Best known were Charlotte Hill and Milam. The latter's dam was Grecian Whip, perhaps the most recognized of Kentucky Whip's daughters. Many thought the famed quarter horse Steel Dust traced to Kentucky Whip.[29]

Early Texas may not have had many Thoroughbreds, but it already had plenty of horses. Wild horses abounded in West Texas. The new arrivals often gazed in amazement at the vast number of feral horses they saw. Travelers in the first half of the nineteenth century often rode for days without losing sight of the scattered herds. An early settler recalled that "a company of rangers to which I belonged, when in pursuit of Indians in the country between the Nueces and the Rio Grande rivers, met with a drove of mustangs so large that it took us fully an hour to pass it, although they were traveling at a rapid rate in a direction nearly opposite to the one we were going." He continued by noting: "As far as the eye could extend on a dead level prairie, nothing was visible except a dense mass of horses, and the trampling of their hoofs sounded like the roar of the surf on a rocky coast."[30]

Texas was natural horse country, as these wild animals did well on the native grasses. The Spanish settled in what became San Antonio in the early 1700s, bringing Spanish stock with them. Comanches and other Plains Indians raided the new arrivals, stealing horses and other goods, and when settlers from the United States first encountered them, the American Indians were already skilled horsemen. Mexican laws regulated the capturing of these wild horses, a tradition that settlers to Texas eventually followed. These were purebred Spanish horses, as the Americas had no horses before the arrival of the Conquistadores. The nutritious grasses kept them strong, and they would eventually make their way into the pedigrees of Texas quarter running horses. Sometimes a particularly nice mare might be bred to a Thoroughbred stud.[31]

Although Spanish law prohibited capturing the animals without a permit, that did not stop determined horse traders from the United States in the late eighteenth century. Philip Nolan is perhaps one of the most famous to bring these horses to the breeders east of the Mississippi River, making several trips into Spanish Texas to do so, and violating Spanish law at the time. He went to San Antonio in 1795 where he obtained 250 horses that he drove back to Natchez, selling the last one in 1796. In June 1798, Vice President Thomas Jefferson wrote him saying he understood there were "large herds of horses in a wild state in the country West of the Mississippi," and he was "desirous of obtaining details of their history in that state." He had been told that Nolan could give him "interesting information" about their existence. In November 1799, Jefferson received a letter telling him Nolan had just brought 1,000 horses to New Orleans, evading arrest by the Spanish authorities on his trip. Unfortunately, Nolan's luck did not last. While on an illegal expedition to Texas, Spanish troops intercepted him near the present site of Rio Vista in 1801 and executed him for his illicit activities. How many of the horses Nolan brought to the United States ended up bred in Kentucky and Tennessee is lost to history.[32]

As pioneers moved west, their animals sometimes escaped from wagon trains and joined the free-roaming herds. The word mustang soon became identified with these feral horses—the Spanish word being *mesteño*. The Llano Estacado, a treeless plain of West Texas, proved a perfect grazing range, but early western settlers saw wild mustangs from as far south as the Rio Grande and as far north as Canada. Many early immigrants brought with them Thoroughbreds, and they soon discovered that the better mustang mares often crossed well with their bloodstock. These mares prevented too much inbreeding with the limited number of American horses that came with the early colonists.[33]

Mexicans easily caught these animals and sold them to the new arrivals for low prices. One visitor from Ohio noted that the Mexicans take "great pleasure" in their horses, "which are raised in great numbers in the neighborhood of San Antonio and form the principal article of commerce in the hands of the natives. Many of them make the breeding of horses an exclusive business. . . . These animals answer well for broods when crossed by the Spanish or American horse. The issue, called the Mexican horse, may be purchased as low as five dollars and seldom brings more than twenty-five." The visitor, however, pointed out that the price may be cheap "but in a comparative view does not afford the best bargain." He may have been referring to riding these animals rather than using them for breeding. Amos Parker, who visited Texas in the mid-1830s said mustangs, when broke, only sold for $6 to $12.[34]

Mexicans captured these feral horses on the western prairie. Riding grain fed horses in the chase they could often wear down the wild horse that lived off the land. The locals, continued the Ohio visitor, used a "lasso or lariat. The skill of the Mexican in the use of this instrument exceeds belief. He will dart like a falcon into the midst of a drove of mustangs, single out the one that pleases his fancy, and at the distance of twenty or thirty paces throw the lariat with unerring certainty." They preferred capturing mares since they served for breeding purposes, and when she was caught the process of controlling her was called "kneed" by the locals. That meant cutting a tendon to prevent escape. Some of these wild animals, when caught by Plains Indians, also served well as race horses between the various bands.[35]

With the arrival of settlers from the United States the importance of horses in Texas changed. Often new settlers came with a knowledge of racing and a desire to bring that expertise to their new home. Turfmen were a close-knit community in the sense that men who bred blooded horses knew other men who did the same east of the Mississippi River. As an old saying noted, "A man who rode good horses was usually a good man" meant that a man who raised fine stock was probably a gentleman. These were men who could afford to import the best bloodlines, and often their homes reflected this wealth. Thoroughbred racing was a way for like-minded men to meet and discuss the merits of the various stock.[36]

When Stephen F. Austin brought the first colonists to Mexican Texas many settled along the Gulf Coast, and that region would become the cradle for the infant industry of raising bloodstock. Texas soon boasted of some fine plantations where horse breeding flourished. In Brazoria County, wealthy planters built elegant houses and spent their money buying expensive horses. John Greenville McNeel was one of those. Four McNeel brothers, J. Greenville, Sterling, Leander, and Pleasant, all owed handsome homes situated near the Gulf of Mexico. The home of J. Greenville, Ellersly Plantation, was a large two-story brick residence of twenty-one rooms with galleries the entire length of the house supported by massive pillars. Inside could be found marble hearths and mantels and the ceilings had intricate ceramic medallions. With mahogany and walnut furniture, it was considered the one of the finest homes in Texas in its day. Visitors would gather to enjoy a good time, dancing, riding, and fishing. At one point J. Greenville owned a stallion valued at $6,000, suggesting that he probably bred mares at his stable. But hardships following the Civil War resulted in McNeel selling his home and likely his horses too.[37]

McNeel settled in a part of Texas distinguished by the wealth of many of its inhabitants. Eventually fields of rich sugar cane spread though the region, particularly Fort Bend, Brazoria, Matagorda, and Wharton counties. The profits made here allowed breeders to purchase the finest bloodlines from owners in the United States. Another plus that Texans enjoyed near the coast was that the climate provided the perfect venue for racing. Normally promoters divided the season into two halves. The calendar opened in the spring and closed in early summer. The fall campaign, which generally began in late September lasted until November. But as tracks began to appear in far South Texas, many could hold winter meets. Even in the northern part of Texas, enthusiastic sportsmen might spend the Christmas and New Year's holidays at the races if the weather remained mild.

Brazoria County provides a snapshot of the lifestyle of the wealthy along the coast. On the Lake Jackson Plantation of Abner Jackson there was a lake with a man-made island in the center said to have cost $10,000. He also owned some 300 slaves and probably several horses. John H. Herndon married the heir to the Calvit Plantation where he "had a large stock of cattle and fine stock of Arabian horses," and racing was a favorite pastime. On the Bingham Plantation started by Francis Bingham on the Brazoria/Fort Bend county line there "were balls, dances and parties, fish frys, barbecues, 4th of July orations, horse racing, of which they were fond, and the chase. Each plantation had its pack of hounds." Most of these plantations disappeared after the Civil War with the end of slavery and decline of the local sugar industry.[38]

During the 1820s and 1830s the settled regions of Texas began to take on the appearance of a civilized country—new towns appeared, roads were built, and plantations prospered. Frontier conditions still prevailed, but the wealthier settlers enjoyed a few luxuries, among them fine horses. Most of the small towns, including the Mexican communities, already had racetracks. Nacogdoches in East Texas had the first known American-style track in 1805. A traveler coming from Louisiana in the mid-1830s wrote: "We passed two race-courses by the road side" as he crossed the Sabine River into Texas heading for San Augustine. By this time the main racing centers along the coast could be found at Velasco and eventually in Galveston, but organized racing in South Texas was advertised at San Felipe, capital of the Austin colony by 1832, with an announcement for the spring races appearing in a local paper that year. Organizers scheduled the first day's festivities for any horse, mare, or gelding, the distance one mile and repeat. The second day's racing was for any creole of Texas, one mile and repeat, and the third day was a mile race for Spanish horses. In North Texas the racing center became Clarksville, founded in the early 1830s, but it had stiff competition from the course at the small town of Boston, around forty miles east.[39]

At the same time, racing underwent many changes in the United States. An American innovation—the dirt track—replaced the traditional grass course patterned after those used in England. This new type of track originated at the Union Course on Long Island, which opened in 1821, when the grass (as seen in England) was "skinned" or turned over to produce a dirt surface. This became the model for future tracks, and times usually ran faster on dirt tracks than on grass. Constant moisture was necessary to keep a prepared track from becoming hard. Ideally, the saturated earth beneath the surface was springy and resilient, providing excellent footing. Tracks along the Texas Gulf Coast would eventually adopt this innovation, although some were sand.[40]

For those new settlers unable to afford bloodstock, they raced short distance or quarter running horses. This was the horse that went west with the frontiersman, a saddle horse that could be ridden or used on the farm as a workhorse. Frontiersman did not have the luxury of spending large amounts of money to import stallions from England, or even breed native mares to expensive studs. They needed a horse that could be used for work and play. One that a farmer could ride to town, but still might match race a neighbor on Sunday. These animals were more heavily muscled than Thoroughbreds and generally not as tall. More compact, later defined as a "bulldog" type of conformation with heavy hips, they served as a work horse during the week and a race horse on weekends. In contrast, the Thoroughbred, usually tall, lanky, and fine boned, was carefully raised by men of money who could afford to improve the breed to run long distances. As newcomers arrived in Texas in the 1820s and beyond they brought a wide variety of horses, but no matter whether their horse was bred to run or raised to be a saddle horse, there was always a man ready to test his animal's speed against anyone who challenged him to a race. Texas became the home of a variety of horses, from sleek Thoroughbreds to the horses ridden daily by new settlers to the feral horses on the Llano Estacado, the Staked Plains of West Texas.[41]

In 1840, the editor of the Houston *Morning Star* explained what he saw as the difference between a Thoroughbred and a scrub, a horse of inferior breeding and conformation, in a highly biased editorial. The "high spirited" Thoroughbred "imparts some of its fire and mettle to his rider. When mounted on a noble animal, our conceptions are bold, and we feel nerved for feats of high daring; but astride of a scrub, our mental operations are spiritless, and creep along as slug," as a result of "the dull animal we are riding. We may safely assert that the reckless exuberant valor" of the courageous rider "would have oozed out at his heels, in spurring a mustang; and we are inclined to believe, that even a coward might fight bravely, if well mounted." He went on to add: "The raising of serviceable animals for plough nags may be encouraged variously; but the turf alone furnishes the thorough breed [Thoroughbred]. . . . We are glad to see that this subject, the raising and training of fine horses, is attracting so much of the notice of our planters. Texas ought to rival the world in this respect."[42]

In these early years Thoroughbred racing provided entertainment for men of wealth—lawyers, doctors, politicians, and large landowners. These men did not always devote their lives to the breeding and racing of blooded horses, but enjoyed the race meets held a few weeks each year. Because it was a sport for the upper class, it often merited attention in local newspapers. It had redeeming qualities that men who engaged in cockfighting, dog fighting, or scrub races for their enjoyment did not. All involved gambling, but Thoroughbred racing could occur alongside gala events for the ladies, with men in fine suits and women in imported dresses. Cockfighting and other rough sports belonged to the lower classes that could not afford anything more. In Texas, as in other parts of the South, the common man's amusements and the rich man's pleasures took different directions with money making all the difference.

An Alabama native described the specific kind of well-to-do Southerner who frequented jockey clubs or hunted foxes as "great on horse-flesh. His conversation runs chiefly on dogs and horses, horse-trappings and the like; and he himself much affects jockey caps, and other sporting articles of costume, and fills his house with wood-cuts of all the celebrated racers, as well as with whips, saddles, bridles, spurs, etc., etc. Besides, from association so constantly with jockeys and grooms, he soon learns all the slang phrases peculiar to jockeydom and rattles them off most volubly on all occasions." As soon as immigrants from the United States moved to Spanish-speaking Texas, men from the South who admired purebred horses began to emulate what they had seen in states like Kentucky and Tennessee. But the common man also had his opportunity to race, local tracks sprung up in Texas almost as rapidly as the houses the settlers built for their families.[43]

"Racing was almost as universal an amusement as shooting matches, a characteristic feature of every pioneer celebration," wrote one historian. "Every owner of a horse was confident of its prowess and eager to match it against all comers." Racing was at a zenith of popularity in the early nineteenth century. According to one expert, the "names of the kings and queens of the turf were then truly 'household words,' familiar to everybody everywhere." Public interest in racing was at a degree "unequaled, before or since," and all social classes enjoyed the sport. Unfortunately, political events in Europe cut off trade with England and from 1806 until 1830 the importation of Thoroughbreds dropped dramatically. That did not stop the sport from attracting devoted followers though, and in 1823, when racing enthusiasts in the North challenged owners in the South to a race at New York City's Union Course, some estimated the attendance at 60,000, including it was said, future president Andrew Jackson (although some historians have disputed the number in attendance). There in May they saw Sir Henry, the entry from the South, lose to northern-owned American Eclipse in four-mile heats: 7:37, 7:49, and 8:24 seconds. Besides the $10,000 purse, probably ten times that amount changed hands between bettors.[44]

The North-South rivalry reflected the general atmosphere in the United States as slavery slowly emerged as a political issue that widened the gulf between the two sections. The jockeys riding southern horses were often slaves, as were most of the handlers, trainers, grooms, and general stable hands. Still, the racecourse was one place white Northerners and Southerners could put aside their growing differences and enjoy the festivities. In the late 1820s, Monsieur Tonson was the talk everywhere, especially in his home state of Tennessee. His sire, Pacolet, traced back to the Godolphin Arabian and dam, Madam Tonson, to Fearnought. It would eventually be recorded in *The American Stud Book* that his dam did not have the "requisite number of crosses to constitute a thoroughbred, but she was one of the most celebrated brood mares of America." That, of course, is a tribute to horses of American ancestry, since most Thoroughbreds traced back to English imports. Monsieur Tonson, foaled in 1822, was one of the first horses born and bred west of the mountains to successfully challenge the belief that Thoroughbreds from the western wilderness were not equal to those of the East. His spectacular come-from-behind finishes prompted the catch phrase among race-goers: "By gar, M'sieu' Tonson come again."[45]

Wherever Southerners moved there were soon Thoroughbreds and long-distance heats, as well as quarter horses and short-distance sprints. As more immigrants arrived in Texas they imposed their customs upon the frontier and reshaped the environment to fit southern patterns. Their pastimes reflected southern virtues and vices—hunting, fishing, dancing, cockfighting, card playing, gambling, drinking and, of course, horse racing. Almost every family owned a horse, and a man with a fast one often invited anyone who claimed a faster one to prove it on a frontier track. But as more settlers with money moved to the Gulf Coast small local tracks failed to satisfy the most devoted. Those seriously interested in promoting the sport eventually imported quality horses bred for speed, and planned to replicate American style racecourses, often employing English bloodlines to do the trick. After Texans won their independence from Mexico in 1836, organized Thoroughbred racing, characterized by jockey clubs and carefully constructed tracks, began to appear as new towns emerged and older ones increased in size. This new breed of Texas turfmen wanted to reproduce what they had enjoyed back home.

2 Racing on the Frontier

The 1830s

From the beginning Texas beckoned to the adventurous, and many of the new settlers who answered the challenge to tame the frontier came from the racing centers of Kentucky and Tennessee. A visitor observed that the racing of quarter horses was "a great favorite of the middling and lower classes; and they have a breed of horses to perform it with astonishing velocity, beating every other for that distance with the greatest ease." Southerners had a strong attachment to their horses, and an Englishwoman observed that in Louisiana the "pleasure-taking citizens rode fast horses everywhere and 'thoroughly enjoy[ed] themselves.'" Riding was a natural extension of the southern love of horses, and children learned at an early age. "No sooner was a young Southerner 'rid of his bib,'" said one observer, than he was "mounted a-horseback; and this was not a hobby-horse either, . . . but a genuine live pony. . . . By the time he is five years old he rides well." This often matured into an enjoyment of racing as an adult.[1]

A horse was a necessity for both work and sport. Even though pedigrees were important for those animals used in formal racing, the accuracy of any pedigree was in direct proportion to the knowledge and integrity of the owner. Pedigrees of horses often read much as the owner wanted—proper bloodlines were claimed for handsome colts of dubious ancestry. It would be decades before there was any official registry to verify an animal's bloodline. Lying about a horse's breeding in a frontier society where men carried a gun and did not hesitate to use it, however, could have serious consequences, or at the very least, end in a dispute that went to court.

As a result, information about Thoroughbreds and their breeding soon began to appear in print. Pedigrees of the more notable stallions had from time to time been published in periodicals, and in 1829 John Stuart Skinner of Baltimore began monthly publication of the *American Turf Register and Sporting Magazine*. Its success encouraged William T. Porter and his brothers to start a weekly publication and, in 1831, the *Spirit of the Times* appeared. Various horsemen kept personal breeding records, but in 1833 Patrick Nisbett Edgar published the first stud book, often noted as much for its omissions as for its contents. Sir Archy is absent and some critics believed that Edgar ignored horses owned by men he disliked. These publications, however, did much to unify a sport that was spread across the United States. Turfmen found a way to communicate with others interested in the sport. Subscribing to the *American Turf Register* or *Spirit of the Times* meant a horseman in Texas could keep abreast of races in the States and stay up-to-date on the best bloodlines. He no longer felt isolated on the frontier. Also, much later, in 1868, Sanders D. Bruce published the first volume of *The American Stud Book* giving Thoroughbreds a degree of authenticity. But only in the 1890s, when The Jockey Club purchased the rights to this work, did the registration of Thoroughbreds become centralized in New York City. Some of Texas' finest horses appeared posthumously in these volumes.

Although Texas was on the periphery of the sporting world, it occasionally merited mention. In the early days of the Republic a visitor from Mississippi commented in the *American Turf Register* about a race he had seen on Christmas Day at Richmond, Texas. "I was struck with the spirit of the people for racing," he noted. He believed that Texas would be one of the greatest racing countries in the world, but, he added, they "lack horses very much."[2]

That, of course, was not true. Texas was a land rich in feral horses, and horses with Spanish blood often made their way into many Texas pedigrees. But well-to-do Texans were eager to acquire English bloodstock as were their neighbors in the United States. One of the most impressive to be imported in

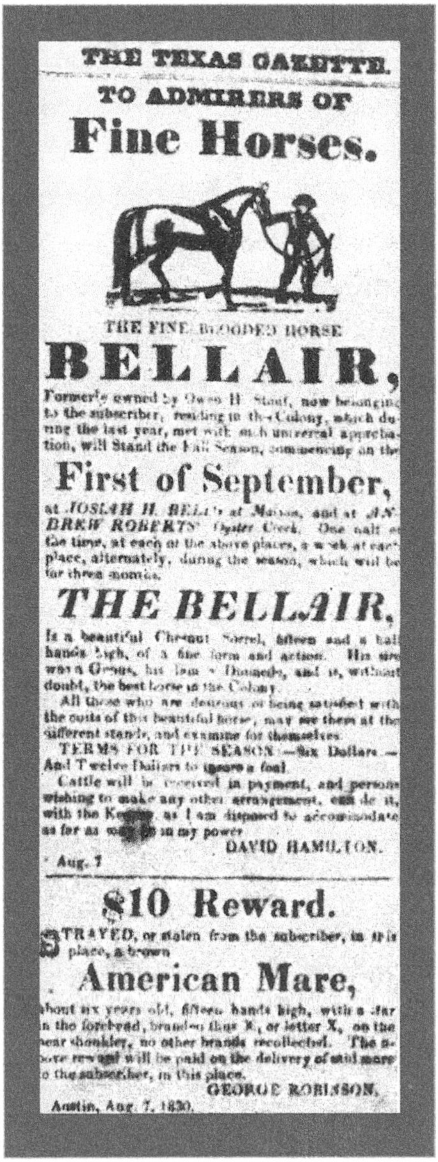
THE TEXAS GAZETTE.

TO ADMIRERS OF

Fine Horses.

THE FINE BLOODED HORSE

BELLAIR,

Formerly owned by Owen H. Stout, now belonging to the subscriber, residing in the Colony, which during the last year, met with such universal approbation, will Stand the Fall Season, commencing on the

First of September,

at JOSIAH H. BELL's at Marion, and at ANDREW ROBERTS' Oyster Creek. One half of the time, at each of the above places, a week at each place, alternately, during the season, which will be for three months.

THE BELLAIR,

Is a beautiful Chesnut Sorrel, fifteen and a half hands high, of a fine form and action. His sire was a Genius, his dam a [illegible], and is, without doubt, the best horse in the Colony.

All those who are desirous of being satisfied with the colts of this beautiful horse, may see them at the different stands, and examine for themselves.

TERMS FOR THE SEASON.—Six Dollars.—And Twelve Dollars to insure a foal.

Cattle will be received in payment, and persons wishing to make any other arrangement, can do it, with the Keeper, as I am disposed to accommodate as far as [illegible] in my power.

DAVID HAMILTON.

Aug. 7

$10 Reward.

STRAYED, or stolen from the subscriber, in this place, a brown

American Mare,

about six years old, fifteen hands high, with a star in the forehead, branded thus X, or letter X, on the near shoulder, no other brands recollected. The above reward will be paid on the delivery of said mare to the subscriber, in this place.

GEORGE ROBINSON.

Austin, Aug. 7, 1830.

Bellair was the first stallion advertised in a Texas Newspaper. *The Texas Gazette* (San Felipe de Austin), August 14, 1830.

the 1830s was Leviathan. A full sixteen hands high, he was a peculiar shade of red or mahogany. Sold to well-known turfman James Jackson of Alabama, Leviathan stood at the stable of George Elliott in Gallatin near Nashville, Tennessee. By 1840, Leviathan's colts were among the best in America. He headed the sire's list numerous times, and in 1838 became the first stallion in the United States to sire the winners of more than $100,000 in one season.[3]

At the height of Leviathan's popularity Samuel A. White, who came to Texas from Tennessee in 1830, brought a stallion by Leviathan to his home on the Navidad River in South Texas. White bred the stallion to eighty well-selected Mexican mares, and his experiment resulted in what one person said was "the best horses that we have ever had." A letter written to the *Austin City Gazette* stated: "This matter is now beginning to attract the attention of the farmers in this section, and I have no doubt but that there will be a sufficient number of horses raised on the La Vaca and Navidad to supply the whole of Western Texas within a very few years." The writer claimed that the "half-breeds will rate with or above the American animals. I would propose to distinguish the half-breed by the cognomen of the '*Texian Horse*.'" They were "said to combine more of action, hardiness, and kindness of disposition than any other kind." Not everyone agreed about that assessment of Texas horses. British diplomat Francis Sheridan, when visiting Texas in 1840, judged them through the highly critical eyes of one used to the stock seen in England, and decided that Texas horses were "of a very inferior description, though capable of great endurance. They are a ragged, cow-hocked, rat-tailed set and the truly fastidious would hesitate e'er he attended a badger bait on the back of one." Unfortunately, it is not known what horses Sheridan saw that elicited this response.[4]

Leviathan's bloodline was not the only one to reach Texas. James Jackson of Alabama imported another English stallion that had widespread influence. Glencoe, foaled in 1832, had been highly successful in England. He was a powerful chestnut that stood sixteen hands high. He passed into the hands of Alexander Keene Richards, a leading Kentucky breeder, who kept him until he died. Since breeding mares was as important as racing their offspring, Richards was known for his fine breeding stock. He inherited a large fortune, a reported income exceeding $200,000 per year. He was a lover of blooded horses, as were many people, but unlike most, Richards had both the means and the money to indulge his fancies. He obtained a herd of choice brood mares and bought the aged Glencoe. Through the years some of the greatest race horses were in his stables. Important to Texas, Richards shared many of his bloodstock with his relative in Fort Bend County, Dr. George Feris, and Feris even named a son Keene Richards Feris. By the 1850s the two men were experimenting with a Thoroughbred-Arabian cross that would eventually give Texas a horse remembered as the "Feris Arabian."[5]

George Achille Feris became known far and wide for his importation of Arabian stock. He had been born in a center of horse racing, Lexington, Kentucky, in 1817, to European parents. Feris graduated from Georgetown College before attending Transylvania Medical College where he received a degree in medicine. Described as tall, straight, and commanding, he arrived in Galveston in 1837 with "twenty-five cents in cash and no acquaintances." He quickly made himself known to prominent businessman Thomas F. McKinney, who helped him get a job as a doctor in the port of Galveston. In 1838, Feris settled in Fort Bend County. His love for Thoroughbreds endured throughout his life, but he developed an equal love for Arabians that set him apart from most Texans.[6]

Feris's ties to Richards make the Kentucky breeder an important part of this story. Born in 1827, Keene Richards, as he was known, was reared as an orphan by his grandfather, Dr. William B. Keene, at Blue Grass Park, a large plantation near Georgetown. In a description of Blue Grass Park years later a contemporary wrote: "Mr. Richards' place adjoins the handsome village of Georgetown, and for fertility and beauty it is one place in a thousand. It embraces about 300 acres with private track, stabling, and all the conveniences requisite for rearing and developing the race horse. The training stables are constructed on a grand scale, with sixteen boxes 12 by 15 feet and a covered walk around the structure for walking exercise at any season without going from under cover. The paddocks contain five acres, and each has running water and is furnished with a stable, all convenient of access, and safe." The plantation was partially destroyed during the Civil War, and Richards's Thoroughbred stock was put up for auction after the conflict ended. Nothing remains of Blue Grass Park today.[7]

Richards's horses raced throughout the South, but one southern track stood above the rest, and would have more influence on Texas jockey clubs than any other. The Metairie Race Course at New Orleans opened its gates in March 1838, and after a few seasons it became the most important in the South, a position it maintained until after the Civil War. The course was a regulation mile with fifty yard stretches and its stand held 5,000 spectators. Both the club and stables attracted owners and fans alike. Texans held a strong connection to the Louisiana city since it was an easy voyage from the Texas coast to New Orleans, the largest city on the Gulf Coast. Beginning in the late 1830s, steamboats, schooners, and sloops ran more or less regularly from New Orleans to Galveston.[8]

For those Texans with the money to pay passage, a trip to the Crescent City could be an enjoyable experience. One woman reported: "The Captain a gentleman—always at the head of his table—set out in the best style—silver forks, or what looks like silver—large & small, with ivory knives. White waiters, neat & orderly—French Cook . . . & Bedding the finest & whitest linen—water closets—& lady-like chamber maid, every thing nice." The wealthy paid for expensive first-class cabins with all the luxuries, but their slaves ended up sleeping near the horses and any other belongings their owners brought for the trip. The less fortunate passengers booked tickets in steerage.[9]

Steamboats from New Orleans also provided passage for many seeking to make a new home in Texas, though not everyone wanting to start anew in the Republic could afford the expense the trip entailed. Another alternative was by river steamboat. When the Red River had enough water for navigation, families could come up the river to Shreveport from Alexandria and Natchitoches, Louisiana, and then cross into Texas. Jefferson, a small town in East Texas, became a welcome center for immigrants from the United States. Some steamboats did not make much effort to be fancy, were often dirty, and turned into disagreeable experiences for those who chose this way to travel. One could also simply walk, ride a horse, or bring wagons from Natchitoches to San Augustine and Nacogdoches, crossing the Sabine River into Texas by ferry. One of the most impressive to come overland was Jared E. Groce of Alabama, who made the trip in 1821–1822 with his entourage. He rode a Thoroughbred horse and was accompanied by more than fifty covered wagons with his belongings, along with herds of horses, mules, and other farm animals. Not surprisingly, he eventually became the richest man in Texas.[10]

At a time when more immigrants arrived in Texas, bringing with them expensive horses, racing was changing back in the States. Large racecourses on the East Coast gradually adopted the prepared dirt track, and proprietors began charging admission to cover the cost of maintaining the ground. More and more tracks that had been merely roped off along either side of the final quarter mile stretch erected wooden rails. At first the rails ran along both sides of the stretch; then they were extended around the lower turn, and eventually around the entire oval. The next step was to build stands for spectators, although an extra admission fee was frequently charged for the privilege of sitting in them. Most of the fashionable people preferred to drive to the races in coaches, barouches, or other suitable vehicles, and remained seated in them while watching the races from along the rails. Part of the charm of this arrangement was that gentlemen might ride among the carriages to pay their respects to the female occupants. At first the schedule included only one race a day so that spectators could return home before dark. It soon became common for two or more races to be on offer, but the length of the races and number of heats run limited the starts a horse could make in a season. Three or four starts often composed a campaign, although Thoroughbreds with exceptional endurance and soundness might race ten or more times a season.

Thoroughbred racing was becoming more formal throughout the United States at tracks with jockey clubs. Rules began to regulate the weight a horse carried, depending on the age of the horse with the date of birth always calculated as May 1, regardless of actual day of foaling (until after the Civil War when it changed to January 1). Moreover, a horse was not considered a race horse if he could not go a full mile, and races were also for two, three, or sometimes four miles. Rules regulated rest times between heats. For example, a horse entered in mile heats, the best three out of five starts, was allowed to rest twenty minutes between each race. For two-mile heats, the entrant could rest for thirty minutes, and for three-mile heats there was a thirty-five-minute break before repeating.[11]

A superior horse could disqualify opponents by "distancing" them. A line was measured back from the finish, and a stand or pole erected at that point. Horses whose heads did not reach this pole by the time the leading horse arrived at the winning post were declared "distanced." A common distance for a heat of one mile was sixty yards from the finish line. For two miles it was 100 yards; for three miles it was 130 yards; at four miles it was 150 yards. For one-mile heats, the best three in five, eighty yards was considered a distance.[12]

It was a gesture of sportsmanship on the part of a winning owner to allow his opponent to "save his distance." This meant that the winning jockey pulled up his horse and crossed the finish line at a walk to permit slower mounts to reach the distance pole in time. One reason for this was the desire to save the slower horses for the next heat in order to have the opportunity of betting against them. Nor was it always beneficial to demonstrate too much superiority, since that could mean being assigned heavier weights in the next heat, and this often meant changing the odds for the bettors.

Gambling was a chronic ailment in the South, and Texas was no exception. A visiting German observed that "the wagers are sometimes quite large, single bets . . . amounting to as much as five hundred dollars." This extreme wagering often resulted in quarrels and fights that could have fatal results. A visitor in 1837 noted, "Texas is going to be one of the greatest racing countries in the world, to be racing and betting the way they do now." Betting, which started as stakes put up by rival owners, evolved into selling individual entries in an auction on the larger racecourses. Since heat racing depended on the outcome of more than one heats, it was losing favor to short distance races where there was a winner recognized immediately at the finish line.[13]

Organized racings did not fully develop until after the Texas Revolution ended in 1836, for political problems with Mexico discouraged racing enthusiasts. In

1834 and 1835, nevertheless, the village of Columbia located on the Brazos River in present Brazoria County, had a track where match races between two speedy horses were run for purses as high as $500 to $1,000. In 1836, P. R. Splane publicly offered to wager $10,000 on his horse against any others for 600 yards or one mile. Frontier racing often encouraged questionable practices, including jockeys throwing races to benefit one side or the other, and after the fall races in Houston in 1839, the editor of the *Morning Star* observed: "The sports of the turf are being reclaimed from the hands of jockies [*sic*] and gamblers, and are now under the control of gentlemen." Unfortunately, because of the stakes involved in gambling, that practice did not end, and would be a problem all throughout the nineteenth century.[14]

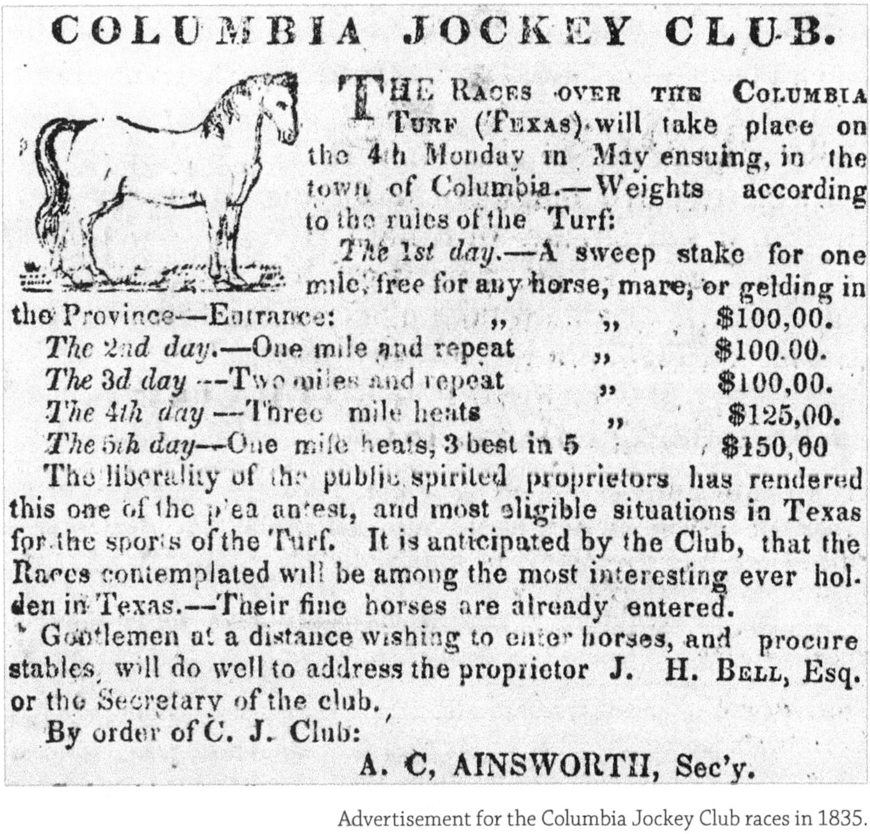

COLUMBIA JOCKEY CLUB.

THE RACES OVER THE COLUMBIA TURF (TEXAS) will take place on the 4th Monday in May ensuing, in the town of Columbia.—Weights according to the rules of the Turf:

The 1st day.—A sweep stake for one mile, free for any horse, mare, or gelding in the Province—Entrance: „ „ $100,00.
The 2nd day.—One mile and repeat „ $100.00.
The 3d day —Two miles and repeat „ $100,00.
The 4th day —Three mile heats „ $125,00.
The 5th day—One mile heats, 3 best in 5 $150,00

The liberality of the public spirited proprietors has rendered this one of the pleasantest, and most eligible situations in Texas for the sports of the Turf. It is anticipated by the Club, that the Races contemplated will be among the most interesting ever holden in Texas.—Their fine horses are already entered.

Gentlemen at a distance wishing to enter horses, and procure stables, will do well to address the proprietor J. H. BELL, Esq. or the Secretary of the club.

By order of C. J. Club:
A. C, AINSWORTH, Sec'y.

Advertisement for the Columbia Jockey Club races in 1835.
The Texas Republican (Brazoria), April 11, 1835.

One of the first known records of horse breeding dated to 1838, two years after independence. The leather-bound manuscript carried the label: "S. C. Robertson. Horse book," and was kept by Maj. Sterling C. Robertson. He was one of the organizers of the Texas Association that asked permission of the Mexican government to bring settlers to Texas, and later served as *empresario* of Robertson's Colony. As one of the signers of the Texas Declaration of Independence, he later sat as a senator in the First and Second Congresses of the Republic.[15]

The horse operation was a family affair. Robertson's finest stallion was Black Douglass. Although his breeding is not known, the mares he covered carried the blood of Diomed, Dungannon, and Truxton, to name a few. In 1833, Sterling Robertson's brother Eldridge Blount Robertson advertised "a fine bay mare, nine years old, for sale; she was sired by old Sir Archie [Archy], her dam by imported Knowsley; grand dam by imported Diomed," with the price only $500. Breeding records were kept in the major's own handwriting until May 1840, when his son took over. Elijah Sterling Clack Robertson continued to raise fine horses after his father's death in 1842 from his home in Salado. One mare, Ellen Douglass, foaled in 1839, raced at the Washington-on-the-Brazos course.[16]

Although Texas had tracks in almost every county, one of the first of any merit was upstream from the coast on the Brazos River at Velasco. Located in Brazoria County, Velasco grew rapidly. In the rich sugar growing region, wealthy plantation families used the town as a summer resort. With regular shipping routes to New Orleans and Galveston, Velasco prospered. There was Velasco Female Academy as well as a school for young men. British visitor Francis Sheridan observed that "Velasco is by no means a gigantic town, as it numbers no more than between 20 & 30 irregularly built huts & houses. Nor does it afford much gratification to a lover of the Picturesque situated as it is on a low sandy beach w^{h} [which] soon merges into a flat shrubless, prairie extending as far as the eye can reach. There are a few houses on the left side of the river, . . . but the greater part locate on the right." There was no church and "the good Christians of the place are content to offer up occasional devotions in each others houses.

As some sort of recompence there is a Court House, on the top of w^h [which] floated the Yankee Colors as well as those of Texas." A hotel accommodated visitors, and the town had all the amenities needed to welcome travelers. The Velasco Jockey Club, organized in 1838, named its course New Market after its counterpart, Newmarket, in Petersburg, Virginia, and it adopted the rules of that course. *The Weekly Picayune* in New Orleans announced in April 1838 that the "citizens of our neighboring Republic pay considerable attention to the improvement of their blooded stock. Fine horses are raised and the sports of the turf are to be enjoyed in their full vigor. . . . The races over the New Market course. . . . [are] only two to three days run from this city—so that we may expect to see crowds going down upon the Columbia and other vessels, to enjoy the pleasure of the trip, together with the excitement and interest of attending the New Market Races in Texas."[17]

The Velasco Jockey Club officers were all prominent Texans. The president was Branch T. Archer, a doctor and native of Virginia who served as a delegate from Brazoria to the Convention of 1833, as one of the commissioners to the United States in 1836, and in the First Congress of the Republic. The secretary of the club was Edwin Waller, a Virginian who was a signer of the Texas Declaration of Independence. First vice-president was Gen. Felix Huston, a swashbuckling Kentuckian who lived in Mississippi before moving to Texas to become commander of the Army of the Republic. He possessed a volatile personality that earned him both warm friends and vehement enemies. His notoriety may have resulted from the fact that he tried to kill Gen. Albert Sidney Johnston in a duel in 1837 after Johnston superseded him as commander of the Texas army.[18]

The other officers included second vice-president Gen. Thomas Jefferson Rusk from South Carolina, who was a member of the Second Congress. Third vice-president was William Harris Wharton, who was the first Minister of the Republic of Texas to the United States. Wharton married Sarah Ann Groce, the only daughter of Jared E. Groce. Wharton also built one of the first frame houses, calling his plantation "Eagle Island." A Texas "island" was "a clump of forest wood in the midst of a prairie" and Wharton's home was built amid live oaks on a horseshoe shaped lake of about fifteen acres. One newspaper correspondent described it as a "mansion" with a garden that grew 500 varieties of imported "exotic plants," tended by a Scottish gardener. A cousin of Stephen F. Austin, Mary Austin Holley, visited the Whartons, and later wrote that they had "a great many beautiful books and other curiosities—centre table, woolen damask curtains—sofa, silver pitcher, white china &c &c. I hated to leave such an agreeable place."[19]

One of the moving spirits of the Velasco Jockey Club was Thomas Jefferson Green. Born in North Carolina, he married Sarah Wharton, a cousin of William H. Wharton. Sarah died in 1835, but Green moved to Texas on the eve of the Revolution, where he was commissioned a brigadier general. Francis Sheridan described Green as "Velasco's presiding genius," who lived in the finest house in town. When Sheridan received an invitation to dine with Velasco's elite, he noted that the guests had "better manners & conversation" than he could have anticipated in such a remote location. Green was often responsible for advertising the races and gala events scheduled at Velasco. Mary Austin Holley wrote: "There is to be a great Ball at Velasco tomorrow (22nd) night—being the period of the races. All the world, who can move, *wind & weather permitting* are to be there. . . . Everything available for dresses in Texas has been bought up for the occasion." Decorations and food arrived from New Orleans and ice from Boston, Massachusetts. The ball was held at the Archer House. Since it was only a two or three day run from New Orleans to Velasco, the race promoters expected a large crowd from Louisiana. "The gentlemen dress remarkably well—The clothes being all brought from N York ready made & of the newest fashions," she added. "I expect it will be a great occasion one at least I have never seen. The steamboat plying constantly on the Brazos, will fetch and carry the people."[20]

The races in Velasco attracted men with money. Since it was located near the coast, the town was a center for trade. The racetrack provided entertainment, and women could watch the festivities from the Archer House

Observatory. In February 1839, Green invited a bachelor friend, Dr. Ashbel Smith, to attend the spring meeting of the Jockey Club, pointing out that "many fine women & horses are in attendance all ready." As another inducement, he promised Smith "one week of raceing [*sic*] and frolic in this town. . . . I will assure you a display of fashion and beauty; you may find a wife among our girls." If this did not stir his interest, the writer simply offered to provide a bed, plate, and a stall for his horse. Smith, who died a bachelor, was an ardent supporter of horse racing.[21]

One man frequently seen racing at Velasco was Alabama-born David Randon. He was reputed to be part American Indian, although there is no way this can be verified. Racing was a sport where it was common to see trainers and jockeys who were slaves, but not as common to see one part native. In any case, Randon was described as "a very thrifty, sporty fellow and gave his worth [in 1850] as $33,000, a fortune for those days," and his occupation as "farmer and racer" at his home in Fort Bend County. In 1838, Randon raced horses with impressive pedigrees, including a gray filly Black Eyed White Girl by Pacolet, dam by Sir Archy, that he raised from a colt. The mare later appeared in *The American Stud Book*. Being included in the *Stud Book* was the highest honor a Thoroughbred could receive at that time. Randon was successful as an owner and a trainer, and his wealth increased substantially before his death, which occurred sometime before 1867. His plantation in Fort Bend County was valued at $297,300 in 1860, a sum that included sixty-nine slaves. This amount, of course, would have been significantly reduced by the freeing of the slaves after the Civil War ended. Randon was a regular on the racing circuit, bringing entries to Columbia, Richmond, Velasco, Houston, and Galveston. He often raced against Shelby Smith. Smith frequently brought Charlotte Hill to the track, a bay mare foaled in Texas in 1833, whose dam was by Cook's Whip. Charlotte Hill later appeared in the *Stud Book*. The list of Thoroughbreds raced by Randon and Smith is impressive, and a small example of the horses seen on racecourses along the Gulf Coast.[22]

A neighbor of Randon, Churchill Fulshear Jr., also had an interest in racing. His father was one of the early settlers of Texas, and in 1844, Churchill Jr. sold 654 acres on the northeast corner of land he inherited from his father to Randon for $4,000. Junior's vast real estate holdings were valued at $30,000 in 1850. For about twenty years he operated a track near present-day Pittsville in Fort Bend County, and local lore says it was called Churchill Downs. Since Churchill Downs in Louisville opened it 1875, and writings about Fulshear's track are all after that date, it is probable that the name of the Texas track became popular around the time that the Kentucky track gained fame. He was active in the sport, and so fond of his horses that he built stables for them on the lower level of his home. Fulshear died in 1892.[23]

Galveston also had a popular track. Galveston Island had a long history, tracing back to the first European explorers, but in the early 1820s served as a base for the Louisiana pirate Jean Lafitte. By 1838, investors began selling town lots, and the legislature soon approved incorporation. American-style horse racing was not far behind. In July 1839, Thomas Green received a letter from Edwin B. Settle, secretary of the Galveston Jockey Club, thanking him for his patronage of the forthcoming stake races, adding that "we doubt not Colorado will make a good showing." The sweepstakes, set for Christmas Day, included Green's entry Colorado (by Tallyrand). In the fall of 1839, Dr. Ashbel Smith wrote a friend that the races would begin in December, saying "much attention is now turned to fine horses and they command good prices." One horse competing in Texas was Fyldena, a mare foaled in Alabama by imported Fylde. By 1840, J. H. Learned owned the mare, and was so certain of her speed that he challenged any horse then in Texas to match her for $5,000.[24]

Alabama breeders often did business with Texans. Dr. Robert W. Withers of Greene County, Alabama, a well-known breeder, kept detailed records of what he thought important—births and deaths of his family and slaves and, of course, his race horses. The market in Texas had not felt the effects of financial strain resulting from the Panic of 1837 when Withers hoped to send several blooded horses to Texas. The noted northern trainer Isaac Van Lear brought the horses from New York, and the two men agreed to transport them to Texas for resale. But a disagreement ensued between the partners, resulting in Withers's charge that the horses were either unsound or broken down.[25]

Withers was General Green's connection in Alabama, and he depended on Withers to buy and ship him available race prospects. Transporting horses by steamer was not an ideal way to deliver them unscathed. Francis Sheridan watched the process at a Texas port and noted, "the Method adopted for getting the animals on board is simple & imposing. Two planks extend from the deck of the Steamer to the shore—the animal has his legs tied,—a cord is passed under his shoulders & having been thrown down he is dragged on board across the planks." It is quite likely that Withers made sure his Thoroughbreds were treated with more care than the boarding Sheridan witnessed, because he wrote Green in August 1839 that he owned some of the finest colts in the country by Fylde, Luzborough, Leviathan, and others, which he thought could even "Eclipse the fame of 'Star of the West.'" Bred and owned by Green, Star of the West was a gray mare foaled in 1834. She was by Bertrand, dam by Tiger Whip, and she later appeared in *The American Stud Book.* Withers hoped that the market would hold in Texas, for he planned to send the colts to Houston by way of Shreveport. Withers and Green shared an interest in fine horses, but Green left Texas in the mid-1840s, dying in North Carolina in 1863, and Withers died in Alabama in 1854, leaving his lands in Texas to his wife to use for the support and education of their children.[26]

Galveston quickly became the main center of racing along the coast, and Thomas Freeman McKinney was the dominant figure behind the sport. McKinney, called the "Father of Texas Thoroughbreds," did more than any other man to introduce and promote purebred horses in the first half of the nineteenth century. In the 1830s he formed a partnership with Samuel May Williams.[27]

According to a contemporary, McKinney stood five feet ten inches tall and weighed about 170 pounds. Muscular and broad shouldered, he was "no ordinary man, bold and outspoken, generous, warm-hearted, enthusiastic and devoted to his friends and a bitter enemy—of strong partialities and prejudices, he could see no faults in friends and no virtues in enemies." His temper was quick, "often unreasonably so." Francis Sheridan was struck by McKinney's gawdy appearance. Often considered one of the "Barings of Texas" (the Baring financial firm was famous in Great Britain), Sheridan first saw McKinney attired in a black-edged frock coat made out of a scarlet blanket and picking his teeth with a Bowie knife. On further acquaintance, however, Sheridan found him to be "far superior to the general run of Texians & acknowledged by all to be a very honest, charitable & worthy man. He has been the making of Galveston." McKinney's personal habits led Sheridan to observe: "Among other eccentricities of this remarkable man was one which I much admired. He never had any fixed hours for grubbing—always eating when he was hungry & drinking when dry. His Partner followed him strictly in the latter—but then he was always dry."[28]

McKinney and Williams prospered. The firm owned wharves and warehouses at Velasco and Quintana, on opposite banks of the Brazos River. McKinney was president of the Quintana Jockey Club. His passion for racing kept the firm in the horse business even though his partner did not share his enthusiasm. In the late 1830s the firm transferred its center of operations from Quintana to Galveston, a thriving little town of more than 2,000, where the men owned a warehouse, wharf, and two lots. They also owned an interest in a tavern, rent houses, and the Tremont Hotel, the largest hotel in Texas until it burned down. Another major investment was the Galveston racecourse covering 140 acres. In 1840, Francis Sheridan, noted that "considering that the horses must put up with Sand instead of Turf, a very good race course it is. Being a circle of about a mile & a half, perfectly flat & railed all round. The racing stables w^{h} [which] are not *exactly* as good as those at New Market are a short distance from the Beach & between it and the race course. Here we saw some very fair specimens of the American racers, & an English Stallion, called 'Stafford.' Of course, the most animated conversation took place as to the relative merits of English & American Horses and the knowing ones of Galveston were loud in their expressions of hope that England would accept a challenge to run a horse against the famous American horse 'Boston' [at] 4 miles & stakes unlimited." In typical British fashion, Sheridan concluded: "I joined in the hope, for great as the advance as to breeding may be among the Yankee horses, they are a long long way behind us, & in my humble opinion ever will be." When Sheridan first arrived in Texas he judged the horses he saw as "a cross between a goat & a Jack Ass," but revised that opinion somewhat when visiting the Galveston course. About the same time the Houston *Telegraph and Texas Register* printed a story of American pride for their horses. When an "emigrant Yankee" in England was asked by a British jockey if he had ever seen such "remarkably swift horses in America," the American proudly replied: "Swift . . . why I guess we have—I *seen* a horse at Baltimore, on a sunny day, start against his own shadow and beat it a quarter of a mile at the first heat!"[29]

McKinney came by his love of horses honestly. Born in 1801 he was the grandson of Charles McKinney, who immigrated to Virginia in the 1750s, and raised and raced horses on the Virginia-North Carolina border. This was a region where neighbors owned both Thoroughbreds and quarter horses. Charles moved his family and his horses to the Bluegrass region of Kentucky in 1784. Thomas followed in his grandfather's footsteps in his love of fine horses. He left home in his early twenties and eventually ended up in Nacogdoches where his mother's brother ran a trading post nearby. By 1828, he settled in the area and married Nancy Watts. Sometime the following year he bought a slave named Cary, later known as Cary McKinney, who became skilled in handling horses. Slaves not only served as jockeys, but often trained them as well. Thomas and Cary cemented a relationship around their similar interests.[30]

Prosperous men like McKinney certainly hoped to emulate the British success with race horses, but unlike the British, who made slavery illegal, McKinney used slaves to train, manage, and generally take care of his string of horses. After he relocated to Galveston, he helped Cary acquire three town lots. On one of them Cary opened a livery stable with seven horses and three carriages. Matilda Houstoun, a British visitor in 1844 complained, "There is not much variety of amusement in Galveston." Yet she praised the modes of transportation. "Horses were to be hired in plenty, and not very bad," she added. "[T]here is a certain Captain Cary, in Galveston, who keeps, what is courteously termed, a livery stable. He is a free negro, who with great labour and perseverance saved up money to the amount of $1,000, and purchased his freedom." McKinney allowed Cary to hunt and sell game to raise money, and both McKinney and Williams supported a bill in the Texas Congress that allowed Cary to petition for manumission. But the Fourth Congress passed an act that prohibited free blacks from living in Texas without special permission forcing Cary to post a $1,000 bond in order to stay. His service as an express rider in the Texas Revolution helped him obtain permission to remain in the Republic, one of only two freed slaves to achieve that goal. The legislature was probably influenced by McKinney's support, since he loaned the government $99,000 to finance the Revolution. Horses could be rented from Cary for fifty cents per day, carriage included, that could carry the ladies to the racecourse if they chose to go. Unfortunately, little is known of Cary's part in training McKinney's race horses. Cary died sometime after 1846.[31]

McKinney's love of horses had personal consequences too. In the late 1830s he and his wife Nancy separated. At some point he met Anna Gibbs, whose mother, a widowed Boston teacher, opened a school on the island in 1838. Anna was young, just twenty when the school opened, and she was described as a "vigorous athletically inclined young woman who loved horseback riding." Since McKinney kept several horses at his home and built his track nearby, it was almost inevitable that they would meet. In 1842, at age forty-one, McKinney caused a huge scandal by divorcing Nancy so he could marry Anna, some seventeen years his junior. At a time when divorces were rare, he needed to petition the Congress of the Republic for permission as well as appear before a district judge. McKinney's friend, President Sam Houston, approved the petition on the grounds of mutual abandonment for more than two years. McKinney and Gibbs married in September 1842.[32]

A visit to the Galveston racecourse often meant seeing one of McKinney's horses in action. Two days before Christmas in 1839 McKinney's stallion, Osceola, raced there. Osceola was by Wild Bill and his dam by Timoleon, the "Pride of Virginia." Timoleon was by Sir Archy and McKinney was so proud of that fact that he bought a painting of Sir Archy, which hung above the fireplace of his home in Galveston and later, when he moved to the Austin area in 1850, hung over the mantel at his home on Onion Creek. In April 1839, Osceola ran at the New Market track at Velasco, along with his other Thoroughbred, Tom Thurman. Both stallions can be found in *The American Stud Book*.[33]

Shelby Smith was another name often seen on the racing programs, pitting his horses against the string of David Randon, McKinney, and other Texas Thoroughbred breeders and trainers. In 1833, he moved from Kentucky to Texas where his mother, brothers, and sisters soon joined him. Shelby did not come directly with his family to Texas, but stopped off in Louisiana. Soon after he arrived in Texas, however, he and his twin, Jack, gained a reputation as "breeders of racing stock and were known as sporting men although most of the horses they contested were the wiry mustang ponies." This statement, in a book published in 1912, is not exactly accurate as records indicate Shelby Smith often raced horses with Thoroughbred blood.[34]

Smith lived near Houston, the site of one of the most notorious racecourses in Texas. Francis Sheridan recalled in 1840 that the "most uncivilised place in Texas is I believe Houston the former Capital—I have heard & read of more outrage & blackguardism in that town during my stay on the coast committed there, than throughout the whole of Texas. It is reckoned unsafe to attend the races there, or indeed to reside in the Town a week after them, so desperate is the Bowie-Knifing & pistoling on these merry making occasions." He may have visited the track in April 1840, when an unfortunate shooting occurred there. Sheridan added that at "the last meeting of these '*gentlemen sportsmen*' one man was shot dead, a lady in the stand narrowly escaped with her life, & a general stabbing concluded the day's diversion." Sheridan recalled that "the feelings of some gentlemen had been so hurt, that they were seen for days afterwards bobbing round the corners of the streets, to avoid the shot of or gain a favourable opportunity of shooting an acquaintance." All social classes carried Bowie knives, although Sheridan though it was more prevalent in Houston than anywhere else in Texas he visited. Everyone was armed, either with pistols or Bowie knives, and it was unheard of to go about without a weapon, he added.[35]

Racing enthusiasts certainly did not want negative publicity. They organized the Houston Jockey Club in October 1838 and Shelby Smith, a member of the rules committee, was among those accused of the shooting at the track in 1840. The newspaper at Brazoria reported that Smith shot a gambler named Vance. The Austin paper implicated Smith's brother and reported an affray between Shelby and Jack Smith on one side, and John S. Vance and a Mr. Patterson on the other. Another version came from the German-speaking immigrant, Gustav Dresel. In his description of the events "the wealthy planter Walker made a bet with the gambler Vance, the stakes being the horses on which they were mounted. Walker lost. He contested the bet. A dispute ensued. Walker shot a bullet through Vance's heart. The latter's few friends drew their pistols, and in a few minutes seven of the shooters were more or less seriously wounded. Walker was arrested and indicted by the district attorney for murder, but set free under [a] five-thousand-dollar bond. But since Vance had no lawyer to represent him, the matter was dropped."[36]

Violence often accompanied gambling disputes, and although incidents in Houston made the newspapers, no racetrack was immune. The Houston *Telegraph and Texas Register* reported another killing in 1842 when Flournoy Hunt was shot by a man named Black near Harrisburg, and the paper wrote: "The quarrel occurred at the RACE TRACK." The article continued to say that "no less than three persons have been killed in broils at the race-tracks within three years. Mr. Syms at Nacogdoches, Mr. J. Vance in Houston, and Mr. Hunt at Harrisburg. Terrible, indeed, is that sport which is so often stained with blood."[37]

Gustav Dresel worked at the warehouse on Buffalo Bayou owned by the proprietor of the Houston track. Dresel remembered L. C. Stanley as a passionate gambler who, as joint owner of a secret gaming table, had won $15,000, which he invested in land, buildings, and slaves. He put his property in his wife's name in order not to lose it gambling, a not uncommon practice at the time because of Texas community property laws. Despite his propensity for betting, Stanley invested wisely, and soon after winning $3,000 at the table bought out his partner in the racecourse.[38]

Despite its reputation for violence, the Jockey Club at Houston hosted lavish social events. At one club ball the ladies' tickets were printed on white satin, and generals Sam Houston, Albert Sidney Johnston, and Sidney Sherman were in attendance. Dances were held for every possible occasion and the larger races provided an opportunity to enjoy the society of the ladies. Music could be provided by a single violinist or slaves fiddled to provide the entertainment. The following description of a ball in Galveston probably mirrored the ones at the elite jockey clubs: "There was an elegance and refinement about it belonging to older and more favored cities, a grace shown by the many beautiful women present, not only as regards dress but all the accomplishments which must adorn the sex."[39]

Sam Houston knew how to throw a ball and he did frequently as governor. But he was also an astute judge of horseflesh. He imported a son of Sir Archy to Texas in 1839 whose dam traced to Janus. Foaled in Pennsylvania in 1828, Copperbottom (also seen as Copper Bottom) arrived in Galveston by way of New Orleans and was ridden to Chambers County. Later he went to Huntsville and finally Hopkins County, where he stayed until his death in 1860. Father Benedict, a French priest who arrived in Galveston in the late 1840s, noted that on Sunday afternoon slaves matched their owners' Copperbottom horses in races along the beach. The stud made his name with his short burst of speed and is considered the first quarter running horse to achieve fame in Texas.[40]

Another Sam Houston—not the general—competed on the track. The colt was foaled in 1835, his sire was Kosciusko. Owned by David Randon, the stallion proved more successful as a sire than as a race horse and he later appeared in *The American Stud Book*, although apparently under the name Sam. Those familiar with General Houston's fondness for strong drink understood why one of this stallion's colts carried the name Big Drunk. Naming a horse after a famous person or family member was an American custom, and one rarely seen in England. A historian of racing, John Hervey, born in 1870, thought the "excellent and tasteful British custom of avoiding markedly personal appellations" for a colt's name far exceeded the American "ridiculous and tasteless practice" of honoring family and friends.[41]

Since most jockeys at large meets were slaves, they were not yet accorded the honor of having their names included in the day's program. In fact, there was no mention of jockeys, black or white, because in long distance heats the jockey was not as important as he would one day become in short distance races. While the training was usually assigned to slaves, as a matter of personal pride and pleasure, an owner often directed the preparation of his horses. Friends occasionally took each other's horses into their stables and ran them under their own colors and in their names, leading to much confusion concerning ownership. David Randon, for example, raced General Green's horses as well as his own; Col. Willis Alston raced those belonging to both McKinney and Col. Tod Robinson; and Shelby Smith raced those of D. Mitchell and John Fawcett along with his own. Adding to the confusion, actual ownership changed frequently.

Among the founders of the Houston Jockey Club was George Feris, who would later be known for his Arabians. Included in the Feris papers is a diagram for a track, and it is likely that the Houston course was quite similar. The total length was one mile, although the outer ring measured one mile, twenty-two yards. The area of the track encompassed thirty-eight and one-fifth acres. Each side of the track was 440 yards or a quarter of a mile, which made it suitable for short sprints as well as distance races. In fact, the first known race specifically advertised as a "quarter of a mile" was at Houston in the fall of 1840. Informal quarter mile match races became a frequent pastime but when the Houston course offered this special event, it was during the week preceding the regular distance races.[42]

In Texas, match races had been popular even before settlers from the United States arrived. Sprints, which might vary from one-eighth to three-fourths of a mile, were between two competitors. The course laid out was two parallel paths from fifteen to twenty feet apart, and a dash to the finish line decided the victor. The quickness with which the contest was decided added to the excitement of the crowd, for much money or property changed hands on such tests of speed.

"Fun and frolic were the ruling passions of the hours," wrote Dr. John W. Lockhart from Washington-on-the-Brazos. In 1840, this former capital counted about 250 residents and fifty to 100 non-residents, "principally gamblers, horse racers, etc., for this was a great resort for such characters," observed the doctor. John W. Hall owned a track on his land two miles south of town, where many races were run. Well-off men wagered cash on the outcome, while the less affluent bet livestock or anything else of value. Farther north on the Brazos, at the village of Bucksnort near present Marlin, quarter mile matches and heavy betting were common. In the next decade Bucksnort earned a reputation for its short distance racing.[43]

Races were almost always certain to draw crowds, for they provided an opportunity for men to discuss not only the entries, but topics ranging from the weather to politics to the occasional Indian raid. Many political deals were closed at the track. Early Texas politicians knew that racing was to their benefit, for captive audiences could be found enjoying the sport. At the Myrtle Turf Course on Spring Creek, about twenty miles north of Houston, the races in July 1839 provided a venue for candidates for office to harangue the voters. The *Telegraph and Texas Register* reported on July 31: "There was a 'feast of reason and flow of soul' recently up at Spring Creek, consisting of a *horse race*, three *stump speeches*—one from a candidate for the senate and two from candidates for the lower house. We have not learned which was the more interesting to the people, the *race* or the more *windy* performance of the candidates." Secretary of the Myrtle Turf Jockey Club was James W. Henderson, a native of Tennessee who would later serve as governor of the state of Texas.[44]

Legislators worried about the popularity of gambling, but not on horse racing. A visitor to Texas in 1837 noted that gambling happened "to such a disgusting extent at all times that Congress, during the spring session, passed a law making it highly penal to play. But as those who passed the law were most active in breaking it, the law itself was of little consequence any further than it afforded the gambler the double satisfaction of knowing that he was breaking the laws of God and those of man at the same time." Branch T. Archer, who served in the Texas Congress when the law passed, also served as the first president of the Velasco Jockey Club.[45]

Most Texans did not consider gambling on races in a derogatory sense. Even match racing on local tracks had customs that entrants carefully observed, and informal rules that Texas courts often enforced. In spite of the safeguards, gambling fever proved strong, and many a Texan often regretted his part in the diversion. "Does your horse carry double?" was a question voiced from Kentucky to the Texas coast as racing often involved participants losing horses, saddles, bridles, hats, boots, or just about anything of value.

Although racing prospered along the Gulf Coast, the eastern part of Texas also had racing that developed independently. While many immigrants came to Texas by Gulf steamers, others made the journey overland in wagons or on horseback, and a few simply walked, generally taking the road from Natchitoches, Louisiana, to San Augustine and on to Nacogdoches. One of the earliest tracks could be found near Nacogdoches. In the mid-1830s Amos Parker visited a man who lived on the banks of the Neches River forty miles from Nacogdoches, whose house was near a racecourse. The "gentleman told me there were frequent races on it," Parker recalled, and that "he had himself won twelve hundred dollars on a bet, a short time before."[46]

By the 1830s, racing reached the little settlement of Douglass, about fifteen miles northwest of Nacogdoches. Spectators came from as far away as San Augustine, more than sixty miles, to attend the races. A frequent competitor there was William C. Sparks, who was always ready to match one of his horses. In August 1839, he wagered $1,000 in Texas money on his horse Rabbit Head against Joseph S. Ables's Little Bill for a dash of 600 yards. Sparks, described as a "perfect little dude" with red hair and blue eyes, frequently used a black jockey named Little Jack. Douglas was apparently a popular place to test an animal's speed as well as socialize. German-speaking immigrant Adolphus Sterne recalled traveling there in July 1843 as "all hands are gone to Douglass where a big Horse race is going to take place the candidates are all there—no doubt to make very fair promises!!"[47]

San Augustine was another site of a racecourse. Antonio Leal had come to the area in the eighteenth century and built pens for the mustangs he and Philip Nolan caught in Texas in the mid-1790s. It was in the heart of the "Redlands"—the country between the Sabine River and Attoyac River—and took its name from the color of the soil. A popular saying "there is no God in Texas," referred to this no-man's land, for the district was a haven for fugitives from justice. This strip gave refuge to desperadoes who drifted across the Texas border and settled among the respectable citizenries. The absence of law made it a sanctuary for anyone evading justice. It was no surprise to see betting on the races and other types of gambling extensively practiced, "mostly on the Sabbath day," recalled William P. Zuber, whose family lived there in 1830. He remembered his mother's warning, "William, don't drink any of that water," as they ferried across the Sabine River into Texas. Later he was told that "when a man drinks Sabine water, he becomes a thief." Thieves were in abundance in the district, and it was not uncommon for horses to disappear only to reappear on the market in Louisiana. Despite this situation the residents of San Augustine formed a jockey club and raised $1,400 to build a racecourse. The club advertised its first spring meet in 1840, boasting that many of the horses entered had come all the way from New York. Several large stables of horses were in training for the event, and the animals were the talk of the town.[48]

American-style horse racing had grown in popularity in Texas in the previous two decades, and although there was a financial panic in the United States in 1837, Dr. Ashbel Smith, surgeon general of the Army of the Republic, wrote in December that "times here are very easy—money plenty—and the people much better satisfied, I will venture to assert, than our brethren in the United States." Throughout the 1820s and 1830s the political climate in the United States was favorable to horse racing. Those states of Kentucky, Tennessee, Alabama, Mississippi, and Louisiana now raised fine stock instead of importing Thoroughbreds from Europe, although British imports could still be found in the region. Andrew Jackson was president from 1829 until 1837 and his devotion to the turf was well-known. It was not surprising that he installed several of his race horses in the White House stables. Even though Jackson's horses raced under the name of A. J. Donelson, their ownership was no secret. Not since the time of Washington and Jefferson had racing been so generally identified with, and promoted by, national figures. As more settlers from these states arrived in Texas, so did their love for racing and fine horses.[49]

Although the Panic of 1837 did not have immediate repercussions in Texas, organized racing relied on men of substance and property for its main support. By April 1840, Dr. Ashbel Smith wrote that Texas currency was worth only sixteen cents on the dollar. By July, Smith observed that "times are terribly hard I think every body almost must break and go to work." In September, he wrote that he would gladly sacrifice a part of his valuable holdings in order to obtain cash. But there were no purchasers, because there was little money in circulation. An early historian of wealthy Brazoria County plantation owners noted: "During the 1837 'panic' cotton was piled on the banks of the Brazos at Brazoria for nearly a mile, with no sale. Times were very tight, and but few could pay their taxes. . . . A cow pony on the prairie unbroke was worth one plug of tobacco." Still, in 1838 the *Spirit of the Times* observed that the "great reduction in the price of cotton and sugar has not prevented many gentlemen in the South-west from engaging in breeding and importing fine stock." That was true in Texas too. Horse racing gained a foothold in the Republic and survived the economic downturn without any lasting ill effects. The *Spirit of the Times* reflected this growing love of the sport in a column headed: "Jockey Club in Texas!—We shall hear of one in Astoria directly."[50]

3

Times are A-changing

The 1840s

The oft-quoted claim that "Texas was a heaven for men and dogs, but a hell for women and oxen," certainly seemed true as immigrants flocked to this nascent country on the Gulf of Mexico. Women talked sadly of homes and friends left behind, and of the hardships and privations of living with danger a constant threat in this new land. The Republic of Texas offered countless opportunities for those dissatisfied in the United States, but men outnumbered the women in the early years emphasizing its male-dominated society. Economic hardships following the Panic of 1837 continued into the early 1840s, and as prices fell and credit tightened many Americans, seeking a means of escape, packed up and headed west, bringing entire families. "Gone to Texas" or simply "GTT" chalked on abandoned cabins throughout the nation meant that the former occupants hoped for a fresh start elsewhere. What they would find in the newly founded country was an often-challenging environment unlike what they left behind. In 1839, Edward Stiff, a Virginian who moved to Houston, described the capital of the Republic as a "Roaring Frontier Town" with about 3,000 people, but he estimated not more than forty females. The men all carried "the savage Bowie-knife, which as if by common consent, was a necessary appendage to all." The town was a "wild and woolly place peopled by a colorful assortment of characters of every conceivable description, from the most worthy to the reckless and feckless. Many were adventurers hoping to make a fortune." Yet for the thousands of people moving to the Republic, Texas offered a chance at a new life, a new beginning, in a new country. A chance to tame this rugged wilderness.[1]

The decade of the 1840s was a time of change. There was a sharp decline in the number of adventurers who came for the purpose of fighting Mexicans. Many of the "Gentlemen loafers," who had been "only too ready to avenge fancied insults—returned to the United States, moved on to new frontiers, died of drunkenness, or went to work." After Texas became a state in 1845, the number of family units arriving increased, and the population began to see a rise in traditional family values as more towns built permanent structures for churches and schools. While racing was still popular, drinking and gambling fell into disfavor in this new atmosphere, two popular pastimes at the races. In 1839, the Reverend William Allen made a temperance speech in Galveston's Tremont Hotel, and in February he helped found the Texas Temperance Society in Houston. A local paper reported, "*grogshops, which in the low country of Texas, are but the portals to the grave*." This seldom translated into criticizing "gentlemen" from enjoying a drink during a day at the races in larger towns or enjoying a shot of whiskey at spur-of-the-moment sprints on local tracks.[2]

Although Texas felt the effects of the depression later than the United States, organized racing declined in the Republic. Many of the early promoters either left Texas or curtailed their racing activities for various reasons. The settlements of Velasco and Quintana lost much of their importance after the firm of McKinney and Williams relocated to Galveston. McKinney, who owned the track at Galveston, began to liquidate his interests on the island in 1842, and by the early 1850s moved to his ranch across the river from Austin in Travis County, his wealth much reduced after helping finance the Texas Revolution. Also, among those tired of life in Texas was Thomas J. Green, who successfully promoted the races at Velasco. He eventually returned to the place of his birth, Warren County, North Carolina, and purchased Esmeralda, a 900-acre plantation, where he continued to breed Thoroughbreds until his death in 1863.[3]

Other early promoters of horse racing disappeared from the scene. John W. Hall, owner of the original track at Washington-on-the-Brazos, died in 1845. Dr. Ashbel Smith, a prominent supporter of the tracks at Galveston and Houston, was in Europe as *chargé d' affairs* to England and France from 1842 until 1844. Shelby Smith, another well-known turfman, vanished from the racing annals in southern Texas; he later died in Mississippi. Col. Willis Alston, who raced horses for Tom McKinney and others died near Brazoria in 1841. Alston murdered a prominent physician who criticized the way he killed a man in Florida. A mob intended to lynch Alston but, according to one of several versions of the incident, a pistol went off in the confusion and during the excitement, Alston was killed.[4]

Another reason for the decline of racing was that the Republic was virtually impoverished. A leading newspaper reported in 1842 that "A general gloom seems to rest over every section of the Republic, and doubt and sorrow are

Washington Races.

WASHINTON, June 7th, 1845.

WE, the undersigned, do agree to run a Race; one mile and repeat, over the Washington Course, on the last Thursday in November next.

Advertisement for the races at Washington in 1845.
National Register, Washington, Texas, July 3, 1845.

depicted on almost every brow." L. C. Stanley, owner of the Houston course, went to New York City, and newspapers reported few races around Houston between 1841 and 1843. Upon his return in 1844, he organized races early in January and again in the spring, but in April the track was in such bad condition that the payouts were small. In September 1841, Adolphus Sterne of Nacogdoches wrote, "no money, no Business, except the grog shops," but in early February 1842 he noted that the "Grog Shops all Shutt up *no Cash*," and "times have never been so hard in Texas, like they are now, I have never known the *want* of two bits until now,—!!!!!" Since grog shops and saloons generally outnumbered other businesses in towns, and drinking, gambling, and racing went hand-in-hand, it was clear times were tough in Texas. One firm that carefully handled its finances was McKinney and Williams. In 1844, wholesale money prices showed ninety to ninety-five cents in specie for a dollar of McKinney and Williams notes, and only fifty to sixty cents for Texas "exchequers."[5]

Taxes also discouraged those fond of the turf but short of money. Horses kept exclusively for racing were taxed at three dollars each, while those used in "any mechanical art or branch of industry" carried only a ten-cent tax, with four exemptions allowed. The increased taxes hit track owners particularly hard, for they often paid a considerable sum for each recognized racecourse. In 1840, the Houston paper announced that an act of the Republic of Texas Congress on January 16 levied a tax of $100 on tracks. Only theaters, billiard tables, and nine or ten pin alleys paid higher taxes, with billiard tables coming in at $250. With little money in circulation, any tax proved onerous.[6]

Organized racing suffered another blow as continuing problems with Mexico in the early 1840s kept many of the men who supported jockey clubs busy trying to keep the Republic afloat. Annexation to the United States in December 1845 only created another set of problems that eventually led to war with Mexico the following year. Texas leaders found little time to devote to frivolous pursuits, and spending a day at the races became a luxury few prominent Texans enjoyed. Sam Houston served as President of the Republic from 1841 until 1844 and as US senator from 1846 until 1859. Other influential Texans who frequented the races in the 1830s spent their time worrying about what the future held as Texas went from an independent Republic to the twenty-eighth state in the Union.

Meanwhile, racing became increasingly popular on the frontier, for there one could own a race horse or a quarter mile track without being harassed by government tax collectors. The average man gave little thought to politics. Bucksnort, a small village opposite the falls of the Brazos near present-day Marlin in Falls County, was the site of frequent short-distance races. There were few inhabitants between Washington-on-the-Brazos and the village. Bucksnort consisted of some outbuildings, a general store, a school, a blacksmith shop, a stagecoach stop, and of course a saloon and a racetrack with a stable. It was primarily a way station for travelers to and from Torrey's Trading Post near Waco. Tradition says the name Bucksnort was the idea of a drunk customer in the saloon, and a visitor from Ellis County recorded that in 1844 it was the only place between Nashville-on-the-Brazos (in present-day Milan County) and Dallas where a man could go to buy food and supplies. A visitor to the area noted: "To hear people speak of racing on the extreme outposts of civilization, sounded peculiar to me, but . . . I actually saw a race track which had been recently used. Later I had other occasions to observe, that the love for this national sport asserted itself in these places, far removed from civilization."[7]

Since few detailed descriptions of scrub races exist, it is important to look at each extant example not only for racing rules and customs but also for the hype surrounding each event. One such account, published in the *Spirit of the Times* in the 1850s, gives a vivid description of this form of entertainment and of the type of town that promoted scrub races. Bucksnort had all the requirements necessary for frontier horse racing. On a cool October day in the 1840s (the report does not give a specific year), some 200 people crowded into the village to see a quarter mile race. In the general store there was music to entertain the visitors. Dancing, drinking, and a variety of noises accompanied the merriment, all increasing in intensity as the afternoon wore on. The conversation ranged from inquiries after stray ponies to capturing horse thieves to Indian raids. The race was, however, the main topic on most minds, for Col. Baron de Kalb Pierch's horse Rolette was matched against Keeno Cook's Slidin' Jenny. Rolette seemed to be a slight favorite.[8]

It was to be a gala affair. In mid-October Pierch wrote to his friend, Luke Lightwood, a lawyer practicing in the town of Crockett, inviting him to come the following weekend in order to arrange Pierch's legal affairs and, at the same time, to attend a "real full deck race." Money was short, so Pierch wagered $1,000 worth of land certificates against horses of equal value put up by Cook. The colonel was an adventurous rogue worthy of mention. Pierch claimed he served with Andrew Jackson at New Orleans, fought in the Texas Revolution, scouted against the Comanche, and ran for the state legislature. Born in the 1790s, he spent his early life in search of adventure. One of the spectators noted that he had known Pierch for a long time, and once lost a yoke of steers and three yearlings on a horse of his in a questionable race. Pierch was too uncertain in sporting matters to be trusted, he concluded. Keeno Cook was another matter. Unlike his rival, he was a man of few words and reserved in manner. His serious contemplation was at obvious variance with the "boisterous deportment" of the mass of the assemblage.[9]

The day of the race provided entertainment for all. Many passed their time at the general store while the entrants worked out the preliminaries. There were "sounds of music and dancing, accompanied by a variety of fancy noises, in the way of Indian yells and the various cries of wild beasts peculiar" to this region emanating from the interior of the building. Spectators gathered early in the morning and as was the custom, judges needed to be selected for both the starting and finishing lines. If there was to be a handicap, it needed to be ascertained which horse got the advantage at the start, and by how many feet, so that this information was available before any betting began. In addition, the horses staked by Cook had to be properly valued, and this process elicited "much profanity and rough sarcasm upon the part of Colonel Pierch directed toward Keeno Cook, who bore them with a tranquility of manner." All of this took the entire afternoon, and preparations for the actual race did not commence until evening. In an unusual decision Pierch and Cook would act as their own starters. In sprint races the starter was often more important than either the trainer or jockey. A horse could gain a twenty-foot advantage on an opponent at the word "Go," and in a race lasting only twenty seconds or so, the advantage was obvious. This was known as "getting the bulge" on one's opponent.[10]

There was trouble from the outset. Rolette tore loose from Pierch and took off down the path. When the judges yelled "No start!" the hapless jockey tried to restrain the frantic steed, but his sharp spurs came in unlucky contact with the horse's sides. Rolette broke his girth and sent his rider head over heels onto the turf. Because of this unexpected accident, Pierch decided to ride Rolette himself, with the proprietor of the saloon serving as his starter. The colonel, who dressed in a manner befitting a victor, divested himself of his "long-tailed blue" coat and "low quartered shoes." He tied his brow with a red cotton bandana, then encircled his waist firmly with his suspenders. His contrast to the tidy garb of a jockey club rider was almost comical until he vaulted into the saddle, when his masterly handling of the horse indicated that a professional now held the reins. This added new life to the betting. At the word "Go," Cook's horse jumped a length ahead of Rolette.[11]

Despite the rough start, the race lived up to expectations. The track sank into a depression, then rose to an elevation beyond. Rolette caught up with the mare. "Look at Pierch," exclaimed a spectator, "standing high in the stirrups, and thereby showing several inches of clear daylight between him and the seat of the saddle—his elbows flattened to his sides, his knees firmly pressed against Rolette's shoulders, he is lifting him at every bound." As the two dashed down the track, Rolette drew several lengths ahead of Slidin' Jenny. Pierch's friends and backers shouted in a "maddening frenzy of joy" as their favorite approached the finish line.[12]

But frontier races were nothing if unpredictable. "Well said the wise man," wrote an observer, "the race is not always to the swift," for at that moment a "huckster" chanced to see a delinquent customer on the opposite side of the track. Thinking this was his opportunity to collect his debt, he scampered across the mare's path and onto the grass that divided the two race paths, amidst cries of "lay down" and "go on." For one second, he hesitated, bewildered, then plunged into the path of Rolette, who hit him squarely in the back. The horse floundered and fell against an old man and young boy mounted on a mule. Slidin' Jenny swept by "like a storm, and passed through the poles a winner amid the shouts and yells of the crowd."[13]

Pandemonium broke out. Unfortunately for the peddler, the fall had not injured Pierch. The huckster tried in vain to make a hasty exit, but the crowd hemmed him in until Pierch was able to confront the unhappy fellow. "Now, what did you git in my horse's path fur? Don't tell me about not meaning anything; you was hired to do it—*hired*!" shouted Pierch as he attacked the peddler "tooth and nail, being stimulated thereto and encouraged therein by the shouts of the bystanders." The poor peddler was mercifully saved when spectators pulled Pierch from his victim.[14]

In typical frontier style and being a seasoned politician, Pierch conceded the race. A short time later, completely composed, he mounted a stump in the center of the commons to address the crowd in the language of an unsophisticated Texan, "I've come to the conclusion, feller citizens, ov raisin' no squabble about the matter, but to give up the stakes. It weren't Keeno's fault, who's a good feller . . . but though he won by accident, yet he won the race. Ef we were in his place, I expect we would most proberbly be for keepin' the money too. . . . Whippin' the cuss [the peddler] has put a bad taste in my mouth; less all go back to the grocery and licker." Thus soothing his backers who decided to "avail themselves of his general invitation," all returned to the store and the barrel of whiskey.[15]

Bucksnort and its track did not last long. Dr. Frederick Roemer, a German speaker visiting Texas about this time, remembered Bucksnort in a depressed condition. His host for the night was a friend of his companion. At his home they dined on the simplest supper he had eaten on his entire trip, consisting of nothing but "cornmeal mush and cold milk." Their host was noticeably embarrassed, and Roemer learned later that the man had once been wealthy, but because of his passion for racing, for which he kept expensive horses and bet large sums on them, he suffered financial ruin. Roemer said the same misfortune happened to other residents of the little village. Bucksnort was apparently a lively racing center in its heyday, but by the early 1850s the town was on the decline.[16]

Judging by court records, the match race between Rolette and Slidin' Jenny was more typical than unusual. But except for the wagering, quarter mile match racing had little in common with the distance races of several heats. The races at recognized courses were governed by jockey club rules, and were largely tests of the animal's speed, endurance, and training. The owners of distance horses were generally men of substance who were expected to be above cheating in order to win. That, of course, was not always the case as unscrupulous owners and trainers could be found everywhere.

Still, quarter mile racing was different. Although there were certain customs that were at least superficially observed, these races attracted men determined to win any way they could, and who developed many tricks to enable their horses to defeat faster ones. This was not unique to Texas, for the same type of men enjoyed quarter mile racing in colonial Virginia. One by-product was the multitude of disputes regarding races that went to court, and much of what we know of early short distance races comes from those records.

The popularity of match racing traced far back into history, and Texans enjoyed the sport as much as those past generations. In December 1842 spectators watched Diddle and Moll-row, both small American horses standing barely over fourteen hands high, take to the track. Englishman William Bollaert, visiting his Scottish friend Robert Robson at his castle near Columbus (complete with drawbridge and moat) and known as the Scotch Hermitage, was among the 200 to 300 fans who braved the cold weather to enjoy the festivities. Robson, a wealthy Scot who immigrated to Texas, accompanied his guest to the site, about one mile from the Hermitage.[17]

Bollaert was a sophisticated traveler and, having arrived in Texas in 1842, wanted to soak up the atmosphere of the Republic. He noted that following "the battle of San Jacinto, cities and towns were founded with rapidity, and amongst other public improvements races and race courses were established." Even "planters and farmers have formed courses on their lands, thus affording pleasure to the settlers and the means for improving the breed of horses." Bollaert also kept a journal he hoped one day to publish, and a frontier race was quite an experience considering that his prior knowledge of the sport centered around races he attended in England. Bollaert watched the crowd carefully as spectators considered the two entries and placed bets. Since money was scarce and seldom used in betting among the common folk, cattle, horses, slaves, or land changed hands and a barrel of whiskey was readily available to encourage the wagering. The race was 600 yards, with the two parallel tracks about twelve to fifteen feet apart. This was considered a "crack race," but the cold weather prevented "the aristocracy and their families" from attending. Bollaert noted that in contrast to the expected rabble he saw "no rifles, pistols, or bowie knives," and the only person the worse for his liquor was the owner of Diddle. In contrast, Moll-row's owner was seen riding up and down, speaking to no one, apparently concentrating on the outcome of the race.[18]

Diddle seemed to be the favorite. His jockey, attired in nothing but shirt and drawers, tied a "kerchief" around his brow and mounted his horse (in contrast to the formal attire Bollaert was accustomed to seeing jockeys wear back home in England). Moll-row's rider kept on his trousers, but since he weighed in too heavy, had to forego the use of his saddle. The track was muddy so a swift jump at the start was all important. The jockey on Diddle had trouble settling his mount, but the "skittishness and jumping" about was blamed on the jockeys trying to gain an advantage for the start. The sprint ended quickly, around twenty seconds, with the favorite losing. Diddle's owner was by that time too inebriated to be aware of his loss. Some thought there were dirty moves on the part of the jockeys about halfway through the race, but the course judges were unanimous in declaring Moll-row the winner. As the crowd dispersed, those who lost on Diddle began to plan for the races scheduled for the following day. As one observer commented to his downcast friend, "I hope you'll have better luck tomorrow, long races—none of these jumps." Whether or not Bollaert attended the races the next day is unknown, but the extremely cold weather may have kept him away. His stay in Texas ended in 1844, not only because of ill health, but because of the British opposition to the annexation of Texas by the United States.[19]

Further north, in Brazos County near present-day Bryan, a race was arranged in September 1844 between a horse promoted by E. C. Chandler and John H. Galbreath, and one belonging to Henry G. Hudson. According to a witness, the Hudson horse ran off the track at the start and went some forty feet before being brought back by his rider. The impression of the spectators was that Hudson's jockey pulled the horse off course deliberately. Galbreath later bragged that he paid his opponent's jockey $15 to throw the race, but when Hudson's rider followed Galbreath to Wheelock, a little town east of the Brazos to collect the debt, Galbreath sent him to Chandler for the money.[20]

Chandler refused to pay and denied any knowledge of wrongdoing. He said the race was fair "so far as he knew." He admitted that Galbreath made the race for him, but he had put up the main stake and agreed only to give Galbreath part of the money won. Chandler went on to assert that Galbraith was a "worthless fellow, and capable of offering and making a bribe." He admitted, furthermore, that the Hudson horse would have won if he had not bolted from the track. It was, however, impossible to prove that the jockey threw the race on purpose. Cases such as this often ended up before a local judge because of the absence of any supervising body on frontier tracks.[21]

Disputes did not stop small town racing from growing in popularity. While southern Texas suffered under the effects of the depression, Clarksville, near the Red River in North Texas was a growing community. In 1842, the town boasted of nine cotton gins, four gristmills, and three tanneries. By 1843, racing was in full swing there, and it was probably one of the most active locations for the breeding of fine horses. American horses were popular, and the offspring of Leviathan were especially admired. Richard Miller, who lived in Bowie County, advertised his stallion Lycurgus as "got by Priam, the noblest son of that unequalled horse, the imported Leviathan." His advertisement boasted that Lycurgus, "Nature's Master Piece," stood near Clarksville. Lycurgus carried the blood of Leviathan, Sir Archy, and Fearnought on his sire's side and his dam traced back to Diomed. *The Northern Standard* reported Lycurgus' "movements would make the hunter's mouth water," and "for catching Indians or Mexicans, he is the very *dandy*. Come and see, and judge for yourselves."[22]

Another popular spot to test an animal's speed could be found just outside of Clarksville. At the Dayton Grove Track in December 1844 the Berkshire Boar, owned by James Bourland, took on Rackmaroleon, owned by Alfred Bailes. The stakes were $1,000 a side, and the importance of the wagering was indicated by the fact that it required an hour before they had a clean start. Rackmaroleon gained an early lead, but the Berkshire Boar had no trouble in overtaking him and crossed the finish line thirty to forty feet ahead "under a tight rein." No one timed the race, but an observer noted "if it had been, it would have been to criterion of the speed and power of the Boar." After his loss, Bailes purchased the winning horse. Berkshire Boar had previously been known as the Flying Dutchman and, wrote a reporter, "is certainly one of the best put up nags that we ever looked at." A number of famous Thoroughbreds carried the name Flying Dutchman. Duplicate names were not unusual for the time but would be eliminated when registrations became official at the end of the century.[23]

Bailes was so sure of the speed of his new acquisition that on Christmas Day 1844 he issued the following challenge in *The Clarksville Standard*:

> **TO THE OWNERS OF ALBERT GALLATIN**
>
> I understand that you say, you can beat the Berkshire Boar seven hundred yards—This is therefore to inform you, that I say the Berkshire Boar can beat

> Albert Gallatin, the said distance of 700 yards with catches on each, for five hundred or one thousand dollars over the Boston Course.
>
> **ALFRED BAILES**
>
> *December 25, 1844*

The owners of Albert Gallatin probably welcomed this opportunity, but unfortunately the results of that race are unknown. The stallion belonged to brothers, G. W. and J. C. Hart, who owned a farm a little more than a mile southwest of Clarksville. The stallion carried the name of a former US secretary of the treasury. Foaled in 1840, he was fifteen hands three inches high and a dark bay with black legs, mane, and tail. He traced back to Sir Archy. J. C. Hart published an extensive pedigree in the local newspaper and challenged the world to prove otherwise. J. C. also served as secretary for the Clarksville Subscription Club—the local jockey club. During the fall races the Harts' stallion was "publicly bantered," and J. C. felt the need to answer. The owners of three well-known racers claimed their horses could beat Albert Gallatin. Hart responded by saying, "Albert Gallatin can tear the hind sights off of Tom Marshall, one mile, mile heats, or a dash of two miles." To the supporters of the stallion James K. Polk he said that "Albert Gallatin can knock the sand out of James K. Polk's gizzard," and to the owner of Woodpecker he claimed, "Albert Gallatin can make him raise his hocks from one mile to two mile heats, or a dash of three miles." Hart ended by saying, "I was not disposed to banter on my horse, had he not been bantered first, but knowing as I do, the blood that flows through his veins to be that of old Sir Archy, I am disposed to back him on the above assertions." If nothing else, this exchange probably ensured a good turnout at the track for those who wanted to see which would prove the better horse.[24]

Devotees of the sport enjoyed not only the contest at the track, but also followed with equal fanaticism the exchanges in the press, and the Clarksville paper promoted the races by printing provoking articles. One titled "A Challenge" issued by C. E. Hilburn in November 1844 and involving Albert

Gallatin read: "Hart & Co. are hereby informed that my horse Woodpecker, can take their horse, Albert Gallatin, two miles heats over the Boston track, on the 1st Monday in May next, for a negro boy worth six hundred and fifty dollars, and three hundred and fifty dollars in cash. The objection I have to the Clarksville track is, that it is too muddy in wet weather and too hard in dry." Hilburn's stallion Woodpecker stood fifteen and a half hands high and was a blood bay that traced back to Diomed on his sire's side and to Blackburn/Cook's Whip on his dam's. It is unknown if the Harts accepted this challenge, but by May 1845 Woodpecker was apparently owned by Thomas D. Lee and standing at stud. He alternated weeks between John Robbins farm, ten miles west of Clarksville, and John Sikes farm, ten miles east of Clarksville. There was a $10 fee for a single breeding and $20 to ensure the mare was with foal. His owner accepted mares from March 15 until June 15.[25]

Albert Gallatin apparently changed hands too, and by the end of the decade belonged to the president of the Webber's Prairie Jockey Club, "Black" Tom Moore, and his friend, Samuel Wilson. Moore earned his nickname because of his dark complexion and jet black hair. He arrived in Texas in 1827 and built Moore's fort near Gilleland Creek about 1831. The fort, named for him, was around thirteen miles from Austin. Moore and Wilson agreed to a match race with J. A. Lorane's brown mare Promise by Red Bull and out of a mare by imported Luzborough. The race was to be one-mile heats for $1,000 a side, $500 in cash and $500 in American horses. At some point Wilson refused to run the race because he believed the surety of Lorane in the forfeit note was not good. In fact, he assigned different reasons at different times for not wanting to compete. A witness testified that when abiding by the customs of racing, to entitle one of the parties to the forfeit from the other, it was incumbent upon him to appear at the place on the day agreed on, with the amount of money or property to be put up on his part, and trot or lead his horse around the track. On the day of the race Albert Gallatin was nowhere to be seen, but Lorane ran his horse around the track, and then sued Wilson and Moore for the forfeit. The defendants argued that to entitle Lorane to the forfeiture it was necessary for him not only to appear at the place and time agreed upon but, to have the amount stipulated in the wager ready to stake. According to the witness, Lorane did not have either the money or the American horses with him when he galloped the track alone. Wilson and Moore's argument proved futile, however, for a jury awarded Lorane the amount of the note, plus interest incurred in the five years of litigation.[26]

Webber's Prairie, located near Austin, was the site of a popular track. Later renamed Webbersville, it was known as "Hell's Half Acre," because of the "community's lawless and immoral reputation" in its early days. The printed *Rules and Regulations of the Webber's Prairie Jockey Club* in 1849 was only nine pages, but it covered some of the more important procedures like starting, which was done by the tap of a drum. It also stated that one duty of the judges was to "see that the riders are dressed clean, and in jockey style" rather than informally as one saw at scrub races. It was a steward's duty to "preserve order, clean the track, keep the crowd from the horses when coming to the stand after the close of a heat; and to exercise vigilance to prevent disorder, detect foul riding, or any other misconduct." But when compared to rule books in modern times, the authors only covered the basics.[27]

The rule book provides a unique look at racing in Texas in the 1840s. It states races of the jockey club would be held each spring and fall, and that the Austin paper would publish the results. A secretary would keep a book where details of each entry could be found, including the name of the owner, name of the horse, color and age of the entry, name of sire and dam, and a description of the rider's dress. Horses could be disqualified if there was a question about the truthfulness of the information, specifically the age, but if there was a doubt and if the animal won, then the owner had sixty days to provide testimony proving his case before being awarded his winnings. One significant note is that the word "nag" was frequently used interchangeably with "horse" and was not a derogatory term. While the modern definition of nag is a horse that is old or in poor condition that was not the case in the nineteenth century.[28]

Texas had not lost its reputation for lawlessness on the day in late December 1845 when it joined the Union and state officials raised the Stars and Stripes in the capital of Austin. One authority on Thoroughbreds claimed that the first blooded stallion of true renown arrived in the newly born state around this time. Rodolph, a bay foaled in 1831 in Woodford County, Kentucky, was by Sir Archy Montorio (Sir Archy of Transport), whose sire was Sir Archy. His dam was by Haxall's Moses. He traced back to Blackburn/Cook's Whip. She was one of the most distinguished Kentucky matriarchs of her day. Rodolph ran only seven races, winning all, but he made his reputation in a Kentucky versus Tennessee match in Louisville as a five-year-old in four-mile heats. Rodolph

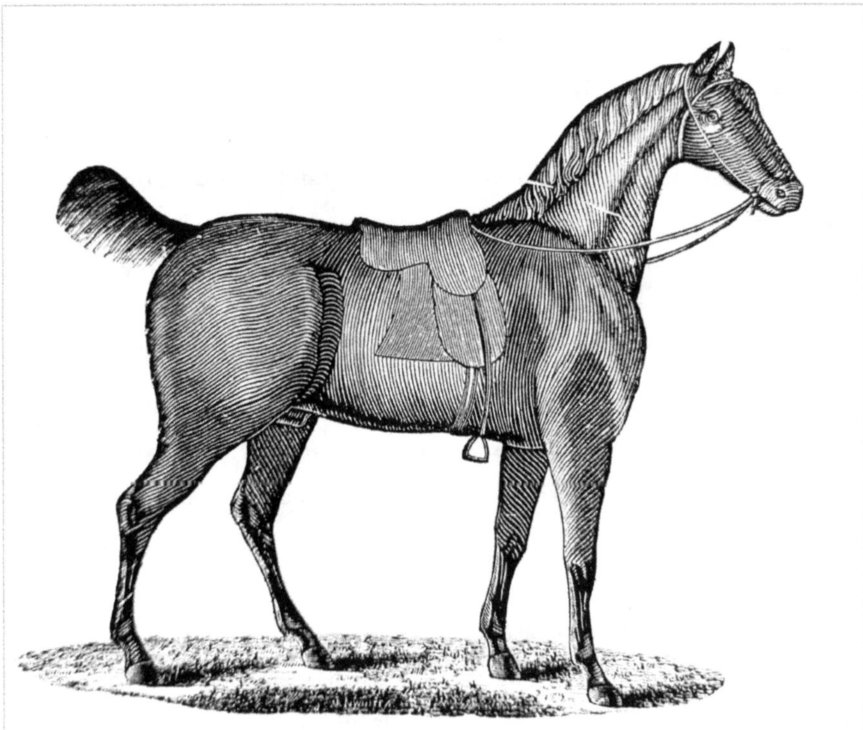

A saddle or quarter running horse in 1841. The Thoroughbred was not heavily muscled like the saddle horse used for sprint racing. This characteristic would become more pronounced as the century ended. Richard Mason, *The Gentlemen's New Pocket Farrier*, 1841.

distanced his opponent in the first heat over a track deep in mud. So convincing was his victory that no horse would match him the following year. He stood fifteen and a half hands tall but failed as a sire in Kentucky and was soon sold. Where he arrived in Texas is unknown.[29]

Even though times were changing in Texas, the breeding of fine horses remained a priority for some of the more devoted. These men came from all over the United States. One who raised blooded horses in Lavaca County hailed from New England. Amasa Turner, who was born in 1800 in Plymouth County, Massachusetts, decided to visit Mexican Texas in 1835. He joined the Texas army and when he planned a visit to see his family back east, Turner received instructions to recruit as many men as he could on his trip. In New Orleans he raised 100 men to fight in the Texas Revolution, arriving in Velasco in January 1836. He fought at San Jacinto and after serving in the Texas army from January 1835 until August 1837, he received 1,280 acres of land. As a civilian he was collector of customs for the Port of Galveston, and in 1837 built the Galveston Hotel. He also owned a plantation in Harris County and divided his time between Houston and Galveston until he moved to Lavaca County in 1848. There he raised purebred horses, something he had apparently being doing for several years. He earned praise for being the "most extensive raiser of fine horses in Western Texas. He has invested a large capital in the very best blood to be procured in the country." Most of the horses he bought came from Tennessee, but unfortunately their bloodlines are unknown. Turner believed that West Texas, which at that time was not very far west because the Indians still controlled much of the state, was "admirably adapted" to raise blooded horses to the "highest perfection." The author of a brief article in the *Victoria Advocate* went on to add his own opinion by concluding: "The day will soon arrive, when the useless herds of Spanish horses will be driven from the country, by the infinitely more valuable American horse. Would that the day had already arrived." Little did the writer know that some of those wild Spanish horses, when bred to American horses, would produce a cross that the cowboy often rode in the last half of the nineteenth century. But it was men like Turner and others who made this possible.[30]

Thoroughbreds remained popular in East Texas too. W. W. Holman, in San Augustine County, owned a stallion, Leviathan, sired by imported Leviathan. Holman was a wealthy farmer from Kentucky and once raced his stud against Claiborn Howard's filly for a single dash of a mile. Leviathan won, beating his opponent by around thirty feet. Sometime after this race Leviathan was taken out of state and did not return until the spring of 1846 when he was advertised again standing at stud at Holman's place three miles west of San Augustine. His pedigree was impressive. His sire, imported Leviathan, needed no introduction to horsemen and his dam, although unnamed, was described as the "finest looking animal in America, and possessed the finest action, and could have been sold for $1500 at 20 years of age." She had been brought to Tennessee by a "celebrated rogue by the name of Jacob Jones," who said she was an Eclipse mare and later evidence proved this was true. Those interested in breeding would have to hurry, as Leviathan was leaving San Augustine at the end of the season. Since a fee was not mentioned, it is safe to assume that Leviathan's services did not come cheap.[31]

East Texas also provided fertile ground for raising and racing purebred horses. In 1841, John D. Nash, who served as sheriff of San Augustine County, ran an advertisement for a Thoroughbred named Proclamation that would stand at his home, four miles southwest of San Augustine, for a $25 fee or $50 to ensure a foal. The thirteen-year-old stud traced back to Diomed, stood sixteen hands high, and was a dark chestnut. Cattle or corn would be taken in payment. But East Texas, although not on the frontier, was a rough area. At one track located a mile west of San Augustine, W. H. Landrum was ambushed while returning home from the races. Although struck by four bullets, he survived. The editor of the *Red-Lander* wrote, "we trust that it was not one of our citizens who has been guilty of so base an act; and that we may not lay under the imputation or suffering such a monster to exist among us, we trust that energetic and prompt measures will be adopted to discover the offender."[32]

San Augustine was also the site of short distance match races along with regular jockey club events. At the local track in November 1845, Sheriff Nash matched his roan against a man named Shanks, whose horse Blackhawk was by Glencoe. It was to be a mile dash for $400 a side. The next race reported in extant papers was not until 1848, and it was at the track owned by William Hollis, a forty-eight-year-old farmer from Tennessee. The Red-Land racecourse was to be the site on October 31 where Nathaniel Vice's bay Curley and Walter Krather's bay Little John would meet. It was for 600 yards and $1,000. For November 1, Hollis planned a match—mile heats for $1,000, between William E. Long's sorrel gelding Simon and Sheriff Nash's brown mare Purity. The following day, on November 2, regular jockey club races would begin and would last three days. But the main events were the two match races, and Hollis believed the "race between Simon and Purity will excite the most intense interest." He also provided stables, boarding, and anything else needed at the track. Unfortunately, which animals won these races is lost to history.[33]

Still, the annexation of Texas opened old wounds with Mexico. The Republic of Texas claimed the Rio Grande as its southern border, while Mexico insisted it was the Nueces River with its mouth at Corpus Christi. American President James K. Polk accepted the Republic's claim to the land between the Nueces and the Rio Grande and ordered Gen. Zachary Taylor to move his command there in mid-1845. Taylor soon counted more than 3,000 men in camps around Corpus Christi. When war was declared in 1846, thoughts of organized horse racing all but disappeared as many Texans hurried to join the fighting. Some 5,000 to 7,000 Texans enlisted in the army in the summer of 1846, and even Gov. James P. Henderson took a leave of absence to command a division of volunteers. These were often the same men who raced on Texas tracks and many crossed into Mexico mounted on Thoroughbreds. Others rode quarter running horses. These recruits came from all walks of life, some of them as ready to fight Mexicans as they had been to fight each other at scrub races over a disputed outcome. "Them Texas troops are the damndest troops in the world," Taylor was heard to say. "We can't do without them in a fight, and we can't do anything with them out of a fight." One cavalryman wrote, "A more reckless, devil-may-care looking set, it would be impossible to find this side of the Infernal Regions," adding that "with their uncouth costumes, bearded faces, lean and brawny forms, fierce wild eyes and swaggering manners, they were fit representatives of the outlaws which made up the population of the Lone Star State." The war lasted until 1848 and jockey club racing ended in South Texas during the months of fighting.[34]

One to head for Mexico was well-known race horse Ball Higgins. He had "been entered in races in eastern Texas and had won considerable money for his owners." The stallion, noted for his "extraordinary powers of endurance, his sagacity, and his rascality," carried a man in the campaign at Monterey and accompanied his owner by water to Veracruz. The horse apparently did not enjoy the trip by ship, for he attacked an Irishman meddling with the animals. One report claimed, "the old scoundrel pitched at him, open-mouthed," and took the man's ear off "clean as it could have been done by a pair of shears; then chewed it up, and swallowed it. . . . We boys couldn't help laughing." This story has all the indications of a tall tale told by soldiers once they returned from war, but it did emphasize that high-strung Thoroughbreds made the trip to Mexico with the soldiers from all over the nation. Riding Thoroughbreds into battle was a mark of distinction, and a way to separate the officers from the common soldier, who was not as well mounted.[35]

At the close of the war several companies of US soldiers arrived to take over defense of the state against the still-hostile Indians. In 1849, military authorities decided to build a line of forts for the protection of the settlers. The coming of the army brought a new supply of blooded horses into the state, for many of the officers owned Thoroughbreds. Since most of the soldiers were from east of the Mississippi River, they marveled at the difference in racing on the frontier. Frank H. Stone, a surgeon with the army, had an opportunity to witness frontier racing firsthand, and indeed began participating in match racing while temporarily stationed at Presidio de San Elizario near El Paso. Stone, who owned a sorrel horse called Tom, had never raced or tried his horse for speed, but he soon learned that Tom was one of the fastest in the regiment, and matched him against "Bowman's mare." Captain Bowman brought this mare from San Antonio where she was thought to be the fastest horse in the state, having won many races. The race, held in December 1849, was for a distance of 600 yards with $50 going to the winner. Stone rode his own horse, but Bowman asked a Mexican to ride for him. Stone recalled that "there were some officers down from Santa Fe and several from El Paso to see the race," which his horse won by twenty-seven feet.[36]

Stone's Tom quickly won the reputation as the fastest horse in the region. Priced at $175 before his win, Stone refused to take less than $300 for him afterwards. He felt that he would have no trouble selling his steed because there was a Mexican in Chihuahua who owned a horse he thought could not be beaten. Texans were eager to find a horse capable of accepting the challenge, and it is possible that Tom was bought for that purpose.[37]

The war with Mexico had an unexpected but positive impact on Texas racing. Soldiers loved a good race when not actively campaigning. The soldiers who came to fight often rode purebred mounts from east of the Mississippi River, and many of those volunteers decided to make Texas their home after the war ended. America's favorite pastime began to grow again, but now it was in the new Lone Star State, a state with a bright future.

At the same time, the 1840s had not been kind to racing in the states east of the Mississippi River. The economic downturn in 1837 had repercussions well into the next decade, and the cost of the war with Mexico placed an added strain on the government. The price of fashionably bred Thoroughbreds dropped and stud fees fell accordingly. In 1839, eighty different stallions were advertised in the *Spirit of the Times*, with stud fees ranging as high as $150. Ten years later, in 1849, only two stallions were advertised, and their stud fees were $25 and $30 respectively. The same trend happened in racing. In 1839, there had been 153 race meets reported across 106 different tracks. In 1849, the *Spirit of the Times* reported only thirty-eight meetings held on twenty-seven different courses.[38]

Perhaps the highlight of the decade was a renewed North versus South rivalry. In May 1842, the southern champion Boston lost to the New Jersey-bred, five-year-old mare Fashion. Named "Queen of the Turf," Fashion won by thirty-five lengths for $20,000 a side. Southerners, of course, immediately wanted a rematch. That rematch of northern and southern horses would be held at the Union Course on Long Island in May 1845. The northern champion would be Fashion; she would be eight years old by that time. But she would not face Boston again. The southern entry would be a six-year-old named Peytona. Originally christened Glumdalclitch (for the giantess in Dean Swift's *Gulliver's Travels*), Peytona was an Alabama-bred chestnut. She came from the stable of the late Irish-born James Jackson, one of the most renown and respected breeders in America. He imported both Leviathian and Glencoe to his Forks of Cypress plantation. Although Jackson died in 1840, his nephew Thomas Kirkman inherited the horses, and brought Peytona to the match in 1845, which would be for $10,000 a side.[39]

Peytona was a daughter of Glencoe and out of Giantess, by Leviathan. At almost sixteen hands three inches tall she had a long stride not matched by many horses of the time. Prior to the race, well-known northern trainer Isaac Van Leer trained the mare in Mobile, Alabama. When she left on the thousand-mile journey to Long Island in February 1845 she went part of the way by steamboat, part by railway, and part trotting behind a wagon. The trip took a month and Southerners turned out along the route to cheer her on. On the northern side, Fashion was the fad of the day. She had all sorts of feminine wear named for her, such as bonnets and gloves, and her name adorned northern steamboats, theaters, and hotels. An estimate of the crowd attending the race ranged between 70,000 and 100,000. Overcrowded ferries and trains carried fans heading to the event. When it was all over, Peytona edged out Fashion to win, with the time of the two heats 7:39¾ and 7:45¼. This was the fifth time that horses from the North and South met, and it was the last of major importance. Sectional differences in the 1850s made having another North–South rivalry impractical. Northerners took solace in that Peytona had a northern trainer and was ridden by a northern jockey. Texas had a connection to Peytona, as she eventually passed into the hands of Keene Richards, who along with George Feris in Fort Bend County, raised Arabians. Richards bred Peytona mainly to two Arabian stallions he brought from the Middle East. One of her colts was Transylvania, by the Arabian Massoud. Transylvania was later bred to War Dance, Thomas Jefferson "Jeff" Wells's stallion that spent part of the Civil War years at Tom McKinney's farm near Austin. Although Wells lived primarily on his plantation in central Louisiana, he also owned land in Texas which he visited frequently.[40]

The ties between horsemen in the Lone Star State and those in Louisiana, Kentucky, Tennessee, Mississippi, and Alabama became especially significant. The economic crisis of the early 1840s hurt tracks in the Northeast, and the center of racing shifted south to New Orleans where the Metairie course eventually took top billing. Texans always felt a special bond with New Orleans, since it was just a short steamboat voyage from Galveston, and the pleasures found in the city made it a frequent destination for those who wanted to enjoy the cosmopolitan atmosphere and attend the races at the same time. Frequent showers made the ground perfect for dirt tracks. One authority believed that at this time the New Orleans racecourse was "the best kept and most carefully worked and prepared in America," citing abundant evidence in contemporary sources. One other early track, christened the Eclipse, was built in 1837 around six miles upriver from the city. On race days there was train service every half hour and steamers transported fans for twenty-five cents each. The stands reserved for the ladies had carpet and cushioned seats. The parlors and other private rooms featured drapes of silk and velvet, mirrors, and paintings. Chefs provided the best Louisiana cuisine.[41]

When Metairie opened in 1838 it surpassed all others. The owner erected an outer fence twelve feet high, and "on a scale of magnificence surpassing any thing of the kind in this country." A "splendid pavilion" was two stories, and around 250 feet long and thirty-seven feet wide. It housed three apartments, one for the ladies, one for club members, and one for "transient persons." Several large stables accommodated the horses. The whole affair was built in "such a manner as to throw every course at the North completely into the shade." Going to the races was still a "pastime for gentlemen and ladies," wrote a historian of New Orleans in 1895, "not a business for professionals." There were crowds in the hotels and as racing enthusiasts headed for the track there was the "whirl of carriages and cabs and vehicles of all kinds along the shell road." Then there were the jockeys, "petted and spoiled like ballet-girls—and the horses!" Once the races ended for the day fans enjoyed dinner at Moreau's, Victor's, Miguel's, and other places serving New Orleans fare. Male race patrons could end the night at the various saloons on St. Charles Avenue and St. Louis Street smoking cigars and drinking whiskey. The proprietress of the Texian Hotel, No. 72 New Levee, advertised a ball beginning at 5:00 p.m. in March 1838 and no doubt she did the same during race week. Texas largest cities could offer nothing like this—the state was still too unsophisticated and the towns with jockey clubs too small to support such luxury. New Orleans was the closest location for a real vacation with a wide variety of attractions that could not be found anywhere in the Lone Star State. It was here that Texans with the means and money headed in the antebellum years and Metairie survived as the South's premier track until the Civil War. While this sounds like the ideal holiday, visitors needed to remember that a racetrack could also be a dangerous place on occasion.[42]

The city of pleasure offered something for every man. There was cockfighting, prize fighting, and for those with "exotic tastes" there were "encounters between bulls and bears, wild animals and reptiles—and even one between a dog and an alligator." Many of the turfmen who made New Orleans the racing capital of the South were not native to the state, but outsiders who relocated to Louisiana for a variety of reasons, such as Jeff Wells and Richard Ten Broeck. The horses they raced were not Louisiana bred but foaled in Virginia, South Carolina, Alabama, Kentucky, and Tennessee. Ten Broeck, who hailed from one of the most distinguished Dutch families in New York, was at this time the uncrowned king of the sporting world. The first horse he raced in New Orleans was probably in 1844 but by 1847–1848 he took over management of the

Bingaman Course in Algiers, across the river from New Orleans, but also the Bascombe Course in Mobile. He soon acquired an interest in Metairie. Some of the most famous racers of the forties came to New Orleans.[43]

Another who was instrumental in Louisiana becoming the capital of the racing world in the South was Duncan Kenner. Born in New Orleans in 1813 he became a politician of note as well as one of the nation's leading breeders. Living upriver from New Orleans, he named his sugar cane plantation Ashland—where he counted around 500 slaves—after Ashland, the Kentucky home of noted politician Henry Clay. Construction began in 1839, with the structure completed in 1841. At sixty feet square, the two-story domicile has twenty-eight columns in the antebellum Greek Revival style. The home has been called the "grandest and largest plantation house ever built in the state. The walls were "adorned with paintings of horses, and the grounds included a racetrack." He both bred and raced horses on his estate. He was also one of the founders of the Louisiana Jockey Club and the New Louisiana Jockey Club, remaining involved in racing until his death in 1887.[44]

Texas in the 1840s could not rival the glitter of New Orleans. The money made on the sugar cane plantations in southern Louisiana meant that the rich could indulge in blooded horses and enjoy some of the finest tracks in the nation. Many wealthy turfmen had connections in Kentucky, the Thoroughbred capital of the South. Texas turfmen frequently enjoyed the races there, and men like Texan Tom McKinney became friends with like-minded Louisiana horsemen, especially Jeff Wells and Duncan Kenner. While it is impossible to know how often they made the steamship trip to New Orleans, it is safe to assume that when Texans wanted culture and entertainment as well as a few days at the races, they headed to the Crescent City. Texas had racing, but not the kind of racing seen at Metairie, nor the quality of horses running in New Orleans. Thoroughbreds from throughout the South came to New Orleans to test their speed.

Louisiana was where the famous mare Reel made her name. Foaled in 1838, she was sired by Glencoe at the plantation Forks of Cypress, Alabama, belonging to noted horse breeder James Jackson. Her dam was Gallopade. She produced three outstanding mares, Reel, Fandango, and Cotillion. Reel's first race was at Opelousas in November 1841, under the colors of Jeff Wells, who bought her as a yearling. Her owner took her to New Orleans where, in December, she came in first in front of four competitors. She continued to impress spectators with her speed the following year. But at five years old her leg gave way in a race and Wells decided to retire her, breeding her to Leviathan. After giving birth to three foals, she was sent to the Kentucky farm of J. R. Gross where she was boarded with the rest of Wells's horses. There she remained, producing a total of thirteen foals. All were fillies except three. Reel is considered one of the greatest broodmares of the nineteenth century; she passed on not only her speed but her color—eight of her foals were gray. Her connection to Texas was that she was the dam of War Dance, probably one of the best-bred stallions to spend time in the Lone Star State. When war broke out in 1861, Wells sent War Dance to his place in Texas for safekeeping.[45]

The 1840s saw the birth of two towns in North Texas that would eventually become major centers of horse racing in the last half of the nineteenth century. In the late 1830s John Neely Bryan, a native of Tennessee, settled on the banks of the Trinity River, and by 1841 founded a settlement that became the city of Dallas. In 1849, the US Army established Fort Worth on the West Fork of the Trinity River, although settlers had already moved into the area in the early 1840s. Soon other towns emerged where scrub tracks flourished, some of the better known were McKinney in Collin County, where William Davis donated land for a townsite in 1849. In Denton County, created in 1846, the town of Denton eventually became the county seat, and to the south of Dallas was Waxahachie, where Emory W. Rogers gave land to establish a seat for Ellis County in 1850. As more families moved west after the end of the war with Mexico, this region would develop a budding horse racing culture. Quarter running horses came with the new arrivals. Many of the animals that made the trip tied to wagons or ridden on well-beaten trails from the north had been foaled in the states of Tennessee and Kentucky and therefore often had

Thoroughbred blood, although few could claim to be purebreds. Racing was as important to the new arrivals as taming the land they now claimed as home. Thoroughbred racing would eventually be found in the Dallas-Fort Worth area, but the quarter running horse dominated early on.

As the decade ended, racing in Texas began to take on a new look. While Thoroughbred racing remained the choice of those who could afford bloodstock, sprints became increasingly popular among average Texans. Racing picked up again in the South after the lull caused by the economic crisis early in the decade and the war with Mexico in the later years, while the North continued to lag behind. In 1849, the Union Course in New York hosted only one regular race meeting of three days, and Pittsburgh fans saw only a handful. The ones in Pennsylvania were held in defiance of a state law that prohibited racing. Penalties could mean the seizure and confiscation of the horses. Opposition to racing, with its evil of gambling, spread throughout the Northeast. But in Texas, the number of short distance races increased. As new settlers headed for this land of opportunity they built homes, brought their livestock, and watched the line of settlement push westward. Informal races, always popular on the frontier, suited these new Texas farmers and stockmen who did not own expensive horses and did not build carefully prepared tracks. In the next decade, sprint racing became the chief equine amusement across the Lone Star State.

4

On the Way to War

The 1850s

Antebellum Texas had a strong southern influence in its character but with a definite western twist. Violence was part of a society where Comanches and Kiowas still raided the outlying settlements and new arrivals soon heard stories of horrific Indian attacks. While people in the larger towns began enjoying sophisticated cultural entertainments, horse racing remained the most popular sport. Texans loved the sacred trinity—racing, gambling, and drinking—and those closely connected pastimes could be found almost everywhere. Distance racing with Thoroughbreds dominated the tracks in the cities, while sprint racing remained popular on the frontier. As the population increased from 212,592 in 1850 to 604,215 ten years later, the line of settlement moved steadily westward determined to claim the land that the Plains Indians called their own. Tracks could be found in every new settlement. The sheer size of Texas meant every man owned a horse, and almost all were willing to test his steed's speed against any challenger.

Racing remained just as popular in the states to the east. In early 1850, the famous race horse Boston was found dead in his stall, but his last colts, foaled a few months later, included Lexington, a horse destined to influence the history of the American turf, and also Lecomte, Lexington's rival in the outstanding race of the decade. Lexington won his first two starts in 1853 under the name of Darley. Among the spectators was Richard Ten Broeck. He and his partners purchased Darley, renamed him Lexington, and shipped him to Natchez.

Lexington (1850–1875), who carried the blood of Sir Archy, sired War Dance, the famous Thoroughbred who spent the Civil War years at Tom McKinney's ranch near Austin to avoid confiscation by Union or Confederate troops. Henry William Hebert, *Frank Forrester's Horse and Horsemanship of the United States*, New York, 1857.

In 1854, promoters arranged a race at the Metairie course to settle the question of regional supremacy. Planned as one of the richest races of the era, the Great Post Stakes called for $5,000 subscriptions, with an additional $1,000 for each starter. Organizers invited every state to propose an entry, but on the day of the race, only four horses took to the track. Lexington represented Kentucky and his half-brother Lecomte ran for Mississippi. The other two, Highlander by Boston and Arrow by Glencoe were from Alabama and Louisiana, respectively.[1]

Lecomte's owner was Jeff Wells of Rapides Parish, Louisiana, a well-known breeder of Thoroughbreds who also owned land in Texas. He wanted his horse to represent Louisiana but Duncan Kenner's Arrow was the official entrant from that state. Wells arranged for Lecomte, whose dam was Reel and his sire was

Boston by Timoleon, to represent Mississippi instead. Wells once wrote that he would run Lecomte against "any horse in the world, any day, any distance, for any amount of money." Wells, born in 1806, was not only wealthy but benefited from social and political prestige. The Wells family owned two plantations in Louisiana—Wellswood and Dentley—south of Alexandria, and more than 200 slaves. He and his brother Montford ran Wellswood, one of the largest sugar cane plantations in the Bayou Boeuf region. Wells named the colt for his friend Ambrose Lecomte, who was a planter and horse breeder near Nachitoches. One way American Thoroughbreds differed from the British was in the naming. The British preferred using classical, mythological, or names from fiction, while Americans liked to name colts after family members, friends, or famous people. As a result, any "distinguished person of either sex who could not point to some high-mettled racer, famous sire or dam, bearing his or her name was to be numbered among the unpopular; while, on the other hand, hosts of men and women unknown to the public, if they happened to be on good terms with an owner, found it easy to achieve a namesake." In a twist on that American custom, the town of Lecompte, Louisiana, was named for the famous race horse and often the stallion's name is misspelled to match the town's misspelled name. Fans of Lecomte's rivals, probably plied with whiskey, mockingly called the horse "Lee Count."[2]

The race went off according to plan and everybody who was anybody, or wanted to be somebody, showed up. Some 20,000 attended. The track was heavy, and the time was slow, but Lexington won two straight four-mile heats. The headline in the *Spirit of the Times* read: "The Great Post Stake. Kentucky Victorious!" Following the victory, Lexington's trainer pulled the horse's shoes off with the intention of turning him out to pasture. But Ten Broeck insisted that the horse run again the following Saturday. In the argument that followed Ten Broeck bought out his partners for an undisclosed sum and matched his horse against Lecomte.[3]

Lecomte was in fine form for the race. For this match Wells hired the best trainer he could find, the well-known slave named Hark. He also thought a change of jockey would help. That jockey was Abe Hawkins, who became one of the most celebrated slave jockeys of all time. He belonged to Wells's friend Duncan Kenner, who paid $2,300 for him to ride his Thoroughbreds. On race day, around 10,000 people came to see the rematch. In the first heat, Lecomte took the lead at the start and held it to the end. In a desperate effort, Lexington's jockey applied whip and spur, but his efforts proved futile. Lecomte crossed the finish line ahead of his rival, covering the four miles in 7:26, a new record that was faster than the one set by Fashion in her match against Boston twelve years earlier. In the second heat, Lecomte repeated his performance, crossing the finish line four lengths ahead of Lexington. Texas turfmen certainly followed the Lecomte-Lexington rivalry because the influx of new settlers brought with them a knowledge of horses and an appetite for racing. The owner of Lecomte, Jeff Wells, was known to many Texans because of his Texas properties.[4]

But in the Lone Star State it was short-distance racing that remained popular in the newly settled regions. In 1857, there was a notable match in Lancaster between the horses of Alfred Bailes and a man named Haley. Lancaster, founded in 1852, was about fifteen miles south of Dallas and that was where Bailes brought a son of Brown Dick to run against Haley's gelding Gray Wonder. Haley was probably Thomas Franklin "Tom" Haley who was known for his eye for fine horses, many of which were iron gray. His farm was a little more than fifty miles southwest of Lancaster, in Johnson County, and traveling meant nothing to men who wanted to breed a mare or watch a good race.[5]

The Young Brown Dick-Gray Wonder rivalry in June attracted a large crowd of dedicated racegoers. Young Brown Dick was a two-year-old set to face Haley's gelding Gray Wonder on a straightaway track of 500 yards for $2,000 a side. Both horses arrived on the appointed day undefeated. According to an observer once the horses started at the word "Go," Brown Dick took an early lead and ran like "a small dog on high rye with two or more tin kettles tied to his tail." Gray Wonder closed the gap as the two neared the finish, but the distance of the race was too short (just over a quarter of a mile), and the gray gelding could not overtake Bailes's youngster. Haley took the loss in stride. As an experienced horseman he knew there would be another day and another chance to test Gray Wonder's speed.[6]

The Haleys were typical Southerners following the familiar routes of others before them as they slowly headed west. The Virginia Haleys fought against the British in the struggle for independence, but after the war the clan migrated across Alabama and Tennessee. Several of the Haleys arrived in Texas in time to fight in the Texas Revolution. In the early 1820s, Richard Haley lived in Shelby County on the Sabine River and sometime before 1850 Richard's father joined him as well as his brother Tom. Born in Tennessee in 1817, Tom Haley was a prosperous farmer by the time he matched Bailes in Lancaster and, like any good Southerner, brought a love of horses with him to his new home.[7]

Tom Haley moved across Texas looking for the right place to settle down, eventually selecting land near the Brazos River in an area still frequented by Comanches in southwestern Johnson County. He was a prosperous farmer, owning fifteen slaves in 1860. It is likely that the male slave who was forty-eight at the time of the race helped with the horses. Haley built a house not far from an old Indian trail that forded the Brazos River, a route that would eventually become a crossing for the Chisholm Trail. He built a racetrack where men, sometimes including cowboys on the cattle drives after the Civil War, came to match their horses and gamble money, land, cattle, or anything of value. Haley constructed a small shed used exclusively for betting at the end of the track where the hopeful gathered to place their wagers and bought whiskey before settling down to enjoy the day's offerings. Women were welcome to sit under the shade of the trees that surrounded the track or watch from carriages. When Haley first settled near the present site of Rio Vista, he brought with him a love and knowledge of fine horses that he not only carried until the end of his life, but his son Charley would continue his father's breeding and raising of quarter running horses and Thoroughbreds, having success with both.[8]

Haley's friend Shelby Stanfield also lived in Johnson County near the Brazos River (in 1866 that part of Johnson County became Hood County). Shelby and his brother Jake worked as stonemasons until they earned enough money to move upriver to the small settlement of Thorp Spring, where they raised race horses. The two brothers moved to Texas from Tennessee, although the family originally came from North Carolina, a region where quarter racing had been popular since colonial times. Shelby Stanfield raised many race horses, including Pid Hart (named for another horseman in Johnson County) and Rocky Mountain Tom. One mare, Corn Stalk, would not line up with another horse, so Stanfield matched her against a stopwatch instead. He was reportedly willing to bet any amount that she could beat twenty-three seconds, sometimes claiming twenty-two and one fourth seconds for a quarter mile, and he won $10,000 in that manner. Stanfield studied pedigrees and he often tried to locate new bloodlines to improve his stock.[9]

Alfred Bailes also entered his horses in races throughout Texas. In the early 1850s he won a court decision against a man named Compton in a lawsuit that arose after a race in Fort Bend County. Compton's horse failed to appear at the place designated for the race. Bailes rode his horse over the course alone, and earned the forfeit based on his loss of time, charges, and expenses incurred in preparation for the race. Bailes was often involved in lawsuits, but in one concerning a race in Williamson County, he lost the decision when it was proved that the parties previously agreed not to run the race. For that reason, there could be no forfeiture.[10]

Men who refused to accept track judges' decisions often sought satisfaction in the county or state courts. Lawsuits concerning disputed races were frequent, and in many instances court records provide the only information available as to the problems associated with them. They generally were the result of racing short-distance horses on small tracks. One example is a race at Canton in Smith County scheduled for August 23, 1851, between the horses of John Randolph and James Moore for $300, payable in property, but with the forfeit to be in cash. Before the race the two men changed the terms of the agreement so that the forfeit could be paid in property and the wager in cash. Randolph, whose horse lost, refused to pay, declaring "the note was given for an object illegal in its character, immoral in its tendency, and contrary to public policy in inducing intemperance and breaches of the peace."[11]

Randolph won but Moore appealed on the grounds that morality was not an issue in the legal question. He argued that even though "horse-racing tends to vice and immorality, breach of the peace, intemperance, &c.," that did not constitute a legal plea. Moore's lawyers pointed out that "many things tend to immorality . . . which, like horse racing, come not within the condemnation of the law." They maintained that it was strictly a legal question and that the jurymen made their "notions of morality the basis of a legal conclusion." The decision, therefore, should be reversed.[12]

William B. Ochiltree, lawyer and legislator, brilliantly defended Randolph. While Moore's lawyers pointed out that racing in England was a national pastime, Ochiltree reminded them that it was carried on in a style entirely different from racing in Texas. In England, he said, the racecourse was kept under rigid control. Rules and regulations were laid down for its participants that kept it a most agreeable sport. The annual Derby in England, therefore was enjoyed by every class, "from the palace to the hut of the chimney-sweeper."[13]

Ochiltree asserted, furthermore, that "the learned Judges over the Atlantic have but little conception of a quarter-race track in America." In the expressive language of Parson William G. Brownlow, he continued, "the quarter-race track is the shortest road to perdition that has yet been discovered, invariably resorted to by the idle and dissolute." Ochiltree did not stop here, adding that "its general concomitant [was] an oxcart and a barrel of whisky, out of the bung-hole of which flows one continuous stream of drunkenness and profanity of the most disgusting character." Brownlow was a well-known Methodist minister and newspaper editor in Tennessee who often made the headlines for his controversial stands on issues. Racing, as Ochiltree laid out his case, was a pastime contaminated by sin.[14]

Ochiltree found little positive to say about short distance racing as seen in Texas. "The argument," he asserted, "that it is calculated to improve the breed of horses, is only applicable to the regular turf-races such as the Derby that I have referred to. Diogenes himself would smile at the idea of such being the result could he but see the competitors in speed upon one of our quarter-race tracks, groomed by Simon Suggs and rode by—." This was a strong condemnation. Simon Suggs was the fictional creation of author Johnson J. Hooper, who published *Some Adventures of Captain Simon Suggs* in 1845. Suggs was an uncouth rascal, whose humorous escapades of pioneer days in Alabama made him famous. After pointing out what he considered the absurdity of some of the races on quarter tracks, Ochiltree declared that the "production of an Eclipse, a Boston, or a Lecomte, are of incalculable benefit, it is true, to the country at large." But of the better known short distance horses, he felt, the production of a Button or Snooks served absolutely no purpose.[15]

Ochiltree's appeal to the court was in vain, for Chief Justice Hemphill concluded that the laws could not fluctuate with the ebbs and flows of public opinion. He ruled that "the whims and caprices of the jury before whom they are presented" should have no bearing on the outcome of the decision, for the danger of a doctrine such as that was obvious. The judge upheld previous decisions that a note which was put up as a forfeit in case of failure to run a horse race was valid and binding on the makers. He added that it was an error to submit to a jury the question of whether or not a contract was contrary to public policy, since their office was not legislative, it was judicial. "It is the duty of both Judges and juries to decide on rights according to the laws of the land, and not on their belief of what ought to be the law." He concluded that the second contract between Randolph and Moore should be upheld. This was not an unusual case, but the rising sentiment against gambling on horse racing was significant.[16]

In the 1850s many Texas breeders upgraded their animals hoping to produce that Eclipse, Boston, or Lecomte that Ochiltree mentioned, and finely bred horses could be found in various parts of the state. Dr. George Feris of Fort Bend County said that his stimulus to improve his breeding stock came during the last battle of the Mexican War. Feris rode a horse by Medoc by American

Eclipse. The mount's first dam was by Amurath, an Arabian stallion brought from Nubia to Tripoli, then to New York. The second dam was by Stamboul, a stallion that he selected from Sultan Mahomoud's Stables in Constantinople and presented to the United States minister. As was customary with such gifts, he was sold for the benefit of the government. Feris remembered the horse he rode in battle "for style, courage and endurance," and that "he took the palm from all others . . . until he was "unfortunately killed by a lance thrust at the battle of Buena Vista." Feris said that he "knew how to appreciate the value of my lost comrade and conceived the idea of supplying my country with the same noble race."[17]

With this idea in mind, Feris said an "interview was arranged between my cousin A. K. Richards and myself at New Orleans to discuss the matter and took place during race week of the Old Metaire [Metairie] Club" in 1855. Richards, recently returned from a trip to Arabia, was enthusiastic about Arabian horses. This meeting with Richards included several other prominent

Dr. George A. Feris thought Thoroughbreds could be improved by crossing with Arabians. He visited the Middle East to find stallions to bring to Texas. L. E. Daniell, *Types of Successful Men of Texas* (Austin: Eugene Von Boeckmann, 1890).

turfmen of the South. All of these breeders, Feris recalled, "except Richards and myself vigorously opposed the fresh importation of Arabians and cited English writers to prove the failure of Oriental lines since the Godolphin and Darley era." Richards and Feris came prepared, however, and "We met this by showing that all (English) importations of modern date were commercial speculations and managed by unscrupulous men who knew no more about horses than I do about Federal politics." Despite objections, Richards went to Arabia again in search of desert-bred horses. This time he was accompanied by his cousin, Morris H. Keene of Kentucky, and Edward Troye, an artist renowned for his portraits of Thoroughbreds.[18]

The trio were gone fourteen months. Among the horses that they brought back from Arabia was Hamdan, a two-year-old gray colt. Richards purchased Hamdan from the sheik of a tribe of Bedouins, whose family had raised the line for more than 300 years. Feris brought him to Fort Bend County in 1859, but the stallion died the same year. "I regard his premature death as a public calamity," Feris wrote. "He was 15 hands high, with the finest head, neck, shoulders, loin and legs I ever saw, but was too light in the quarters. . . . His descendants should be crossed with the heavy muscled *Glencoes*."[19]

Probably to replace Hamdan, in 1860 Feris bought Abd-el-Kadir, a gray horse by Richards's imported Arabian stallion Moklhadi. Known as the "Feris Arabian," his colts were sold to Mexican stockmen for high prices. Druse, a gray colt, sold for $1,600, and Sheik, a two-year-old, brought $3,000. Abd-el-Kadir stood in Texas until his death in 1866 when he drowned in the Brazos River. Feris remembered that Abd-el-Kadir "was my choice of all the stallions" he owned. He "made his mark in Texas by his produce. He was 'par excellence'" and "the grand gentleman of his race."[20]

A long-time Thoroughbred breeder Tom McKinney also continued to raise some of the best Thoroughbreds on his ranch near Austin, and many of his stallions can be found in *The American Stud Book*. Jim Allen, by imported Priam, was one of his most successful studs, and one of Jim Allen's sons, Lytle, was also popular. McKinney was partial to the Monarch bloodline. West

Monarch, stabled in Texas in the 1850s, was the sire of Regent, whose dam was Ella Boston by Boston. McKinney's horses grazed in pastures with stone fences and his trainer, South Carolinian John Van Hagen, lived in a cabin constructed of stone nearby. A two-room structure, built in the early 1850s, Van Hagen's cabin served as the center of the horse raising facilities and its ruins can still be seen at McKinney Falls State Park. There was also a training track, where races took place until war broke out in 1861.[21]

McKinney's horses were very active during the decade before the war. In 1854, the Austin City Jockey Club formed in the state capital and their course, described as "one of the most beautiful in the State," was where his followers could see McKinney's horses run. Van Hagen announced in December 1854 that he planned to accept the challenge of A. B. Burleson to match his bay colt, Thomas A. Moore by Albert Gallatin, against Van Hagen's two-year-old colt Vanthagen over the Austin city course for one mile and repeat. This race

Thomas F. "Tom" McKinney, known as the Father of Texas Thoroughbreds, raised race horses at his home near Austin. He also built a track on his property. Texas State Library and Archives, Austin, Texas.

would be under the rules of the Austin City Jockey Club for $500 or $1,000 and run anytime during May 1855. Unfortunately, there is no information on how this race turned out. Van Hagen also raced McKinney-owned horses at the jockey club track frequently. Without a doubt, McKinney and Van Hagen raced at every meet of the Austin City Jockey Club, but no extant newspapers prove their participation.[22]

An article in *The State Gazette* in Austin in May 1860 summed up McKinney's pre-war contribution to breeding and racing by saying, "For many years, Mr. Thos. F. McKinney, has turned his attention to raising thorough bred horses, and his success on the race track has enabled him to sell at a round figure, such as he was willing to put in the market. Who that witnessed the performance of SAM PATCH, JUDITH and other JIM ALLEN colts on the Austin track last fall, could doubt their ability to meet the best bloods in the older States. SAM PATCH has been purchased by a gentleman who has taken him to New Orleans, where his speed will be tested with the crack nags of the South, over the Metairie Course." McKinney's farm, a few miles from Austin, "has on it many colts of fine promise that will be ready for the fall races. . . . We have no doubt but that he will heartily join us in the invitation to the turfmen to bring up their best nags and a heap of e'm." Furthermore, at "the head of Mr. McKinney's long list of thorough-breds stands JIM ALLEN, by imported Priam, dam, Miss Wilkins. This distinguished race horse was bred by Col. Meriwither, of Kentucky, and made a brilliant turf record." McKinney also owned Ellen Butler, Mary Jordan, and a Glencoe mare, "whose running record in the old States equalled that of any racer of their day."[23]

The *Gazette* also praised local breeders: "We are very much gratified to find that the people of Western Texas are taking a deep interest in the improvement of stock, and we can now boast of having as many fine blooded horses as any State in the Union.—There is no country in the world better adapted to the raising of thorough bred horses . . . than the Western portion of Texas. The rich prairie grasses for summer feeding, and the mild winters, enables our stock raisers to bring it to market at much less expense than can be done in the older States. And if proper attention is paid to crossing, Texas must at an early day supply a large portion of the Northern States with horses, mules, &c, and people should bear in mind, that it is just as easy to raise a fine blooded horse or mule as a *pitching* Spanish pony." The writer, of course, still saw Austin as on the western frontier, and the wild feral horses on the Texas plains as Spanish ponies.[24]

Texas claimed several breeders of note. One in Central Texas was Burwell J. Thompson. Thompson was a sixty-eight-year-old native of South Carolina who listed his real estate at almost $65,000 and personal estate at around $53,000 in 1860. He was a wealthy planter, owning seventy-two slaves. His stable was eight miles east of Waco where he stood Grey Eagle, a son of old Grey Eagle whose sire Woodpecker traced back to Sir Archy. His dam was by the British import Barefoot. In the late 1850s Col. S. A. Atchison brought the young stallion from Kentucky to the Lone Star State. Grey Eagle was "a beautiful dappled gray" seven years old and standing sixteen hands high. Thompson offered his stud for a fee of $25 with mares pastured and grain fed, if required.[25]

The Austin paper ran an advertisement for the races in Waco in April 1855. It noted that there was a jockey club and that "everything will be properly conducted." The club did not write its own rules but adopted the rulebook of the Metairie course in New Orleans. The track "was situated in a beautiful and almost level spot. A horse can be seen at every jump all the way round from a slight elevation. The soil is light—of a reddish color and has an admixture of sand. It will not become very hard in dry nor very muddy in wet weather. Preparations are being made for the accommodation of man and beast. Eating house and stables will be erected and ready for use. . . . To those fond of amusement and sporting of this kind Waco will, no doubt, offer inducements."[26]

The secretary of the Waco Jockey Club was George Barnard. Born in Connecticut in 1818, Barnard was a colorful character. Indian trader and merchant, he arrived in Galveston in 1838. In the 1840s he and his brother Charles set up a trading post near Comanche Peak in present-day Hood County. Despite the US Army's best efforts to remove the tribes to reservations, he may have supplied Indians with both liquor and firearms in exchange for undressed deer skins that he shipped to northern merchants. By the early 1850s Barnard transferred his operation to Waco where, it seems, he became involved in the local jockey club.[27]

Texas horsemen continued to upgrade their stock and three stallions imported into the United States from England before the Civil War influenced their breeding programs. Bonnie Scotland, foaled in 1853 and imported in 1857, was the first of the trio. Standing over sixteen hands high, he would influence not only Thoroughbreds of his day, but also what eventually became the American Quarter Horse. He was judged the "greatest sire ever to stand at Belle Meade," the plantation of William Giles Harding near Nashville, Tennessee. Belle Meade, Harding wrote to the *American Turf Register* in 1836, was "the acknowledged centre of the race horse region. . . . Blood stock here is all the go. To be without it is to be out of fashion and destitute of taste." Harding would buy Bonnie Scotland in 1872 and in 1880, the year Bonnie Scotland died, his colts won 137 races, passing the record of Lexington and establishing him as the leading sire of that year. He also sired exceptional short distance horses, and many famous twentieth-century quarter horses trace to him. Among these were Pan Zarita, Joe Blair, Joe Reed, and Carrie Nation.[28]

The second arrival, Australian, reached America in 1858 as a foal with his dam after Keene Richards asked Richard Ten Broeck to locate a Thoroughbred stallion in England for his Kentucky stud farm. A colt by West Australian was the choice. During the Civil War, however, Richards was unable to remove this stallion from Kentucky to prevent confiscation by Union or Confederate armies, and asked his friend, R. A. Alexander, the owner of Lexington, to take him in because Alexander was a British citizen. The third and last import to arrive before war broke out was Eclipse in 1859, whose influence was also far-reaching.[29]

Planet, foaled in 1855, was known as the "best horse produced in America between Lexington and the Civil War," but the bombardment of Fort Sumter in April 1861 ended racing throughout the South, and thus the career of Planet. He earned $69,700, winning twenty-seven of thirty-one races and placing second in the other four, displacing Peytona as America's leading money winner. *The Texas Annual* of 1878 noted that William Copeland Phillips's Elmonia Stock Farm northwest of Austin boasted of a string of Thoroughbreds that included Foddie Pope by Planet and Silent Friend by imported Australian.[30]

While Texans with the means and money continued to raise and race blooded horses, scrub races involving short distance horses prospered in the years before the war. The *Dallas Herald* observed in November 1858 that "scrub racing, gambling, 'bust head' and rowdyism have reigned supreme in Bonham several days. We venture to say that Dallas has more cause to boast exemption from each and all these vices than any town in the State." Boast they might, but scrub racing was alive and well in the region around Dallas and Fort Worth. Only the coming threat of war would curb the enthusiasm and rambunctious behavior that often accompanied these lively gatherings.[31]

Throughout the state the sentiment for secession was increasing. In the elections of 1857 and 1859, Sam Houston made secession a major issue. Houston, although a Southerner and a slaveowner, was a staunch anti-secessionist, but John Brown's raid on Harpers Ferry, Virginia, in 1859 provoked many Texas editors to espouse the cause of the South. In 1860, Texas voters favored the southern Democratic nominee John C. Breckinridge for the nation's presidency. Texas was now under the control of uncompromising secessionist leaders, and the increasing radicalism of the abolitionists heightened public sentiment for leaving the Union.

Still, the decade before the Civil War produced some of the most famous race horses Texas produced in the nineteenth century. The quarter horse, a horse of many talents, was becoming more common than the Thoroughbred. Many late nineteenth-century quarter horses traced back to three famous short-distance sires: Steel Dust, Shiloh, and Old Billy. They were relatively small and compact.

Short-legged and muscular, the early quarter horse could adapt to both daily work and weekend races on a quarter mile track. Averaging about fourteen hands three inches tall and weighing from 1,000 the 1,200 pounds they had good heads and large jaws. The bulldog or Steel Dust type had small ears and distinctly heavy jaws that tilted out. The best of the breed was of a recognizable type and shared common ancestors. The stories of those ancestors were handed down through the generations, so there is no way to authenticate these tales. The folklore surrounding these three horses made its way into the historical record and is accepted as fact. Newspapers typically only carried results of jockey club meets and local races did not often make it into print. That the owners of Steel Dust, Shiloh, and Old Billy were well-known horse breeders, there is no doubt. There are verifiable facts to prove their existence. And while these three horses also clearly existed, their stories are the stories as told by old-timers who heard them from their fathers and grandfathers.

Because few firsthand accounts describe these three stallions, separating fact from folklore proves difficult. Their names appear in the pedigrees of later race horses throughout the state as seen in articles in local newspapers, thus giving credibility to their widespread influence, but there is little existing primary evidence to authenticate their breeding. Steel Dust would become the most famous of the trio. Ranchman Frank Hastings, who was born in 1860, later observed: "I often think that old Steel Dust must turn over in his grave when his blood is made responsible for some of the broom-tails tacked onto him. It is still a name to conjure with, but almost every horse trader who has not recently joined the church or been rescued from backsliding will declare that his line of equine stock is largely Steel Dust in its breeding. There have been some outstanding Steel Dust stallions used in Texas, but for the most that blood has gone into cow bunch outfits through grade stallions."[32]

Steel Dust arrived in Texas in 1844 as a yearling. The stallion's owners, Jones Greene and Middleton Lee Perry, reportedly paid a high price for him before they moved their families from Illinois to a settlement on the east bank of the Trinity River not far from the village of Dallas. Both men grew up in southern Illinois. Perry, born in Indiana in 1814, was the son of a stonemason from Virginia. His wife Ellen Malinda was the daughter of Thomas McKee Ellis and Mary Witt Ellis. The Perry family moved from Virginia to Indiana before settling in Greene County, Illinois. Middleton, or Mid, visited Texas in 1837. He probably stopped at the home of the brother of his future mother-in-law, who had previously moved to Texas, and settled just south of the Red River in Lamar County. Mid liked the Republic and returned to Illinois for his family.[33]

Jones Greene's family moved from Kentucky to Illinois where they met the Perrys. Born in 1817 in Illinois, Greene married Mary Ann Ellis in 1844, shortly before they left for Texas. She was the younger sister of Perry's wife, Ellen, and arriving in Lamar County after a five-week journey, Ellen and Mary Ann remained with their Uncle Witt in Lamar County while their husbands rode south to look for land. The pair knew they could buy land cheaply in the Republic as the government was handing out big grants to its soldiers. In turn, these veterans were selling good land for twenty-five to fifty cents an acre. By 1845, the two families bought some of the prime land on Ten Mile Creek near the village of Hard Scrabble in Dallas County. They built homes, and the next year were joined by their in-laws Thomas and Mary Ellis and the rest of the family.[34]

The area in which they settled was virgin land for American settlers. John Neely Bryan set up a trading post on the east side of the Trinity River near a natural ford in 1841, and this became the small town of Dallas as more settlers moved to the region. Hard Scrabble was around fifteen miles south. It was a tiny settlement started by Roderick Rawlins from Illinois that attracted settlers from his home state. About the time the Perry and Greene clans arrived Rawlins founded Lancaster nearby and named it in honor of the place of his birth, Lancaster, Kentucky. Ten Mile Creek provided homes with water and the rolling hills with rich black soil proved fertile. Perry and Greene each bought 320 acres on Ten Mile Creek and an additional headright of 320 acres. The Ellis family also acquired 640 acres nearby.[35]

Perry and Greene had high hopes for a new life and for the colt they brought to Texas. They knew they had bought a fine young stallion in the one that trotted behind their wagon on the long trek from Illinois. Steel Dust developed quickly, standing larger than average between fifteen and sixteen hands high and weighing more than 1,100 pounds. He was short-coupled and compact, with bulging jaws and sharp little ears. Heavily muscled, he had the body of a sprinter, although the family primarily used him as a saddle horse. But with racing in mind, the new arrivals soon built a track across from the Ellis home.[36]

Frontier families worked hard, yet they found time for recreation—shooting matches, cockfighting, picnics, house raising, which could be a social event, but especially racing. The informal track laid out across the road from the Ellis place was the scene of many scrub races. Like others in the new land, it was a quarter mile straight track. Located on a flat prairie near a small oak grove, the women could enjoy lunch under the trees while watching the men match their horses. Steel Dust ran his first races on this track, and here he developed a reputation for blazing speed. Spectators came from miles around to see local champions challenged. Families might even spend the day watching the races. Each race was over in less than half a minute, but large sums of money changed hands as well as cattle, horses, land, and slaves.

Judges used various methods to start a match race. One, "ask and answer," involved the starter asking "Are you ready?" When hearing "Yes," he would shout "Go!" Another, called "lap and tap," began after the horses were led about fifty feet back of the starting line, the judge "tapped them off" by shouting "Go!" If too far apart, they began again. One common method was a pistol shot, but for important races in larger towns, chutes built of narrow wooden poles served as the starting gates in an effort to give each entry an even chance. Betting was informal and the owners of the two horses usually worked out their own agreements. The starting and finishing points might be something as simple as a tree.

The reputation of Steel Dust spread throughout North Texas. His fame finally led to a challenge from the owner of another fast horse in Collin County, bordering Dallas County on the north. Monmouth, a high-strung bay standing more than sixteen hands tall, won many races in Kentucky before he arrived at McKinney, thirty miles north of Dallas, on Christmas Day 1850. His owner, Harrison Stiff, was a thirty-year-old recent arrival from Breckinridge County, Kentucky, and migrated to Texas after receiving favorable reports from a brother and nephew who preceded him to Collin County. Nothing is known of Monmouth's breeding, but having come from Kentucky it is safe to say that he carried a large dose of Thoroughbred blood. Stiff traveled by riverboat to Alexandria, Louisiana, where his prized horse was injured while being unloaded. The injury kept Monmouth from competing for a time, but when he finally recovered, he acquired a reputation for speed similar to that gained by Steel Dust south of Dallas. A clash between the two was the only way to satisfy the backers of each. There was also a touch of regional pride associated with each entry.[37]

This would be a North-South race—Texas style—meaning a horse north of Dallas would compete against a horse from south of Dallas. It would bring supporters of each location together to pull for their town's entry and at the same time place wagers that their horse would come out victorious. McKinney was not quite as old as Lancaster. Settlers moved to McKinney just a little later than those around Lancaster and it became the seat of Collin County in 1849. It drew its name from a signer of the Texas Declaration of Independence, Collin McKinney, who also proposed the bill to form the counties in North Texas. William Davis, who owned 3,000 acres, offered 120 for the townsite. The terrain was different from that south of Dallas, the land slightly flatter but still attractive to new settlers from the United States.

The traditional date given for the Steel Dust-Monmouth race is 1855. It was to happen in McKinney and promised to be one of the largest events ever on the Texas frontier. The exact dates of races are impossible to verify, but what is known is that the Steel Dust-Monmouth match was the most anticipated event of its day. The reputation of both horses was well known, and there were rumors that Monmouth could "go faster than a rush telegram on a downhill wire." The Foote House, a local hotel, accommodated the women exclusively where thirty-two women shared the hotel's four rooms. The owner opened a barrel of whiskey on the porch of a neighbor's log cabin and sold a glass full for twenty-five cents. Whiteley's Saloon also kept busy, for it took seven bartenders to serve drinks. A quick nip before the race was part of the attraction. Officials closed the courts in both Sherman and Jefferson to allow people ample time to attend the event. Harrison Stiff had married Mary Ann Nelson, and although she did not approve of racing, she gratefully accepted the money it brought home.[38]

Preparation for the race included finding the right jockey for Steel Dust. Thirteen-year-old Henry Ellis was promised that he could ride the stallion, and he practiced running him every day on the track across from his home. But when his mother learned that the race was to be on Sunday, she piously refused to let him participate. Replaced by Tom McKnight, a black jockey, young Henry, of course, was not happy that he would have to watch as a spectator. McKnight, an experienced jockey, smeared Steel Dust's back and sides with blackstrap molasses to help him keep his seat. This was not uncommon on the frontier, because any trick to help the horse or rider gain an advantage was allowed, just so long as the other owner did not object.

News of the upcoming race spread widely, and the crowd that traveled from Lancaster was vocal in its support of Steel Dust. Led into town guarded by half a dozen men, Steel Dust appeared quiet, almost lazy, to the Monmouth supporters. One Collin County resident jeered that the Dallas County men better do something fast to wake up their horse before race time. Residents did not have the least doubt that Monmouth would prevail. Probably to eliminate any charge of foul play, Stiff generously provided a stall for Steel Dust on his own farm in the New Hope community near McKinney. New Hope, also established in the early 1850s was small, consisting of only a school and church to serve the community. It was around three miles east of McKinney. Both sides, however, took no chances before the race, and kept the horses under close guard.[39]

Race day was everything the fans expected. George A. Wilson, who attended the race, recalled that although there were not more than 5,000 in the whole of Collin County, it seemed that twice that number lined the track. From his vantage point he saw J. W. Throckmorton, later governor of the state, wave his hat to signal the start. McKinney citizens had cleared a straightaway track that measured a full mile. Since there were few other events in this sparsely settled area of Texas, businesses closed in nearby towns so anyone who wanted to attend the race could. While Monmouth was a miler, Steel Dust only ran quarter mile races. The compromise was for a half-mile distance. This was probably one of the largest crowds to witness a match race in Texas before the Civil War. Men, women, children, slaves, and anyone else in the vicinity lined the street that served as the course. Starting time was set for early afternoon.[40]

The two horses appeared ready to run. Both stallions enjoyed a large crowd of supporters escorting them on their way to the track. Arriving at the starting line, Steel Dust no longer appeared lethargic, but was energetic and lively. After much preparation and excited betting, the jockeys maneuvered their mounts to the starting line. As they broke away, Steel Dust and Monmouth sprinted down a hill neck and neck, then disappeared into a draw. Spectators began to climb trees to get a view of the horses, but before they succeeded the two animals came into sight over a rise. Monmouth was taking gigantic strides, but Steel Dust made two jumps to Monmouth's one. Wilson recalled: "Steel Dust was on the left with the little Negro boy lying squat down on his back. Bob (Rudolph) was thrashing Monmouth but I could not see that the Negro boy was doing anything to Steel Dust. Before we could think, they were at the finish line. Steel Dust three lengths in front. Steel Dust turned sharp off the track and plowed to a stop. Old Monmouth kept right on and ran into the thicket, sweeping Bob off his back (the riders rode bareback) and disappearing from view, crashing off down in the woods. I think everybody in the county lost something,"

Wilson glumly concluded. "I was lucky. I only bet a pair of saddle bags but John lost a cow and a mule." The celebrations lasted long after sunset. "There was a heap of cutting up in town that night," he remembered, "but mostly by the Dallas crowd. Most of us slunk off home, poorer but wiser."[41]

One of those who made the trip to McKinney with the Steel Dust backers was John "Jack" Batchler. Batchler moved from Tennessee to Rusk County, Texas, but early in 1855 he relocated to Bear Creek in the southern edge of Dallas County. Two years later he moved to another Bear Creek farm at Bluff Springs in Ellis County just a few miles away. He was a blacksmith by trade and interested in horse racing. He soon made the acquaintance of both Perry and Greene.[42]

One important point of note: the original spelling of Jack Batchler's name was Batchelor and that is how it appears in nineteenth century newspapers and correspondence. But the current family modified the spelling to Batchler and that is how he is identified in modern books about quarter horses, particularly those by the authority on quarter horses, Bob Denhardt. The author will adhere to Batchler to avoid confusion, but it can be seen as Batchelor in quotes.[43]

Steel Dust returned home with his reputation enhanced, but Perry apparently used him only as a stud. He was much older than the average race horse, and normally this would have reduced his ability to win. But when Alfred Bailes, the well-known horse racer, challenged Batchler to a race, the latter was training Steel Dust. Bailes, who raised short distance horses in the Seguin area, was prominent in racing circles. His reputation preceded him on quarter mile tracks, and Batchler wanted the best horse available, so he asked Steel Dust's owners if he could run the stallion. Bailes planned to race his stallion, Brown Dick. A descendant of Bailes wrote in the late 1930s that on a track two miles west of Lancaster the "Unbeatable Brown Dick went down in defeat," beaten by a much older horse. Moreover, there was a quarrel between Jack Lilley and another man over the outcome of the race and during the night, while Lilley slept, he was murdered by an unknown assailant. Such was frontier racing.[44]

Steel Dust was well known in North Texas, and his fame slowly spread when turfmen raced his descendants throughout the state after the Civil War. A rancher in Coke County in West Texas wrote: "We have some very fine running horses here. In this part of the State we have a breed called Steel Dust, that are very fast for one-fourth to one-half mile." Coke County, north of San Angelo, was still largely unsettled when this letter to the editor appeared in the *Abilene Reporter* in 1892. The writer went on to say that this was "one of the best horse countries in the world" where wild horses could still be found. Our "range horses have never been fed an ear of corn or a pound of hay—they hustle their living on the range. With proper feed and care they improve very fast." These range horses, when crossed with Steel Dust descendants, often became the animal that cowboys rode to drive the cattle to market.[45]

Although bred to many mares, only a few of Steel Dust's colts can be verified, but his blood is found in Peter McCue, Rondo, Billy, and Colt Deck offspring. Well-known horseman Jim Brown owned a Steel Dust filly, Pat, whose best distance was 600 yards, but she was killed in a railroad boxcar while being shipped to Brenham. Others of Steel Dust's verifiable offspring owned by Brown were Gray Alice and Rebel, the latter a stallion that was a successful race horse and later as a stud. In addition, Henry Batchler raised Tom Driver, a son of Steel Dust out of a Shiloh mare.

It seems impossible for Steel Dust to have sired all the horses that breeders claimed were his offspring. There were other stallions of similar Kentucky Whip-Sir Archy breeding, and their descendants undoubtedly claimed Steel Dust lineage. But such was his fame that the name Steel Dust was almost synonymous with quarter running horses all throughout the Southwest. The impact Steel Dust had in North Texas was phenomenal. As his fame spread, horsemen throughout Texas bought any animal alleged to carry the Steel Dust stamp. His progeny showed an ability to work cattle as well as run, so Steel Dust breeding suited the needs of Texas cattlemen. These horses moved into the western United States with the cattle drives of the late nineteenth century. Organizers of the AQHA understood the modern quarter horse owed much of his renown to Steel Dust—a horse that left his stamp on the breed. As for his owners, Mid Perry and Jones Greene, they were destined to head for war a few years after the famous match race. Perry would come home from that war, Greene would die before it ended. The Confederate cannons that fired on Fort Sumter in Charleston Harbor in April 1861 heralded the beginning of four long years of conflict, years in which Texas breeding and horse racing suffered significant setbacks.

Steel Dust was not the only North Texas stallion of note. Jack Batchler also owned a fine race horse, Shiloh, that he thought was fast enough to test any challenger. It is not known why he borrowed his neighbor's horse to match Bailes, but there could be any number of reasons why Shiloh was unavailable. Shiloh traced back to Sir Archy, having been foaled in Tennessee in 1844. Shiloh was impressive and considered by many to be the finest horse they had ever seen. He was not very tall and was described as a dark bay with a black mane and tail. It was not long before the owners of Steel Dust and Shiloh arranged a match on the track at the eastern edge of Dallas.[46]

Jack Batchler's son Henry, a boy of seven, recalled that on the day of a scheduled race between Steel Dust and Shiloh late in 1855, Steel Dust was so anxious to start that he reared and struck the side of the wooden chute constructed for the start, running a splinter into his shoulder that disabled him. Batchler rode Shiloh over the track and claimed the forfeit. One of the bets that Batchler won was a gold watch with the initials "J. B." inscribed on the back. Passed down through each generation of the Batchler family, the watch still serves the family as a reminder of the early days of Texas quarter horse racing.[47]

A race between Steel Dust and Shiloh never happened. Steel Dust, like his famous ancestors Timoleon and Boston, was going blind, possibly accounting for his trouble entering the starting chute. The question of which horse, Shiloh or Steel Dust, was the fleetest remained unanswered. Steel Dust never raced again. Shiloh continued to compete for many more years and, like Steel Dust, sired many fast quarter horses. Only one time would their names appear in print together and it was not the famed Steel Dust, but one of his colts. At the Ellis County Agricultural Association First Annual Fair at Waxahachie in mid-September 1858 in Class 11 on the first day the best harness stallion, aged, was "John Bachelor's [*sic*] horse Shiloh." Also in Class 11 the "Best 2 years old stallion" went to Mid Perry's "Steel Dust colt."[48]

At the outbreak of the Civil War, Mid Perry formed a company of cavalry for the Confederacy, and many of the old-timers recalled the soldiers left for war mounted on Steel Dust and Shiloh horses. One man recalled that his father told him that he and a friend rode Steel Dust colts. "Whenever they were shifted to another command, they would match their horses in quarter races. As a result, they always had more money than they could spend."[49]

Shiloh remained in the Batchler family until his death about 1874, which would mean he lived to around thirty. He died after engaging in battle with a younger stallion, and the family buried him in their pasture on Bear Creek. Steel Dust's last years are shrouded in mystery. One account says that the great horse was buried on Mid Perry's farm in 1864; another relates that he was sold for $1,000 to a man who lived near Hillsboro; while still another tells that he was sold for $400 or $500 to a Bill Raburn and ended up in Hood County. Raburn's son said his father sold the stallion to noted horse racer and trainer Jim Brown and he died in South Texas. While there is no way to know which story is true, Brown was known for the Steel Dust colts he raced, and also as a man who bought any horse he thought would improve his racing stock.[50]

The third of the trinity was Billy, often called Old Billy. The history of Shiloh and Steel Dust is well-documented, but that of Billy and his owner is not as easy to pin down. Both Steel Dust and Shiloh earned their reputation in the Dallas area, but Billy, a Steel Dust-Shiloh cross, became famous in southwest Texas in the Guadalupe County/Gonzales County area. The only description of him says he was fourteen and three-quarters hands tall, weighed around 1,000 pounds, and was a dark bay. Sired by Shiloh, his dam was Ram Cat, a daughter of Steel Dust. Billy, foaled about the time the Civil War started, probably came from the Dallas-Lancaster area, but nothing is known about his first owner. According to tradition, his original owner went off to war and left the colt chained to a tree to prevent confiscation by the Confederate government or perhaps because of a fear he might be stolen by horse thieves in the area. The story goes that the colt was in bad shape when his owner returned (or failed to return) at the end of the war. The young stallion had a scar on his neck from the chain that never grew hair again, and his hooves were so long they needed to be sawed off when another Confederate veteran, William "Bill" Fleming, bought him for a reported $580.[51]

Bill (or Billy) Fleming is another name to add to the list of men associated with significant horses in Texas. Born in Georgia in 1830, he moved from there to Mississippi then Texas around 1850. Joining the Texas Rangers, he fought Comanches before going off to fight Union soldiers. He enlisted in the Texas cavalry and was wounded, returning home with an arm and hand so damaged that he was unable to use it again. He may have been passing through the Dallas area when he bought Billy, but his home in 1870 was Guadalupe County in southern Texas. In 1871 he moved to Gonzales County and in partnership with Charles Erasmus Littlefield purchased land on the Guadalupe River at Belmont. He built a dog run style house of black walnut logs and its remnants can still be seen today.[52]

Fleming became a noted breeder after the war. His brand was an ace of clubs. Although friends thought he never married, the 1880 census shows a W. B. junior, with W. B. senior listing himself as a widower. The son disappears from the census, and Fleming remained single the rest of his life. He turned all his attention to raising horses instead. Billy would be the most famous stallion he owned, siring many fast quarter horses in the last half of the nineteenth century. Some of the best foals were when he was bred to the mare Paisana by Brown Dick. At one point Fleming sold eleven horses to some Mexican gamblers for $40,000, but the men lost them in a cockfight the night they reached Mexico. Known locally as "Uncle Billy," he decided at age seventy-seven he was too old to take care of his horses alone and he sold six mares and a stallion, Little John Moore, to his friend William Matthies, a German-speaking immigrant who lived in Texas since coming there with his mother. As Fleming had no family he eventually moved in with Matthies and his family and lived with them until he died in 1911. He was buried in the Matthies cemetery.[53]

From South Texas to the Red River horse breeding prospered in the 1850s. Thirteen miles east of Clarksville in Red River County, A. J. Titus offered at stud Hector, a "beautiful" mahogany bay with black legs, mane, and tail. A full sixteen and a half hands high, he was by imported Priam and his dam traced to Eclipse. In the town of Clarksville, the stallion George Bender was advertised as standing at stud. He was by the celebrated horse Pacific and his dam was by Pacolet. Another, Young Jordan by imported Jordan, was brought from Kentucky to the stable of Capt. Andrew Stapp near McKinney. Young Jordan, purchased by a company for $2,500, was out of Pocahontas. Sired by Sir Archy, Pocahontas brought a reported $15,000 when retired from the turf. Young Jordan was sixteen hands high and a "beautiful red sorrel" that was "very handsome and gay." This is just a small sample of the many advertisements that ran in local newspapers.[54]

By the time the decade ended Mid Perry, Jones Greene, Jack Batchler, Alfred Bailes, Bill Fleming, Tom McKinney, Tom Haley, Jim Brown, and George Feris were among the well-known men frequently seen on the racing and show circuit. In December 1858, the *Dallas Herald* announced the organization of the Dallas County Agricultural and Mechanical Association with plans for a fair the following year. Greene served on the board of directors. Mid Perry and Jones Greene exhibited horses in the show. The Ellis County Agricultural and Mechanical Association also held a fair in 1859, and some of the men who brought entries were Greene, Perry, and Batchler. These names appeared time and again in the press and these men would become legends in the history of the American Quarter Horse. While they started with horses bred for both work and show, it was clear that they were beginning to see their breeding programs as a business. Besides raising horses to race, they sold their animals to the public for use on the farm and in town. In the 1850s, horses often still doubled as the one both men and women rode for pleasure.[55]

The trio of Steel Dust, Shiloh, and Old Billy could be found in some of the best short-distance runners of the mid-to-late nineteenth century. There was no registry at this time, the quarter horse was not yet a recognized breed, but as with other breeds, there was a consistency of conformation and ability. This type of horse was both fast and ready to work on a farm or ranch when needed. The characteristics that men looked for at this time were an ability to live off the land and a rugged power that could be used in day-to-day work or simply as a saddle horse. Speed and endurance were essential, especially when tracking hostile Comanches on the western frontier. When the Civil War came this is the type of horse that many Texans rode as they left home to go to war—an all-purpose animal that easily adapted to the environment.

Horse racing prospered in Texas in the antebellum days, but the Civil War disrupted and reshaped the history of the American turf, including that of the Lone Star State. In the four decades prior to the war, Texas horse racing had grown from an infant industry to a widely popular sport. Antebellum racing in Texas is recorded in scattered newspapers and court records, which are generally fragmentary and incomplete. Jockey club journals and registers, official summaries of meetings, private stud books and breeding memoranda, ledgers and accounts, correspondence and other personal documents, although once abundant, are generally no longer extant. Spur of the moment races often occurred on Sunday afternoons, a bane to the pious who saw it as breaking the Sabbath, as races were accompanied by much swearing and other ungodly activities. Church-going folk objected to both the profanity and the empty pews. Races were not recorded for posterity and there is no way for the historian to verify the accuracy of these accounts, because these stories became part of the folklore that old-timers passed down to their sons and daughters. These major gaps in the history of the turf will always create uncertainties. What is certain is that the Civil War transformed horse racing in both the

North and South. At the end of the war the gulf between distance racers and short distance horses would also tend to separate the very wealthy, who could afford Thoroughbreds, from those of lesser means. Texans who had the money to breed Thoroughbreds continued to do so, but most Texans enjoyed watching sprints, where a fast horse of dubious ancestry could compete. No matter what breed of horse a man owned, however, many of those animals went off to war with their owners, never to return.

5

An Era Ends
The 1860s

War fever hit Texas even before the state seceded in 1861. For months local companies drilled in preparation for a possible conflict. When in April Confederates took Fort Sumter in Charleston harbor the repercussions hit more than 1,200 miles away in Austin. There would be a war. The Confederates would win, of course, and it would not last long—six months at the most. One anxious Texan wrote he feared the "grand, decisive battle would be fought" before he could reach the "seat of active operations." Another recalled, "I was very fearful the war would be over before I saw a live Yankee." As Texans prepared to leave home they did so with all the confidence that this would be an easy victory. Infantry officers and men joining the cavalry would go mounted. The more impressive the horse, the more respect for the rider. No one expected the man or horse to be hurt, there would probably be no actual battles. So many expensive Thoroughbreds and quarter running horses left the state never to return. The more well-to-do new soldiers often took a slave along to care for both horse and rider.[1]

Racing was a popular pastime for cavalry as seen in letters, diaries, and official reports. Soldiers often wrote home not only about their own horses but also about watching races in camp. Randolph Tucker, a cavalryman stationed near Richmond, Virginia, early in the war told his mother: "We have had two horseraces this week gotten up by way of amusement. The soldiers using their own horses. You know we are quartered at the Ashland Race-Course." The

Ashland track, located about twenty miles north of Richmond, was built in the 1850s and an observer in 1860 remarked that he witnessed the meeting of the jockey club and a series of races there. Hundreds of men and women arrived by special trains from Richmond, and crowds filled the grounds near the clubhouse as well as the stands. Moreover, there was "a scene of noise and excitement of betting; the intervals between the races saw the gambling saloons below the grandstand filled to overflowing." The racecourse went bankrupt by the time the war began and the track became a training ground for Confederate cavalry. As soon as recruits arrived to drill for war, they appropriated the track for their own amusement. Gambling on horses quickly became a vice in the military just as it was in society at large.[2]

Organized racing did not completely stop during the Civil War, but it did take a hard hit, especially in the South. There were parts of the Confederacy that became frequent battlegrounds, such as Virginia, and outdoor social activities often stopped. The course at Metairie in New Orleans, Louisiana, often frequented by Texas turfmen, held its regular winter meeting in December 1861, but there were only a handful of owners willing to participate. New Orleans surrendered to Union forces in April 1862, and those civilians owning expensive horses spent much of their time trying to figure out how to prevent their animals from being confiscated by either the Union or Confederate armies. Many owners sent their valuable Thoroughbreds to Texas for safety. Although Union soldiers never occupied any of Texas except along the Gulf Coast briefly, racing as a sport all but disappeared while the men involved served in the Confederate army.[3]

On the other hand, racing increased in popularity in the North, particularly among the soldiers. Officers rarely banned the sport, knowing it contributed to the morale of their men. Unlike the Confederacy, the Union could replace horses easily and their mounts rarely broke down for lack of forage as was seen in the South. One of the best-known Union generals to support racing, and who became famous later as an Indian fighter, was George Armstrong Custer. His enjoyment of racing was no secret. A trooper in Custer's brigade recalled: "At division and brigade headquarters alone was there time for play. Generals Custer and [Judson] Kilpatrick had a race course where they used to devote time to the sport of horse racing." Custer would bring this passion for racing to Texas after the war ended, when he was stationed at Austin in 1865. Custer was not unique among northern soldiers. Late in the war a Union soldier recalled, "Horse racing was still in vogue, and at stated times thousands of soldiers congregated upon an open plain, to witness this exciting sport."[4]

Confederates loved horse racing too, but it could be costly. In the Confederacy a man furnished his own horse, saddle, weapons, and other needed equipment. If the horse was wounded in battle or broke down from overwork, racing, or simply from lack of forage, the soldier had to replace the animal or join the infantry. There was a sense of prestige associated with riding a Thoroughbred, and officers, in particular, wanted the best mount available. A fine horse commanded respect. From privates to generals, Texans preferred to ride. Their penchant for cavalry exasperated Gov. Edward Clark when he tried to fill the quotas that the Confederate government requested. It was very difficult to raise infantry in the state. Clark observed that the Texans' reluctance to become foot soldiers was founded "upon their peerless horsemanship." They were "unwilling, in many instances to engage in service of any other description, unless required by actual necessity." Even English Col. James Fremantle noted that when the war began "it was found very difficult to raise infantry in Texas, as no Texan walks a yard if he can help it." By December 1861, the cavalry leaving the state outnumbered the infantry by approximately 2.4 to 1. What this meant was that many Texas race horses, both Thoroughbreds and quarter running horses, left the state never to return.[5]

Estimates of the horses killed during the war outnumber the soldiers who died in the conflict. Perhaps 1,000,000 horses did not return home, and some of the most distinguished bloodlines in the pre-war days became hard to find. The life expectancy of a horse in a war zone was estimated to be around six months. Horses were in high demand and owners of fine stock hesitated to send their animals into battle. The majority of Texans served in the Trans-Mississippi department, which included Texas, Arkansas, Indian Territory, and the parishes of Louisiana west of the Mississippi River. Battles were not as frequent in that theater, so between fights the men turned to popular pastimes. A Texas cavalryman wrote from Fort Chadbourne on the Indian frontier: "I have bin Horse racesing since I left home. I have Lost one hundred dollars an have got arace to be run on Saturday next [where] I have got dick [his horse] bet on the race and if I loose him I will loose aheap more on the day of the race. I am going to win or loose something."[6]

Racing, and the gambling associated with it, became such a problem in the Confederate army in 1862 that a Texas colonel wrote: "All officers belonging to the Texas Frontier Regiment . . . are hereby required to prohibit gaiming by horse racing . . . whenever the same in any company or detachment shall become a nuisance to the service. If any member of the Regiment should so far lose sight of the interest and reputation of the service as to be caught horse racing or gaiming while on duty . . . the same shall be punished by court martial or otherwise." It was not the racing that caused the problems, although they could be detrimental if the horses were hurt, it was the gambling that raised objections. Even Gov. Sam Houston prohibited racing and gambling in the pre-war frontier regiments, and this continued during the conflict.[7]

Wagering on races was so entrenched in Texas that it was impossible to have one without the other. Col. Henry McCulloch issued an order from Camp Cooper on the Texas frontier that read: "Horse racing and gambling of every description is strictly forbidden, and if any gamblers come to the Posts, or about them, to filch the troops of their earnings, you will order them to stop their gambling or require them to leave at once." One story goes that a Texas cavalryman frequently went around shirtless because he kept losing it betting on his fast horse Dick. Another race horse named Billy, part mustang, was so successful that claims were made he was worth $5,000. This was Texas-style horse racing, the kind of sprints that made Steel Dust and Shiloh

A hurdle race provided entertainment for bored soldiers during the Civil War. Library of Congress.

famous. There were no long races, just short distances to determine the winners and losers and alleviate the boredom associated with camp life.[8]

Enthusiasm for going to war swept across the state. In the village of Lancaster the owners of Steel Dust answered the call to join. Mid Perry raised a company of cavalry, many of the men being mounted on descendants of his famous stallion Steel Dust. Perry was older than most of his recruits, being forty-seven when he enlisted for twelve months in March 1862. Since Confederate soldiers furnished their own horse and equipment, appraisers valued each with the understanding that if lost in battle the government would reimburse the owner. Perry's horse came in at a value of $200. At a time when most horses were valued at $15 to $20 this amount indicates Perry went off to war well-mounted (although one of the two men who appraised his horse was his friend and partner in Steel Dust, Jones Greene). After the expected festivities arranged by friends and neighbors to send their men into battle, the new recruits in Perry's company headed for the fairgrounds in Dallas to learn the fundamentals of being a soldier. Perry's command would become

Company I, Eighteenth Texas Cavalry Regiment. The regiment moved into the Indian Territory where the men first saw battle. They later rode to Arkansas, where they were dismounted by order of the Confederate government in July 1862, possibly prompting Mid Perry's resignation on July 20. Someone needed to take the horses back to Texas and it is possible that Perry, who valued fine horseflesh, thought it was his duty to do so. Whatever his motive for resigning, he was back with the army in early May 1864, just a little more than six months shy of turning fifty. Perry survived the war, dying at home in 1892 at age seventy-seven.[9]

Not all Texans went off to fight, however. Jones Greene, the co-owner of Steel Dust, took a different route to support the war effort. Apparently poor health and eye trouble kept him from active service, but he was remembered for caring for the wives and children of the soldiers at the front. In March 1862, he was working as an appraiser, having valued his friend Mid Perry's horse, among others. He died before the war ended in November 1864 at age forty-seven, but his wife Mary continued to run the horse operation for many more years.[10]

Men stayed home for a variety of reasons. Jack Batchler, the owner of Shiloh, also missed the fighting. Instead, he provided mules for the Confederacy from his farm on Bear Creek in Ellis County. Mules were almost as valuable as horses for both sides. They pulled artillery and supply wagons and did many other needed chores. They died in battle almost as frequently as the horses. Batchler apparently lost around $15,000 during the war, although he seems to have recuperated financially by the end of the conflict. Shiloh was in great demand as a stud. Fragments of the account records for Shiloh for the years 1860–1865 still exist, and among those bringing mares to breed to the stallion during that time was Mid Perry. When the war ended, Batchler recovered nicely, "owning 2,600 acres of land and thousands of cattle and horses" by the early 1890s. He continued racing, but by the 1870s turned to Thoroughbreds. His son Henry brought Kentucky Thoroughbreds to their farm and was one of those to found the Texas Thoroughbred Breeders Association in 1885.[11]

Several well-known Texas turfmen took part in the war. In southwest Texas along the Guadalupe/Gonzales county line Bill Fleming enlisted in the Eighth Texas Cavalry Regiment, better known as Terry's Texas Rangers. Wounded in the Battle of Shiloh in early April 1862, Fleming, known for his stud Old Billy, received a discharge as permanently disabled. The injury to his right arm and hand meant he used his left hand to write and could only scribble his signature. This is probably why he kept no written records of the mares he later bred to his famous stallion, Old Billy. The Eighth Texas Cavalry and Eleventh Texas Cavalry belonged to Maj. Gen. Joseph Wheeler's Corps in the Army of Tennessee where racing was a particular problem. Col. Alfred Roman inspected the corps in late 1864 and noted, "Racing seems to be the favorite enjoyment of the men," he wrote, and was the "main occupation of all men off duty." The "amusement of racing," he added, was often "carried too far." Finally, another prominent horseman, Jim Brown, served under W. R. Wood and later in his father's command. One of Brown's most famous postwar race horses carried the name Rebel.[12]

Tom Haley, who owned the popular track in Johnson County south of Fort Worth, went to war with the "Johnson County Slashers," which became Company C, Twelfth Texas Cavalry Regiment. The new soldiers elected forty-four-year-old Haley as the company's first lieutenant. Among the privates in the company were two of his sons, twenty-one-year-old John Haley and seventeen-year-old Thomas Jr. Fourteen-year-old Charles had to wait another year before his father allowed him to enlist. Only young Allen, twelve, stayed home with his mother.[13]

The Slashers joined the brigade of Col. William H. Parsons, leaving for war in the spring of 1862. In the Texans' second major engagement near the sleepy little town of Cotton Plant, Arkansas, the Slashers' captain was mortally wounded, and Tom Haley replaced him as company commander. But less than two years later, May 1864, Haley was wounded in the regiment's last major battle at Yellow Bayou in Louisiana near where the Red River empties into the Mississippi. Seriously injured, Captain Haley returned home to recuperate.

Apparently unable to recover, Haley died seven months later on February 1, 1865. North Texas lost one of its most prominent horsemen, although his son Charles would continue his father's horse business. Known as Charley, he would eventually make a name for himself in the postwar years, raising some of the finest horses in Texas, both Thoroughbred and quarter running horses.[14]

Another wealthy turfman hurt by the war was Tom McKinney, a guiding light in southern Texas jockey clubs and racecourses. In 1860, McKinney, known as Mac, owned 1,500 improved acres with structures valued at $48,000, including a mill, valued at an additional $10,500. He also owned around 100 horses, 120 mules, 250 cattle, 900 sheep, seventy milk cows, twenty oxen, fifteen hogs, and twenty-one slaves. McKinney opposed secession, but when the state joined the Confederacy, he supported the new government. He was in his sixties when the war began, too old to become a soldier, but he worked as a special cotton agent and took cotton to Mexico to trade with England for weapons for the South. This job resulted in debts he could not pay, and at the end of the war he, like many wealthy Texans, found himself crippled financially. In 1866, the Travis County tax collector counted only forty horses, sixty cattle, and less than 100 sheep at his place south of Austin.[15]

Two Southerners with connections to Texas who supplied many fine Thoroughbreds to the American turf saw their stables displaced by the war. Keene Richards, who frequently raced at the Metairie course, equipped an entire company of cavalry in which, according to tradition, every man was mounted on a Thoroughbred. He remained in Kentucky until he was forced to flee to Louisiana. He took most of his remaining horses to Jeff Wells plantation near Alexandria. A secessionist, despite the fact his brother James Madison Wells was a staunch Unionist, Jeff Wells also equipped and mounted a company of Confederate cavalry. Among the horses Richards brought to Wells's plantation was a chestnut colt with white markings by Lexington. Richards bought him as a two-year-old from Wells. The colt, then known as General Westmore, cost Richards $5,000 in gold, to be paid in full at the end of the war.[16]

At some point between 1862 and early 1864 the colt was brought to Texas to avoid confiscation. The Wells family had extensive land holdings in Central Texas, and Wells was afraid his stable would suffer the fate of his friend Duncan Kenner. Kenner lost all his bloodstock when Union troops raided his Ascension Parish plantation in July 1862. The army confiscated his Thoroughbreds and sold them in New Orleans. Jeff Wells made his last trip to Texas in 1863. He died unexpectedly in July when in Hempstead, about fifty miles northeast of Houston. Only fifty-seven years old, he was buried in Austin County. He may have been staying at the home of his good friend, Leonard W. Groce, in the days before his death. While it is possible Wells brought the colt at the time of this visit in 1863, it is more likely the colt came in 1862 soon after Union soldiers occupied New Orleans. The Wells family owned land in both Austin and Grimes counties (parts of both became Waller County in the 1870s).[17]

Back home at the Wells plantations in Rapides Parish damage was substantial when the Federal army occupied it during a failed attempt to invade Texas in the spring of 1864. By that time, with Jeff Wells dead, the remaining stock in the Lone Star State was under the care of his nephew Jefferson (also known as Jeff). Wells's death may be the reason the colt eventually ended up at Tom McKinney's ranch in Travis County. McKinney was a former business partner of Wells's friend Leonard Groce. In any case, the stud covered a few mares at McKinney's ranch for a fee of $100. It was also during the years in Texas that the younger Jeff Wells bred the stallion to an unnamed mare by Lecomte. The product of this breeding was Lizzie G, the future granddam of Domino, one of the most famous winning race horses in the last decade of the nineteenth century. But after Jeff Wells died, and since Richards still owed for the colt, Wells's estate claimed ownership—leaving James Madison Wells, the Reconstruction governor of Louisiana from 1865 to 1867, as the colt's owner. When the war ended Richards sent the stallion to Metairie where he made his only start in April 1866, and afterwards Richards made his agreed-on payment to Governor Wells for the colt. Renamed War Dance, Richards and his stable returned to Blue Grass Park at Georgetown, Kentucky, where

War Dance stood at stud for $50. Richards lived there until his death in 1881, although much of his fortune was gone. His cousin in Texas, Dr. George Feris, continued to raise and race horses, but Richards was no longer around to supply him with the great bloodlines of the South. Too many Thoroughbreds left for war, never to return.[18]

Since War Dance was probably the most notable Thoroughbred brought to Texas in the first six decades of the nineteenth century he deserves more attention. His sire Lexington was well known. Sired by Boston, Lexington traced to Sir Archy. His dam Reel was known to serious turfmen since she was the dam of Lecomte. Wells believed that a Lexington-Reel cross "would produce something extraordinary." Wells originally named the colt General Westmore, since Wells continued the American custom of naming horses for friends or family, as he had with Lecomte. Gen. Samuel M. Westmore was the adjutant general of the state of Louisiana who frequently raced his horses at the Metairie course. "American bred" War Dance was "the produce of what is usually esteemed the best brood mare and the best horse, on the turf or in the stud, that this country has ever produced," judged a writer for *The Times Picayune* in 1870. War Dance's only race, in April 1866 at Metairie, which he lost, was run under the name Gen. Westmore.[19]

When War Dance stood at stud at Tom McKinney's ranch near Austin he probably received little serious training owing to the uncertainty of racing resuming across the South. He arrived at Metairie sometime early in 1866 where he went into training. By April, he was troubled with a "slight swelling on the right knee, caused by striking it accidentally in his galloping." Many fans believed another Lecomte was in the making, "had not this swelling of the knee occurred, he would have been the favorite at big odds." One of the most famous black jockeys of the time, Abe Hawkins, was to ride him as he faced Gen. Rousseau, a stallion sired by Commodore by Boston. A New Orleans paper reported just a few days earlier that Abe was "probably the best rider on the continent." He "knowns the ropes like a book." Furthermore, "We make these remarks for the benefit of strangers, for all frequenters of the Southern turf know Abe." It would be a three-mile dash for $600. Westmore fell behind in the backstretch, "acting strangely," and looking like he was about to throw his rider. Something was clearly wrong. He would not respond to the jockey and fell further behind. He had pulled a tendon in his right foreleg, accounting for his strange behavior, and did not finish. The deep mud was heavy, probably causing his injury. "The gay and lively racer that pranced as beautifully before a crowd of anxious admirers but a few moments before, was now undone forever." A reporter faulted the track management for not "postponing the racing until the track became passable," rather than "to risk the ruin that Westmore fell heir to on yesterday." He never raced again but became a prolific sire of fine race horses, including Lida Grissom. She distanced the field in a race in New Orleans in April 1870.[20]

When Keene Richards acquired full ownership of General Westmore following the loss, he renamed him War Dance because he came from a long line of race horses named after various dances. His dam, Reel, was named for the popular dance in Virginia. Reel's dam Gallopade was named after a popular British dance. Other colts of Reel were Fandango (1836)—named after a Portuguese/Spanish dance, and Cotillion (1837)—named after a French dance. It was not uncommon to name a horse for dances popular in the United States. According to one source, the stallion, General Westmore, "during the late war . . . took his flight, with others, before the approaching Federal army, and made this war dance even into Texas." The stallion's brief visit to the Lone Star State earned him a name inspired by the Comanches and Kiowas war dances on the western frontier. Wells was dead by this time, but he probably would have approved of the new name.[21]

The number of horses that left Texas in the four years of war and did not return cannot be calculated with any accuracy. Since Texans served primarily in the cavalry, and there were well over 100 various cavalry units raised in the state, the ones that became warhorses totaled in the thousands. At the beginning of the war a typical cavalry regiment consisted of ten companies of more than 100 men each. To this are added extra horses for regimental officers, quartermaster and commissary officers, a regimental wagon master, and teams for the regimental wagons and so forth. At full strength, which was seldom met, each regiment would require well over 1,000 horses. Artillery also required horses as did the field officers in the infantry. Texans also preferred to ride their best horse to war to avoid its confiscation if left at home. Officers wanted to be seen on the finest mount available and the warhorse Traveller became almost as famous as his well-known owner Gen. Robert E. Lee.[22]

Replacing horses was often difficult. Texas soldiers serving east of the Mississippi River were a long way from home. Purchasing a replacement was often beyond the means of a private making $11 a month, even if there were horses to be found. Pvt. William Fletcher, who transferred to the Eighth Texas Cavalry after the Battle of Chickamauga, remembered a near-constant searching for and swapping of horses to keep himself adequately mounted. Riding mules was not unknown. At one point Fletcher described his horse as "badly thumped," and "gave signs of a complete letdown." While Fletcher impressed a number of horses from civilians, his friend John Pipkin rode a Texas mustang of a "mouse color." Fletcher recalled that the animal consumed everything eatable nearby "apparently no worse for the wear. I had often scolded him for the unnecessary hard rides and little care he would give his horse; and when I would get after him he would say: 'Bill, it makes no difference, you can't kill him.'" Mustangs knew how to survive on the open range, and like Pipkin's horse, many would be the sturdy, dependable mounts found herding cattle to market after the war ended.[23]

Inflation resulted in the price of horses skyrocketing. In May 1862 a Texan wrote home: "Horses bear tremendous prices," as his company's lieutenant sold his for $300. In November 1862 a cavalryman in Arkansas informed his wife in Texas: "Dont sell off any more horses unless it is to supply yourself with the necessaries of life. Horses are worth twice as much now as a year ago and if the war continues they will be higher still." Six months later, in May 1863, price increases prompted a Trans-Mississippi trooper to observe: "Horses here transcend all bounds, rating from $25 to $800." R. L. Dunman, who

Impressing horses from civilians during the Civil War was the typical way cavalrymen replaced their mounts killed or just worn out from hard service. Many cavalrymen preferred to ride Thoroughbreds, although Texans often rode quarter running horses of mixed breed. *Harper's Weekly*, December 24, 1864.

served east of the Mississippi River with the Army of Tennessee, recalled: "It was a cavalryman's business to keep mounted, and we had to be a pretty resourceful bunch of young fellows to do this. If our horses were shot from under us, we usually 'managed' to get another one! As a cavalryman I was never compelled to walk but *one* day during the entire war."[24]

One prominent family recognized for its "fine horses" was that of Amasa Turner of Lavaca County, who sent his only son and son-in-law, George Turner and Frank Batchelor, to war mounted on Thoroughbreds he had bred and raised. As a member of Terry's Texas Rangers, Frank complained from East Tennessee in June 1863 that his "fine black horse was stolen and after spending days in fruitless search I was compelled to buy another not worth half so much, giving 260$." He thought of his "gallant steed," then contrasted him with his "present scrubby nag," and was forced to mutter, "this is a sorry sight." He went on to add that there "seems to be a regular gang of horse thieves prowling through the country and some hanging must be speedily done to cure the evil." Fortunately, three Texas soldiers saw his horse and retrieved him from the villain who took him. George, whose sister was Frank's wife, wrote that he was very glad the troopers reunited the horse with his owner, because it "relieves me from the unpleasant necessity of sneaking up into Ky in the double and doubtful capacity of scout and horse thief." It seems, he added, "our boys borrow more than half the horses they are getting from there"—"borrow" in this context meaning "confiscate." For a family that knew bloodlines, riding anything besides a Thoroughbred was unthinkable. George even planned to slip into Kentucky to find a horse for his slave, Lem. Two months later the price of a good horse skyrocketed in his regiment to between $800 to $1,000. Although Amasa Turner lived until 1877, the breeding operation he founded in South Texas declined after both Frank and George died before the war ended.[25]

To some men leaving home their horse was almost part of the family. Sterling Robertson, whose father had started by breeding fine horses decades before the war, wrote to his wife in Salado frequently about his horse, Black Donald, a stallion evidently sired by his father's stud Black Douglass. While stationed at Tyler, Robertson, dressed in black pants, black shirt, six-shooter and knife, and mounted on his black stallion, caused one of his friends to observe that he would "pass for the black knight in Ivanhoe, in appearance, if not in terror to the Yankees."[26]

The requirements for warhorses varied. Cavalry preferred mounts four to nine years old, artillery wanted horses five to seven years. Both looked for animals of at least fifteen hands. These requirements were seldom met and as the war progressed, any horse would suit. Men in the Ninth Texas Cavalry Regiment discovered they could not find replacements for a horse valued at $125 in 1861 for less than $500 or $600 in the later years of the war. Early in 1864 "a decent horse was worth $1,000 and one Captain of the 9th Texas Cavalry had a bay horse valued at $2,000." It was not unusual to see mention of the "Mexican pony" or "Indian pony," referring to the mustangs wild on the Texas frontier as mounts being valued. While a stallion was flashy, he could also be difficult to control around other stallions or mares in heat. More importantly, what was needed in war was a horse that did not shy when the cannon roared, shotguns bellowed, and the smoke became so thick that it was impossible to see. Some horses in the Ninth Texas Cavalry were known to lay back their ears and buck when the bugle sounded. Another important asset was a horse with a comfortable gait for long rides. A high-strung Thoroughbred was showy, but it could have disadvantages if it failed to meet these requirements. Quarter running horses, not as high strung as a Thoroughbred, were the choice of many Texas troopers.[27]

As the war ended in the spring of 1865, confusion spread throughout Texas. Confederate soldiers slowly returned home, only to face shortages and hardships. Many men who left on fine horses walked home, having lost their animals either in battle or when their unit was dismounted. Many of the

Texans captured mustang mares and bred them to stallions that they brought from east of the Mississippi River. *Harper's Weekly*, November 21, 1868.

bloodlines so prominent in the pre-war years died out, never to be seen again in the Lone Star State. When Union Gen. Gordon Granger arrived in mid-June 1865, he installed Federal control statewide. He paroled Confederate soldiers and introduced Texans to the Emancipation Proclamation by making June 19, or Juneteenth, the day that freed any slaves still held in bondage. Two detachments of occupation troops entered Texas overland from Louisiana, and one of those was commanded by a man who loved to test his horses on the track, the passionate horse breeder and racer George Armstrong Custer.

In an unlikely turn of events, it was this northern general who promoted horse racing in the last months of 1865. Custer was a flamboyant personality, but a personality not always admired by the soldiers he commanded. He arrived in Texas from Alexandria, Louisiana, with five regiments of troops that had never served under him before. These were volunteers, men who resented the fact they were not mustered out at the end of the war and sent home. Instead, they received orders to occupy Texas where they soon discovered that the food provided by the army was not always edible. As a result, locals complained to Custer of widespread foraging, and the general used such draconian methods as flogging and head-shaving as punishments. The results were predictable—there were rumors some of the volunteers talked of assassinating him.[28]

Still, he led some of the first Federal soldiers to march across the state, a feat Union troops never accomplished during the war. He encountered little hostility and found the civilians generally friendly. Camping briefly at Hempstead near Houston, he eventually moved to Austin. But he did not make his headquarters in the Capitol building. Instead, he chose the school for the deaf and dumb on the far side of the Colorado River. There he learned sign language from the children, a skill he would later use when dealing with Indians on the frontier.

It was during his stay in Texas that Custer re-introduced racing as a regular pastime. Since the occupation troops did not have a lot to do, races became frequent. Hard up civilians might not have the money to gamble excessively but the soldiers did. Army surgeon Charles H. Lothrop of the First Iowa Cavalry Regiment related a story about races held both in Hempstead and later in Austin. Lothrop wrote in late 1865: "The command remained at Hempstead, endeavoring to obey *un*military orders of the commanding General, horse-racing, etc., until October 30th." On October 21 "occurred the 'celebrated horse race' between 'Jack Rucker,' General Custer's race horse, and a captured horse of Company C, First Iowa Cavalry. It was essentially 'the First Iowa Cavalry against General Custer and his staff.'"[29]

Jack Rucker was not just any horse. He was a bay, thought to have been a Morgan (the first breed unique to the United States), and Custer won large sums of money betting on him at racecourses in the past. Jack Rucker was known for his blazing speed, but also for the fact that Custer was riding him when his cavalry advanced on Appomattox in April 1865. But on the track, the only time Jack Rucker lost was when men betting against him drugged the horse prior to a race. Custer was undoubtedly certain of his victory on this day in Texas.[30]

Custer's confidence was not misplaced when Jack Rucker won. "Large sums of money were 'put up' and lost by the regiment, as was generally believed and openly asserted, by the treachery of the rider (Nicholas LaCosta, a Mexican, and a private of Company C) of the horse 'backed' by the regiment, the rider having received a liberal compensation from General Custer or his friends," recalled Lothrop. "That the race had been 'sold' was so evident that the citizens who witnessed the race were loud in their denunciations of the dastardly act, and had the rider not suddenly disappeared for a time he would have received the punishment he so well merited."[31]

This was not the end of the story. "Soon afterward, by order of General Custer, our 'Company C horse' was transferred to the Quartermaster of General Custer's staff. This, however, did not prevent the regiment from 'getting even' with the General and his staff." It is no surprise that these volunteers wanted revenge as their dislike of Custer was no secret. By November, when the regiment was in the Austin area, "races were of almost daily occurrence," recalled

Lothrop, and he described one arranged to teach Custer a lesson. The race took place on the City track, between a citizen's entry and General Custer's horse, Jack Rucker. A man who was in sympathy with the regiment referred the First Iowa volunteers to a citizen near Austin who owned a horse described as "the fastest and finest" in the state. Since the soldiers wanted to "outgeneral General Custer, a call was made upon this gentleman on the day after our arrival in Austin. After informing him as to our business with him, he very cheerfully entered into the project, and a few days afterward it was announced that General Custer 'had made a race with a citizen.'" After Custer agreed, "the citizen very *innocently* made his way to our camp and informed us of what had taken place. The stakes were $3,000—$1,500 on the part of each. In order to show his good faith and his confidence in the running qualities of his little mare, he proposed to furnish the amount, $1,500, himself, and the regiment might take all the bets they could possibly obtain. The result was the regiment gave the General and his staff an opportunity to again invest. They improved the opportunity and 'put up' all the money they could raise."[32]

The men of the First Iowa considered Custer a vane Eastern Theater dandy and looked forward to seeing him lose. But a few days before the race a soldier called upon the citizen and offered him $1,500 if he would let Custer's horse win. The man responded by saying, "I was not brought up to run horses that way. If your horse is the fastest he takes the money; if my mare is the fastest she gets it." When the day of the match finally arrived the general and his staff, along with their wives, listened to the division band playing, hoping soon to celebrate the victory of Jack Rucker. The distance was 600 yards and, to the surprise of Custer and his backers, Jack Rucker lost to the little Texas mare by more than sixty feet. "Cheer upon cheer went up from the boys and citizens assembled there to witness the race, intermingled with such expressions as, 'How are you, General Custer?' 'Couldn't steal the race this time?' 'Why don't you make your band blow?'—and many other expressions," wrote Lothrop. "It is worthy of note that the band did not *blow*, and the ladies did not wave their handkerchiefs, and that the General and his staff, and the band and ambulances retreated in disorder and confusion."[33]

Like Custer, Texans were anxious to race again. Jockey clubs had not officially dissolved, but when men left the state to fight, they just fizzled out. After the war, many of the men who had belonged were either dead or had moved elsewhere. Times had changed. American horse racing, for all practical purposes, needed to begin anew. The focus on racing in the United States shifted to the North as Southerners began to rebuild their lives. No longer did southern turfmen have slaves to tend their stables. Long before 1861, however, the four-mile race was declining in popularity. The desire was for pure speed rather than staying power. The emphasis centered on dashes of shorter distances. New Orleans gave up its preeminent position in racing to New York, and Texas turfmen, who nurtured the sport in its infancy, now tried to adapt.

While it is impossible to estimate the number of tracks in antebellum Texas, it is safe to say that almost every town or village had some sort of facility, whether an elaborately constructed racecourse or simply two paths suitable for match races. Although the conflict broke up breeding establishments and scattered the bloodstock, it did not destroy the desire for men to test their horses' speed. When Texas emerged from the depression caused by the war, racing would again be a prominent part of the Texas scene.

Yet change would not come without controversy. Thoroughbreds reigned supreme among turfmen, but scrub races with quarter running horses gained ground. The Houston paper printed a letter to the editor in March 1865 summing up the problem. Signed "Fairfield," the letter began: "It appears that the Texas Jockey Club have determined to substitute for the time-honored and popular Biennial Match Race which was to have come off over the Texas State Course on the first Monday in August next, a catch-weight race, differing only from an ordinary Scrub Race, in this, that it is open for the rough-breeds, as well as for common stock of all ages, including three year olds, colts and fillies. The Governor's Plate, honorably contended for in match-races by blooded stock at every biennial meeting since the organization of the club, is the glittering prize to be run for, in the approaching contest. This change of sport by the club is much deplored by all true turfmen, and those who are interested in the success of improved stock. For, if, as has been suggested, many more entries are made, in addition to the fifty-seven already booked, the crowded condition of the track will be such, that some singe-cat scrub, rode by an expert Jeremy Diddler, may, by foul riding, distance the field, and in triumph bear off the much coveted Plate." Fairfield was not the only one to deplore the plan and he had a solution. "To guard against the possibility of such a contingency, I propose that the Jockey Clubs of the several counties in the State, call meetings, to be attended not only by the *initiated members*, but by all frequenters of the turf, and protest against the contemplated change in the character of the race. Each club should also express a preference for some favorite horse, to be entered as a competitor for the golden stakes, with the understanding and agreement among the several clubs, that every horse already entered or that may be hereafter entered shall be withdrawn, except those two which may be backed by the largest number of Clubs in the State. Thus, Mr. Editor, would be insured legitimate sport is a contest between two genuine thoroughbreds, with no danger of either being disgraced by being beaten by any ticky ass, common horse, or *Union Course-singe-cat scrub* that may dare enter the field against them." It would still be decades before quarter running horses, most commonly seen on scrub tracks, became a breed, but times were slowly evolving, and Texas had two distinct types of race horses competing on its tracks.[34]

In August 1865, dedicated horsemen met in Waco. Intending to start afresh, their aim was to form an association for the improvement of the breed. The president was C. A. Hamilton, vice president was J. B. Earle, third vice president was Tom McKinney, and secretary was Robert B. Smith. They planned races on the Central Course at Waco for November using the rules of the Metairie Jockey Club since there was probably not enough money to print their own rulebook. For those who wanted to compete but were short of cash as a result of the war, the price of entering was out of reach. Entrance fees for the heats of one and two miles ranged from $100 to $150. There was even a dash of one mile for "fine saddle" horses. The war had only ended a few months before, but these turfmen seemed determined to return life to normal as soon as possible.[35]

Tom McKinney made the trip to Waco from his home southwest of Austin. It was a ride of more than 100 miles and McKinney, who would be sixty-four in November, was at a difficult time in his life. His business dealings during the war left him in financial ruin. He continued to participate in events around Austin, but it would not be long before his health began to fail, and he wrote to Gen. Albert Sidney Johnston's son a few years later that "My wife frequently has her own cooking & washing to do besides give much of her attention to our stock." No longer with slaves to tend his horses, it appears his much younger wife may have stepped into that role.[36]

Across the South organized racing also suffered the aftereffects of war. The racing of four-mile horses such as Lexington and Boston, so popular before the war, fell into disfavor. Racecourses and stud farms closed in states like Virginia where the destruction had been most severe. Stallions and mares carrying popular bloodlines did not return home from the war. Southern families in the path of enemy armies lost treasured heirlooms, including letters, diaries, and breeding records. Paintings of the great horses disappeared, as did memorabilia such as plates, cups, vases, and trophies, so sought after among antebellum turfmen. Much of southern racing history was lost as the focus of Thoroughbred racing shifted to the northern states.

Perhaps the best example of the effect of the postwar years was the fate of the course at New Orleans. The Metairie track, a popular prewar destination for Texas turfmen, tried to regain its antebellum prominence. Thoroughbreds were short of supply and often had to be shipped from the North. Added to the shortage of horses, a new jockey club emerged, the Louisiana Jockey Club, and built a rival track at the fairgrounds. Metairie tried to compete, but the reign of Metairie as the preeminent course in the South was over. Charles T. Howard, who had been refused membership in the Metairie Jockey Club, vowed to "turn its racetrack into a grave-yard," and when the track went bankrupt Howard bought it and chartered a cemetery on the grounds in 1872. The cemetery has an oval design, like a racetrack, and is the burial place of prominent Confederates such at Gen. John Bell Hood. Texas turfmen who drew their inspiration from the famous track certainly rued its demise.[37]

One Texan who frequently visited Metairie was George Feris. Although he was still at the forefront of the sport, he, like most Texans, suffered from the changes brought about by war. At the end of the conflict, he offered for sale several horses that included the "Feris Arabian" Abd-el-Kadir, eight years old and "the largest of all A. Keene Richards Arabians." Also, the Duke of Elkhorn, a seven-year-old bay over sixteen hands, by Lexington. Others for sale included two mares by Richards's Arabian Moklhadi, another a mare by Richards's Arabian Hamdan, and a number of others were colts of the Duke of Elkhorn and the Feris Arabian. At the conclusion of an advertisement for the sale Feris wrote: "Pedigrees in full, furnished to those wishing to purchase—My negroes have left me & my Breeding establishment can not be kept up, under the new system of Labor. Free negroes & Blood stock will not work together." Since in 1860 Feris reported only two male slaves aged twenty-five and thirty-four years old, he must have depended upon these two men for everything related to his horses, which was typical for the time. Apparently these two men found other work when freedom came.[38]

Feris had no luck in selling all the horses. He wrote that "Abd-el-Kadir remained my property and stood in Fort Bend County until his death which occurred in June 1866. He was drowned in the Brazos river. . . . We will never see another like him." Among Feris's papers is a contract dated October 1867 where Dr. J. A. Gibson agreed to the "use of the Barb Stallion, Bazar, for the season of 1868, I promise to deliver, and give title to Six well formed American mares, bred to the said Barb horse, Bazar." At the end of the season on July 1, 1868, Gibson agreed to send the mares and stallion to Morris H. Keene (a cousin of Keene Richards in Kentucky), or his agent. This was a contract for hire and the stallion was limited to breeding only forty mares. Gibson was a neighbor of Feris in Fort Bend County. Hiring out a stud was a way for Feris to reduce the cost of upkeep and make money at the same time. He was still in the horse business in 1879, as he advertised for sale three horses sired by Arabians.[39]

Feris remained involved in the Houston Jockey Club. The Houston paper reported in March 1866 that "Our friend Dr. G. A. Ferris [*sic*] will visit Houston in a few days, and open books for a Jockey Club. The design of the club is to establish a centre for the thorough-bred stock interest of the State. We trust it will have the attention its importance merits, and that the requisite stock will very soon be secured." The jockey club's Christmas races in 1868 extended across six days and each day was to have two or more races for heavy purses. The local paper announced that the club would "leave nothing undone to add to the interest of the great winter meeting."[40]

Among the Feris papers can be found the booklet, *Racing Rules of the Houston Jockey Club*. Rule 1, found under "Running Rules," says that race horses "take their ages from the first of January." That one statement deserves an explanation. That date caused a divide between the North and South long before war broke out, and for southern turfmen was as contentious as other differences between the two sections. The United States drew its inspiration from racing in England, and Great Britain changed its date for the birth of Thoroughbreds from the traditional May 1 date to January 1 long before horsemen in the United States made that decision. But once it became widespread in England, some in America called for a change, especially in the North. The South refused to accept the January 1 date though, and for a while American Thoroughbreds celebrated their birthdays on two different dates, depending on which section they came from. A southern race horse remained a year younger than a northern horse until the first of May, resulting in confusion and disputes. This remained the case until after the Civil War when the center of racing moved to the North, and January 1 became the official date of birth for all Thoroughbreds competing on recognized tracks.[41]

Feris was not the only Texas breeder to suffer setbacks because of the war. Another racing family to struggle after the fighting ended was that of Tom Haley. Following the war, the Haleys stayed in Johnson County, breeding and raising horses. Although in 1860 Haley's worth was around $20,000, after the war his estate inventoried at less than $5,000 with $1,500 in outstanding debts. Some debts paid included $150 to horseman John Batchler and $17.50 to horseman Shelby Stanfield. In 1868, his sons Tom Jr. and John planned to sell their entire stock of horses to the highest bidder for cash in hand. The mares and colts amounted to an estimated value of about $1,000, yet somehow twenty-one-year-old Charley Haley bought the entire lot for $395. The brothers saved from the auction block many of their father's best mares, and from these well-bred animals would come Rondo, one of the foundation sires of the modern American Quarter Horse.[42]

But horsemen would not let the war keep them down long. In June 1869, the Austin City Jockey Club sponsored races at the Austin City course. The following week races sponsored by the competing Travis County Blood Horse Association were scheduled at J. M. Costley's track six miles south of the capital. Some of the entries in town for the festivities were impressive. At the Austin City stables, "stands Jeff Jennings, a grey colt by Lightning, and Nannie McNairy by Congares," wrote a reporter who visited both sites. "These horses are from the New Orleans stables and are making a tour of inspection of the several race courses in Western Texas." Another, Sandy Walton, was a "fine three-year-old sorrel colt, by Walnut, dam by Epsilon" that had just come from a successful campaign at San Antonio. John Van Hagen brought Geo. Hancock and Belle Warren, but the reporter noted "the first of these has been in the habit of running a *leetle* behind. He is now in the hands of one who will bring every inch of his running qualities into full play." As would be expected, noted turfman Jim Brown, known for specializing in quarter horses, was in attendance and full of confidence in his own entry, Bob Lee. Brown said he would back him against any horse that "don't like to go more than a quarter [of a mile] or a few yards beyond." The reporter ended by noting that anyone who wished to see fine stock and fine racing should not fail to be in Austin next week and the week after. The Austin City track promised to "put up a stand for the ladies that shall be a pleasant place for promenading even when there are no races on hand," and Costley built an "arbor for the ladies. It is a pleasant drive through the prairie, and a trip once will sure to cause another."[43]

The entries from New Orleans made quite a stir during the races in mid-June. On the second day the anticipated race between the Louisiana horse Jeff Jennings, and local horses Sandy Walton and Rock, drew a large crowd, a much larger crowd than the first day's offerings. A firsthand account gave a spirited description of the race: "A fair start was made, the rider of Jeff holding his horse far behind as if he was only trying to see how Sandy and Rock would go through without his interference. The first mile Sandy and Rock were pretty well together, the former running at his ease, well in hand. Going into the second mile Jeff's rider called on him for an exhibition of his speed and gradually he narrows the gap. On the back stretch the gallant little gray from New Orleans sets his Texas backers to shouting, and around the turn he goes at a thundering pace, making it necessary for Sandy's rider to wake up his horse. Rock becomes perfectly disgusted with the wild mad frolic of his companions and drops so far behind that when the distance judge drops the flag, he is too far behind to get scored at it. Sandy wins the heat with Jeff well up." In the second heat "Many of the knowing ones were satisfied that Jeff would win the race, and as they run the first mile close together, when they passed the stand going into the second, Sandy's friends evidently showed less pluck than the game steed on which they had piled up their stamps. The riders were well up to their business; they knew what the horses could do, and by a heavy application of whip, and a smart pressure of the steel, they bring them round the turns and up the home stretch before Sandy's backers have time to hedge all their bets, and he wins after a hard struggle, heat and race."[44]

On the third day, the sorrel mare Nannie McNairy was the only entry in the three best in five-mile heats and all she needed to do was to walk over the track. She "started out in a slow gallop to win the purse. Before she got into the home stretch it looked so much like getting the purse for nothing that she made one plunge to get loose. The bridle broke and she came bursting through the gaping crowd past the stand, and around she goes again through the second mile to run out the third. But she is turned into the prairie and through the woods and is finally brought back without injury to herself or rider." Still, this first meeting of the club was deemed a "decided success."[45]

The Travis County Blood Horse Association sponsored some unusual races in the spring meeting in 1869. There were the expected mile heats, two-mile heats, a single dash of one mile, miles heats (three best in five), a dash of mile for saddle horses only, a sweepstakes for horses and mares not over fourteen hands high, and a consolation stake for horses and mares that failed to win during the week consisting of a mile and a half dash. The rules and regulations of the Houston Jockey Club governed this meet. Tom McKinney served as secretary accepting entries on this occasion.[46]

Both the Austin City Jockey Club and the Travis County Blood Horse Association publicized their races widely. The president of the Austin City club was Tennessee native John D. Nash, who was a wealthy farmer living in Bastrop County, adjacent to Travis County. A prominent member of the Travis County Blood Horse Association was the well-known breeder Tom McKinney, and John Costley, owner of the track, served as secretary. In March 1869, McKinney advertised races at Costley's track beginning May 24 and lasting six days. John Van Hagen, who trained for McKinney before the Civil War, drifted away from racing and claimed to be a retired mill owner in 1870. He no longer lived in the trainer's cabin on the McKinney ranch.[47]

Three years later Texas lost one of its main Thoroughbred advocates when McKinney died in October 1873. Such was his prominence in Central Texas that twenty citizens met with the mayor to plan the ceremony. A horse-drawn hearse carried his body to the capital and the *Austin Weekly Statesman* informed readers that the procession from his residence, six miles south of the city, to the City Cemetery would cross the ferry at Cunningham & Thompson's at one o'clock where his friends could join the funeral cortege. A formal procession formed at the foot of Congress Avenue and all the bells tolled as an honor guard from the Texas Military Institute and its band led the way. On the steps of the Capitol several of McKinney's friends spoke before the procession moved to Oakwood Cemetery for his burial. He was joined by his wife Anna in death in 1896, but the horse operation, one of the most prominent in Texas since the antebellum years, shutdown with McKinney's passing.[48]

Dallas, rapidly becoming the major city in North Texas, also restarted livestock shows shortly after the war and some familiar names resurfaced as participating. In June 1866, the Dallas County Agricultural and Mechanical Association decided to "revive that society, and to hold a Fair during the final week in October next." Fairs included a lot of events other than those involving horses, but to the turfman, it was only the horse shows that counted. Although the author did not find newspapers accounts for that first fair in 1866 or the second in 1867, there is a write-up in the Dallas paper about the Third Annual Fair in October 1868. Some familiar names appear at these events in the later years of the decade. Mid Perry, the owner of Steel Dust, entered some of his horses, as well as at the Fourth Annual Fair in October 1869. The Dallas paper noted that at the 1869 fair J. T. Melton of Collin County showed two mares, a horse and a colt, that "would compare very favorably with the blooded animals of Ohio, Kentucky and Tennessee—Collin county may well be proud of such horses as those exhibited by Mr. Melton. Three cheers for Collin." A Jones Greene is listed as showing in 1868. He was possibly a relative of the Jones Greene, who died in 1864 and who was part-owner of Steel Dust. Also, in 1868, Mrs. Mary Greene, the widow of Jones Greene, won for the best harness stallion three years old and under. After her husband's death it was said she remained on the "old homestead" and managed it "with much success. She is a lady possessed of more than ordinary executive ability, and is highly esteemed in her community." She apparently carried on her husband's breeding business successfully, an unusual occupation for women at the time. The Fifth Annual Fair in 1870 included other men who were also comfortable in the winner's circle: Harrison Stiff of Collin County, whose Monmouth raced Steel Dust, and Jack Batchler of Ellis County, who owned Shiloh. In fact, Jack Batchler and his son Henry took home prizes in several categories, including the sweepstakes for stallions, all ages.[49]

While fairs gave horsemen a chance to show off their animals, they were similar to county fairs in the first half of the twentieth century where everyone participated. Women entered jams and jellies, pickles, butter, and a wide assortment of other items while men showed mules and other farm animals besides horses. What Dallas turfmen wanted and needed was an organization just for racing and in August 1869 they formed a jockey club. By using subscriptions, the organization bought ground and laid out a track on the "edge of the prairie, about one mile east of the courthouse." The first meeting was scheduled for October "when several exciting races may be expected." A committee of five consisting of James Barkley, T. A Lowery (also seen Lowry), G. W. Laws, John C. McCoy, and T. G. T. Kendall received entries for the races held before the fair on October 14 and 15, but stressed it was for "untried horses" only. Reviewing the few issues of the *Herald* that have survived, it appears that Dallas boasted of a very active jockey club that sponsored year-round events.[50]

These postwar races indicate the wide variety of horses running in Texas after the conflict ended. Although more and more organized races included sprints, distance racing had not yet completely disappeared. But much would change in the last decades of the nineteenth century—lovers of Thoroughbreds continued to improve the breed while owners of short distance horses upgraded the quality of their quarter running horses by crossing them with both mustangs with Spanish roots and Thoroughbreds from English stallions. As racing revived in the 1870s, however, it faced new challenges. More and more the public began to object to the violence often associated with drinking and gambling at the tracks. Still, that did not deter Texas turfmen who continued to promote the sport across the state.

6 A New Beginning
The 1870s

Texas in the postwar years was a challenging place to live. It was "notorious for lawlessness and violence." Horse and cattle thieves plagued the countryside, and hostile Indians harassed settlers on the western frontier. Men wore guns, and where armed men roamed the violent death of some was inevitable. The growing pains of maturing from a frontier society to the twentieth century would not always be easy. The population increased from 818,529 in 1870 to 2,235,527 by 1890 with the largest number of newcomers arriving from the states of the former Confederacy. Railroads multiplied, promising a future unlike anything seen before. The little village of Dallas, wrote the editor of a local paper, "seems determined to do all it can in the way of improvement." Even so, the frontier persisted and much of the state remained an unforgiving land without the benefit of law. But whether new arrivals or long-time residents, the love of the turf remained strong. While Thoroughbred owners struggled to reestablish jockey clubs, quarter mile tracks and scrub races rarely failed to find an audience ready to share some whiskey and watch the best horse cross the finish line first.[1]

As the 1870s opened Texas was in the midst of Reconstruction. "Land was without value; cattle were without value; money was as scarce as hen's teeth and infinitely more requisite," recalled John D. Young. Born in Caldwell County in 1856, he added: "Owners were often obliged to sacrifice their stock for almost nothing." Despite the hardships, Texas was growing. By 1870 it could claim two cities with a population of more than 10,000—Galveston and San Antonio. In 1861, the state only noted around 400 miles of railroad tracks. By 1873 that number increased to almost 1,600. Transporting horses was easier than ever for those turfmen with racing in their blood. No economic downturn would keep them from testing their horses on a track.[2]

A man did not need ready cash to compete on a scrub track. All a fellow needed was a horse he trusted and something to wager. Without money to bet, anything would suffice—cattle, horses, hogs, chickens, saddles, bridles, even the clothes on his back. One race that occurred near Giddings around 1871 made an impression on young Sam Hildreth, who later became a Thoroughbred Hall of Fame trainer and owner. As a child Hildreth recalled that with his father Vincent it was "horse, horse, horse . . . all day long, year in and year out. . . . We grew up in a race-horse atmosphere. I honestly believe we knew more about horses than we did about people. When you don't see much else besides a racing barn, and when all the talk you hear is about thoroughbreds, it just naturally gets into every fibre of you." His father, Vince Hildreth, would go anywhere for a race and when living near Kansas City, Missouri, he heard about the money that could be made on the sport in Texas.[3]

What Vince Hildreth heard was of a man in the Lone Star State named Jim Brown who owned some "mighty sweet ones," and "how that little devil" would bet on his horses. Since Hildreth owned a mare that he thought could beat any challengers he packed up his household and headed for Texas. Sam later wrote that "had you been in the country where Missouri hitches up with Kansas, you would have seen the whole Hildreth family and all their belongings on the move, kicking up an awful dust with their four wagons, ten or twelve racehorses, and six or seven riding horses." A racing man like the Virginia-born Vince Hildreth loved nothing more than his "horses and his rovings." His son recalled that "If you think so well of a horse that you're blind to every other thing except that you and he are pals, and that his daddy and his mother were friends of yours and that you know all about his kin and he about yours, then you appreciate the way my father used to feel about Red Morocco his great quarter-horse." When the wagons and horses arrived at their destination in Giddings they found their man. Brown "was a little bit of a whipper-snapper, leather-faced, thin and wiry, and as courageous as they made them, even in that country, where a fellow couldn't get by unless he had his nerve with him. Lee County had the orneriest bunch of horse-thieves, road-agents, and murderers you could find in any part of the South." But Jim Brown, "the runt," told voters if they would elect him sheriff he would clean the county up in no time. He did.[4]

Brown agreed to race his well-known Steel Dust mare Gray Alice against Hildreth's Red Morocco with $5,000 on the line. As news spread cowboys and ranchmen poured into the town with the talk being of the coming match between the Texas and Missouri mares. Betting was heavy, with Gray Alice the favorite. Some of the Texas gamblers, wanting to be sure the odds were in their favor, paid the jockey of the Missouri entry money to disappear, leaving the Hildreths with no rider as race day approached. On the advice of some of the locals, Vince found a replacement before the race.[5]

In his autobiography Sam Hildreth provides one of the best descriptions of a scrub track available. "The race-course," he wrote, "was laid out over a quarter-mile stretch of smooth ground on the prairie. Every horse-owner had his own course and they were all about the same—two narrow pathways running alongside of each other in a straightaway, with a narrow strip of green turf between. They used to make the running lanes by hitching a team of horses to a big iron caldron resting sideways on the ground, and scooping the grass up by dragging the kettle along a straight line. Then they raked the grass from the loose earth, packed the dirt down a little on the sides, and the track was made. Down where the horses started, some of the tracks had fences running about eighty yards along the course to keep the crowds back. Brown's track had rails like that."[6]

The race came off as planned, with 500 or 600 spectators, mostly cowboys and ranch owners. It was an ask-and-answer start. Once the horses were ready "one of the owners, when his horse was headed the right way and close to the starting-line, would yell out, 'Are you ready?' and if the other horse was in position his owner would reply 'Go!'" It was turn-about with first one of the owners asking the question and then the other until the horses were finally positioned correctly. This benefitted the one who got the last word because by the time he yelled "Go," the first owner's horse might have wheeled around or "done some other fool thing." If you were "left at the post, with only two furlongs to go, you didn't have a ghost of a show," added Hildreth. But on this day the two horses managed an even start. Red Morocco led until, as they neared the finish, she hit the grass between the two pathways and shortened her stride. This gave Gray Alice just enough time to pull past and win by a nose. Hildreth claimed the gamblers paid the new jockey of Red Morocco the night before to pull the mare toward the grass and she was not wearing the proper shoes to race on turf. "From the day we set foot in that Texas town," wrote Sam, "we'd never had a chance to win that match race with Jim Brown's horse." Years later one of Brown's former racing partners told Sam that "it would have been like pulling teeth to have got that five thousand if we'd won." But Jim Brown, who was known as a "square man," bought Red Morocco, giving $5,000, a herd of cattle, and some horses to the Hildreth clan before they returned home. When Sam recalled the events some fifty year later, he noted, "I'll never see horse-racing again as I saw it then, out on the Texas plains, where a fellow had to be a smart horseman to win a race and a smarter one to win a bet—and collect it."[7]

Both Jim Brown and Sam Hildreth went on to have successful racing careers. Hildreth was posthumously inducted into the National Museum of Racing and Hall of Fame in 1955. But before he became famous, Hildreth tried his hand at being a jockey. He rode his last race in Dallas in 1882 at age sixteen but when his weight shot up to 130 pounds, he switched to training until he earned enough money to buy his own horses.

These venues attracted a variety of characters, including ones who wanted to make a quick profit. At the Gonzales County Fair in October 1873 around

100 to 150 gamblers could be found in one room. These were transients, men with no fixed abode, and they often frequented brush tracks bringing with them opportunity seekers and vagrants. It was hard to separate legitimate racegoers from those men who only wanted easy money. There were no stands, spectators often sat on horseback to view the match. Respectable women rarely came, and preachers frowned on the events for the gambling and drinking that accompanied the festivities. There were few rules and the two participants typically made agreements involving wagers before the race commenced. Starting the race was still as informal as it had been decades before. One was a simple pistol shot, another "lap and tap." In the latter, the horses began around fifty feet behind the starting line when they turned and began running. If they were neck and neck at the starting line the judge tapped them off by shouting "Go!" If not, they made a fresh start until the judge was satisfied. Finally, most common in Texas, was "ask and answer" as was seen in the race between Red Morocco and Gray Alice.[8]

One man who saw scrub races as a source of income was future outlaw Sam Bass. In 1874, while living in Denton County, he acquired a two-year-old gray mare named Jennie thought to trace to Steel Dust. He witnessed the money that exchanged hands at local races and wanted a part of it. The mare proved a good purchase, because she quickly made a reputation for speed in the region and was soon known as the "Denton Mare." According to one of Bass's biographers the mare's jockey was often Charley Tucker, a young black man who called himself Dick Eidson, because the well-known trainer Reese Eidson raised him. Tucker liked to ride the mare bareback using molasses spread on the animal's back and to start from a small mound. If anyone complained Bass was always willing to give the other horse a slight lead at the start. There are many accounts of seeing Jennie race, but one in Denton County in 1875 turned violent when some of the spectators with money on the mare's opponent challenged the judge's decision to give her the win—by a nose. Horse racing and gambling often led to confrontations that got out of hand. Bass raced his mare from North Texas to the Indian Territory and all the way southwest to San Antonio. What happened to the mare after San Antonio is unknown, but by 1876 Bass was driving cattle to the railroads in the far north. It is likely that Bass sold her when she could no longer win. Having squandered his cash, he and a friend turned to robbing stagecoaches and then trains. Returning to Texas as a wanted man, he became something of a Robin Hood. In the spring of 1878, he and his gang held up stagecoaches and trains within miles of Dallas leading the Texas Rangers to join the pursuers. In July, Bass and his men were in a gun battle near Round Rock where he was killed. Bass and another Texas outlaw, John Wesley Hardin, were two men that one historian decided, "gained the strange sort of awestruck admiration that Americans reserve for truly notorious thieves and killers." Bass and the Denton Mare became famous in Texas, and both were remembered in poems and songs. The cowboy "Ballad of Sam Bass" was familiar to many Texans. A verse read:[9]

> Sam made a deal in race stock—
> One called the Denton mare.
> He matched her in scrub races
> And took her to the fair.[10]

Local races like the ones Bass engaged in often ended in court when one party or the other felt that they lost money because of human error involving the starter. In one case the starter yelled "Go" in such a loud voice that he frightened one of the horses so badly that it refused to take off. The other horse ran the course alone and claimed the victory. The owner of the horse that failed to run the course, William Armstrong, said that since his entry did not start that no race was run. The owner of the winning horse, John D. Walker, alleged "by the rules of the turf in western Texas, when a race is run and a starter selected to give the word, the horses are bound to start at the word '*Go*;' that if one fails to start and the other runs through, the horse running through takes the money." One witness, a Major Hinkle, said he had been familiar with racing and its customs in western Texas for almost thirty years and if a horse failed to start, the owner lost the money. The "parties took the chances that there would be no accident in getting their horses off, and took the chances that the word would be fairly given." In this kind of race at the word *Go* "it is a race, right or wrong." After a long legal proceeding the judge ruled in favor of the defendant, saying "Horse racing is not unlawful. Wagers are recoverable made upon them."[11]

A scrub race could be a spur-of-the-moment affair, as unplanned as a man needing to make a little extra cash right away. Charles A. Siringo, a Texas cowhand who later wrote his reminiscences of life on the cattle trails, recalled that raising money racing was part of his nomadic lifestyle. Born in 1855 in Matagorda County, Siringo signed on as a cowhand as a teenager under cattle king Abel Head (known as Shanghai) Pierce, driving cattle from Austin to Kansas. On one of those trips, he bought a "California pony" with the name of Whisky-peet for $55 with the intention to "take him home and make a race horse of him." He was only three years old and, according to Siringo, a "lightning striker." Sometime in the 1870s Siringo passed through the Indian Territory where a crowd of Chickasaws challenged him to a race. He put up his saddle and pistol against one of their ponies. Riding bareback, he came out ahead, took the Indian pony he won, and set out for Texas. On another trip, as he headed home, he passed through Denton, where he stopped at a "negro settlement" and agreed to run Whisky-peet. He bet $20 and his Winchester (a "fine silver mounted gun") against a $50 horse. Once both parties approved the wager, Whisky-peet took to the track against a "sleepy looking grey." When the race was done, Whisky-peet crossed the finish line at least ten feet ahead of his opponent. But as Siringo rode toward Fort Worth leading his newly acquired horse, three black men caught up with him and said the party that lost the horse had "no right to [wager] him." They claimed the man borrowed the horse earlier that day to ride to Denton. Not wanting to find himself in a sticky situation, recalled Siringo, "I finally let them have him [back] for twenty dollars."[12]

As this and the Sam Bass tale prove, scrub races attracted all sorts—farmers, breeders, cowboys, friendly Indians, ne'er do wells, outlaws, and unscrupulous swindlers. All were part of Texas' unique landscape. At the other end of the social scale were the well-to-do men who ran the jockey clubs in the larger towns. These were the men who ordered their clothing from London, visited the big cities of the Northeast, and spent huge amounts on fine horses and gala events associated with race week in their hometowns. Often the extremely rich were friends with the "robber barons," a term associated with businessmen who acquired immense wealth in the late nineteenth century. Texas was on the fringe of this world, but the coming of the railroad gave the residents a taste of what life was like outside the Lone Star State. Well-known robber baron Jay Gould acquired control of the Texas and Pacific Railroad in 1880. The Texas and Pacific, one of the best known of the early lines in the state, revolutionized racing as horses could now be easily transported to tracks across the nation. Still, Texas was slow to industrialize, and most Texas cities maintained a trace of the frontier settlement well into the end of the century. Houston was one of those urban areas that suffered growing pains.

Houston in the late nineteenth century was a city that could be sophisticated and violent at the same time. A newspaper man, Samuel O. Young, who later compiled articles he published in the *Houston Chronicle* into a book, wrote about the personality of his hometown, a city still in unspoken competition with Austin to be the most important in the state. As a native Houstonian, Young worked as a doctor from 1870 until 1882 when he changed his vocation and began to write for the paper. His stories provide a glimpse of Houston when it was still evolving into the city it would become in the twentieth century. Spur-of-the-moment races had not changed much from the settlement's early days.[13]

Young realized that Houston was rough around the edges before the Civil War and had not improved very much after the conflict ended. It was pure Texan, sometimes displaying a small-town character, and not yet the fashionable city it aspired to be. Out on Buffalo Bayou there was a track for short distance racing. A twenty-four-year-old saloon keeper named Tom Copping owned a "bony-looking gray horse, which he swore could outpace anything that ever came from Pacerville." He said he "was not only willing but anxious to pit him against anything that showed up. He would go against running horses, pacing horses, trotting horses and," wrote Young, "I have no doubt had such things existed at that time, he would have pitted him against automobiles and motorcycles." His faith in his horse knew no bounds. No one took up his offer so after the races one day he "gave an exhibition spin around the track." Once the day's festivities ended, buggies, wagons, carts, omnibuses, carriages, and men on horseback headed back to town. As everyone was leaving, Copping called to a friend driving a buggy with a good horse and offered to bet him $300 to $50 that he would give him a half mile start and still beat him to his saloon (Tom's Saloon) on Main Street between Prairie and Preston streets. The man in the buggy hesitated, then accepted the bet. As soon as the yell was raised to start, Copping's gray balked, rearing more than once when hit with the whip. The surprised rider "was too amazed to do anything" for the old gray, that had "never failed to respond to Tom's call in the most proper and orthodox manner, stood straight up on his hind legs" and "for ten or fifteen minutes they had it up and down all over the prairie." By the time Tom settled him down to run and approached the finish line his opponent was already in the saloon "settin' 'em up" to everyone in the place. Obviously racing down the main streets in Texas towns had not lost its appeal.[14]

Young also related that in 1870 Houston hosted a Texas State Fair, which was initially held at a site north of the bayou, but moved the next year to Main Street where the new location took the name Fair Grounds. Sponsors organized a racing association, and there was "a good race course laid out, and some good races were pulled off every year." One of the horses carried the name Scott Anderson, after Col. Scott Anderson of Eagle Lake and, according to Young, "Scott Anderson was one of the fleetest and best horses that ever appeared on a Texas track." One of his admirers was a man named Gregory, who ran a saloon at the southwest corner of Main Street and Congress

Avenue. At the close of race week, the famous Scott Anderson took the lead in his final race, while Gregory, "waving a handful of bills over his head, shouted: 'One hundred to twenty-five that Scott Anderson wins the race.'" Since there were no takers, Gregory raised the challenge to $600 to $25 when the horse was in the lead "so great that even a blind man could see that he had the race grabbed." Rush Hutchins, a twenty-one-year-old whose father was a wealthy dry goods merchant, accepted the odds, saying "That's a good bet [even] if I lose it," and produced $25 to cement the contract while Gregory gave $600 to a stakeholder. Money had just changed hands when Scott Anderson stumbled and fell, failing to finish. Gregory "accepted his loss gracefully and if he ever kicked himself for allowing his enthusiasm to get away with him, he did it privately, when no one was looking." This kind of impulsive gambling was not uncommon in Texas, or indeed anywhere.[15]

Houston also had formal racing and a jockey club. In 1870, members discussed plans for a four-day race meet to be held in late May. The first two days would be devoted to regular races, the third day would be trotting. The first race on Saturday would be a three-mile heat with a club purse of $1,000, free to all, and the second race was a consolation, free to all the horses beaten in the meet. The consolation would be mile heats, best three out of five. President Gustave Cook publicized the event to jockey clubs across Texas as well as informing the Louisiana Jockey Club, hoping to encourage entries from that state.[16]

While jockey clubs planned their events, short distance racing prospered. In June 1870, there was a race involving Jack Batchler's fifteen-year-old son Jimmy. The *Dallas Herald* noted that the "races to come off at the Dallas Course next Thursday, June 16th . . . are the subject of much conversation with the sporting men of the city and county—There will no doubt be an interesting race or two and a very pleasant meeting." When the day for the "long-talked of and much-anticipated" match race between James Barkley's sorrel mare, Flax Tail, and J. C. Caton's [possibly Clayton] bay colt Ribbon finally arrived the weather failed to cooperate. The night before the race the heavens opened and the rain poured "which rendered the course heavy and unfavorable" for turning in fast times so the judges delayed the start, which was to be at 2:00 p.m., in order to let the ground dry. The attendance was "quite good" under the circumstances. Even though the weather was "bright and warm, the traveling [through the muddy roads] must indeed have been tedious and laborious, which doubtless accounted for the almost total absence of the fair sex, who have hitherto grace[d] our meetings with their presence."[17]

It was 3:30 before the track seemed firm enough and the judges called for a start. The "signal was given to saddle, and the 'jocks' having gone through their preliminary" preparations were ready when the horses made their appearance. Jimmy Batchler (whom the paper described as the "son of 'Uncle Jack'") was astride the mare Flax Tail. Fourteen-year-old Roland Caton [or Clayton] rode Ribbon, a colt "who has previously achieved racing honors upon our track." When the word to start was given, and after two false attempts, "they got well off together, but the colt at once took the lead, which he maintained throughout . . . and came in an easy winner by almost 30 yards." Although young Batchler lost, he would be back in just a few weeks to race again.[18]

In July 1870 there was another much-anticipated race at the Dallas Jockey Club course. This time it was James Barkley's bay horse Reuben and James Caton's [Clayton] sorrel horse Ku-Klux Klan Jordan. Both men were known in the sporting world as "able and experienced trainers." Again, the weather did not cooperate, and before the start a shower fell rendering the track "somewhat heavy." But that did not stop the spectators, and the paper reported the town was "almost deserted" and "vehicles of every kind were in quick demand and all engaged." The day was beautiful although very warm, up to perhaps an hour before the race when the rains came. (The paper also added, in a separate column, that the thermometer on the day of the race indicated 96 degrees in the shade.) But this time the fairer sex braved the heat, arriving before the rain. There was a "large number of ladies," who the writer thought seemed to "take much interest in the race."[19]

The rain did not delay the start and young Jimmy Batchler, aboard Reuben, was ready this time. In the first heat "the two horses got off well together, Jordan in the lead, but on the back stretch Reuben came up and passed him, coming in about 20 feet ahead. Time 1:30. On the second heat, the horses started on the tap of a drum, the sorrel taking the lead, and getting the inside track, leading the bay some distance, until about the beginning of the back stretch, when Reuben gradually and steadily gained, closing up the gap between him and the sorrel, and just before getting up to the home stretch" caught his opponent. Then the unthinkable happened. "Reuben slipped or made a false step with his right hind foot, and endeavoring to recover with his left fore foot came completely down, striking his breast upon the ground, when the rider leaped off. It was evident that the bay could not proceed, having injured himself internally by his exertions and Jordan came in the winner of the heat in 1:25." A reporter, who apparently did not care for the full name of Jordan, wrote, "The Herald gives an account of the races at Dallas, at the course of the Dallas Jockey Club, between Reuben and the Ku-Klux Indian," a play on the name Ku-Klux Jordan, because "we haven't any Ku-Klux Indians hereabouts, or any other kind of Ku-Kluxer that we are aware of." Despite the dire report of the accident, neither horse nor jockey was seriously injured. Reuben was racing again in August when he beat Caton's horse Ribbon in a dash of one mile, and young Batchler grew up to be a well-regarded stock raiser. It was also about this time that jockey clubs began to keep records, as did local tracks. Texas kept its own set of state records, which newspapers published occasionally, especially when broken.[20]

Both promoters and spectators believed the summer races indicated a promising future. The "large number of persons present on the occasion—the numerous bets . . . show that racing is one of the favorite sports of the people of this section; and the absence of all rows and bolsterousness [*sic*] shows the good sense and peaceful disposition of our people. The Dallas Jockey Club may be set down as a permanent institution—a decided success—and regular meetings and fine and interesting races may be expected from time to time when the weather, condition of the track . . . will permit. We hope soon to see the course well fenced and otherwise improved. That it will be so in due time we have no doubt." The October issue of the *Herald* advertised Christmas races to begin on December 22, with a sweepstakes for two-year olds on Christmas Eve. Entry fees varied between $50 and $100. Entries for the Christmas races would be sent to James L. Barkley, a forty-six-year-old Kentucky native. Barkley frequently raced at other venues, and planned to run his filly Lulu Barkley, half-sister of the famous Rebel. Turfman Jim Brown bought the stud Rebel from Mid Perry at the Corsicana races in November 1871. Jack Batchler's "General Hood *alias* Reuben will also be on hand." Corsicana was part of a circuit that turfmen in North Texas frequented, although it is unknown how many towns belonged on the tour.[21]

The races at the Dallas Jockey Club did not always include pure Thoroughbreds as would be seen at tracks in Kentucky or New York. Generally, the animals competing on Texas tracks were a cross between a stud with Thoroughbred blood and a local mare or more rarely, a mare with Thoroughbred blood and a local stallion. In Texas, there were no rules prohibiting entries of unknown breeding at some club tracks. Many Texas breeders raised horses that would not be eligible for entry into *The American Stud Book* of The Jockey Club when it began its official registry in the 1890s. Racing had become more specialized in the state though, and breeders frequently raised horses just to run on the racing circuit. No longer did the same horse that raced on the weekends double as a saddle horse during the week. Texas also bred serious horsemen. Turfman Jim Brown is one of those who raised horses specifically to race. His stud Rebel would sire a long string of winners. Brown not only competed across Texas, but eventually outside the state.[22]

By the mid-1870s as Texas slowly emerged from Reconstruction and control of the state reverted to local legislators, the economy reflected the people's desire for a return to normality. County fairs were one way that people could put behind them the years of hardship and suffering brought on by the war. Although racing was the highlight of these fairs, there were events for everyone. In Marshall in October 1874, there was even an equestrian event for the ladies where they could display their horsemanship. The winner was Mary Turner mounted side-saddle on Sudduth, where she displayed the "grace, skill and beauty" of a winner. As was appropriate in the nineteenth century, women competed first followed by the regular distance races. The contest for a silver cup, 2,000 yards, open to all, was won by Nathaniel Smith's sorrel horse Jordan. Since many horses carried the name Jordan, this one was described as well-known in East Texas. But it was not until after the regular races ended for the day that the real fun began. As dusk came and the women went home to the fireside, the men stayed at the track where they enjoyed whiskey and gambling. There were to be about twenty scrub races for the evening's entertainment. These races were over in seconds, but they were accompanied by much cheering and hurrahs. The more the liquor flowed, the louder the crowd became. The races lasted until it was too dark for the judges to declare a winner. Spectators bet large sums on the outcome of these races, but times were seldom recorded.[23]

Racing in the United States was changing during these years too. The Belmont Stakes in New York crowned its first winner in 1867; the Preakness in Maryland began in 1873; and the Kentucky Derby started in Louisville in 1875. The Derby was still considered a southern race, even though Kentucky did not secede. The run for the roses was at that time a mile and a half distance. The first winner, Aristides, traced back to Lexington on his dam's side and was sired by Leamington, a famous Thoroughbred that came to the United States from England. As was typical, thirteen of the fifteen jockeys were African American. A few months later, in September 1875, Texans staged their own version of racing for the roses. The Dallas paper carried a story about a local race with local entries. The day began with a one-half mile, two-horse match race for $40. One starter was owned by Harry "Henry" Batchler, the twenty-two-year-old son of Jack Batchler. His entry, Warrior, was a three-year-old black horse by General Hood (also known as Reuben) and the dam was by the family's stallion, Shiloh. His opponent was Shoo Fly, a five-year-old by Jordan owned by a Mr. Warren. These were not Thoroughbreds, but they were horses bred and raised in Texas.[24]

Although the race was to begin at 3:00 p.m., it was not until after 4:00 p.m. that they took to the track. The race was an exciting one. Warrior gained an early lead of ten feet but Shoo Fly's jockey "at once plied the hickory," closing the gap. Coming down the home stretch they were neck and neck. "As they neared the grand stand no perceptible difference could be noted in their positions, and the excitement was intense as they flew past the judges stand, both riders punishing the nags severely. The crowd immediately gathered around the stand to hear Col. Miller's decision, and when a dead heat was announced, much satisfaction was evinced, and all quietly acquiesced in it as a good and fair decision. Messrs. Warren & Batchelor [*sic*] seemed both afraid of each other and refused to run the race over again, although they both testified their willingness to run at some future time, for double the money. They therefore declared the race a draw and all bets off."[25]

The second race "excited much interest . . . having been in contemplation for some time, it was looked forward to as a big affair." It was for a quarter of a mile and $1,000. The opponents were Macafee's bay mare Fannie Bates and Jim Brown's gray mare Alice May by Steel Dust. She never lost a race, and Brown offered to give Fannie Bates twenty feet at the start. It was nearly sundown before the horses were saddled and the riders mounted. After half a dozen false starts, the horses finally took off. They went "like the shot out of a gun" and "the race was run almost before the spectators could realize that the horses were fairly off." The Steel Dust mare was "too much" for her opponent and in the final 100 yards "she shot ahead" and won. Local spectators would have known the breeding on both horses, even though Steel Dust had not raced for years. While the stories of Steel Dust may be clouded in mystery, there are verifiable facts as to his offspring. Jim Brown admired Steel Dust, as he owned several of his colts. It is possible that Brown owned Steel Dust when the stallion died.[26]

One of Brown's other mares also carried the name Alice. Gray Alice earned a reputation for speed that crossed state lines. But the unthinkable happened when someone stole the "famous race nag Alice and a fine mule" from Brown's stable late in 1874. "That was the blow-off," wrote a man who knew Brown. "It was bad enough for them to go around shooting up people, but the limit was reached when they swiped Brown's race-horse on him." An angry Brown immediately headed out looking for his prized animals. About 200 miles from Lee County, he found his horse and mule, as well as the men who held taken them. Brown was quick to pass judgement and in a gunfight that followed, he killed one of the gang, wounded another, and the third wisely surrendered. Horse stealing was a criminal offense, and nothing happened to Brown as a result of the murder. A report from Giddings on December 18 published in the Galveston paper stated that two men, a Jones and Edwards from Comal County, each received ten years in the state penitentiary for the theft. Stories such as this about Brown only added to the reputation he already held as a man no one wanted to cross.[27]

The men who made off with Brown's stock were lucky. "If a horse thief was caught red-handed by the owner of the stolen horses," wrote John Young, "he was likely to be hanged on the spot." The Galveston paper noted in February 1878 that there were 750 warrants against horse thieves alone, while hundreds of others probably roamed at large. The capital of Austin was a particular target, and the gangs of thieves "seemed to be organized and succeed month after month in getting away with the horses of farmers, stockmen and city people." There were not enough lawmen to pursue the outlaws, and knowing they were rarely caught without a gunfight, local sheriffs hesitated to act. Owners rarely recovered their horses, unless they went after them. In that case the rustler, if caught, was usually "strung up to the first convenient limb" with the owner claiming self-defense and almost always escaping punishment. The paper estimated that around 100,000 horses had been stolen between 1875 and 1878, although that number is hard to accept as accurate. Smart thieves did not usually go after noted horse breeders, for men who owned expensive stock generally took precautions to protect their investments. The trio who stole Brown's prize race horse should have known they would not succeed with a man of his short-tempered reputation.[28]

Jim Brown was not only a dangerous adversary, he was also a brilliant trainer and owner who eventually became wealthy from his winnings at the track. The excitement of the turf appealed to him, and the spell of the track was in his blood. He was happiest when he heard the thudding of hoofs on the dirt, and he took home a pocket full of money from the bookie. He was described as a little below medium height and not much heavier than his jockeys, yet he gave the impression of being absolutely devoid of fear with nerves of steel. These traits he displayed on the racetrack both in Texas and beyond. A famous Thoroughbred trainer once said, "You can't settle down and be a racing man too; it's one or the other," and Brown would eventually be known as a winning trainer and owner who traveled to tracks far and wide. Born in Alabama in 1839, his family migrated to Texas after living for a short

James Madison "Jim" Brown went from running quarter horses in Texas to Thoroughbreds on the East Coast and Midwest, but he never forgot his roots or lost his love of short distance sprinters. Of all Texas horsemen, Jim Brown captures the story of turfmen from the Lone Star State, both the good and the bad, with a true Texas flamboyance. Courtesy of Chuck Parsons.

time in Arkansas. His father was John H. "Shorty" Brown who helped found San Saba in 1854. The first burial in the Brown family cemetery in San Saba was in the 1870s when one of Shorty Brown's sons and a son-in-law were murdered. Jim Brown and his wife Amanda were in San Saba in 1860 where he claimed to be a stock raiser. By 1870, he was in Washington County listing his occupation as farmer, and by 1880 he was in Giddings where he was sheriff of Lee County.[29]

Brown raced all across the state and the coming of the railroad made transporting his horses easier. Since the railroad made travel faster for owners to move their stock, Brown used it to transport his horses to race meets or just single match races in Texas, and eventually out of state. Unfortunately, he lost his unbeaten racer Pat in a boxcar accident while shipping him to Brenham. At one point he headed for Lampasas to test one of his unbeaten horses against one owned by Solomon Hailey of Llano County named Gray John, a stallion said to be by Steel Dust. Since the actual date that Steel Dust died is not known, it is possible that Hailey's claim is accurate. Gray John was a sprinter, standing fourteen hands three inches tall and proved the better horse that day. It was not surprising that Brown tried to buy Gray John for $2,500 after his loss but was unsuccessful.[30]

Brown eventually made his home in Fort Worth, and before his death owned some of the finest colts in the West. In October 1875, at the Gonzales County Fair, he pitted his Steel Dust mare Alice May against Bill Fleming's Red Rover in a quarter mile dash, which Alice won by nine feet. Red Rover was a sorrel stallion by Old Billy and out of Paisana by Brown Dick. Since Brown later owned Red Rover, it is quite likely he bought him after this race. Brown was known for trying to buy any horse that beat one he owned. Brown epitomized the unique Texas turfman—he was an avid racehorse breeder but with a violent frontier nature that saw him kill more than ten men in his lifetime.[31]

Brown's stallion Rebel helped seal his reputation for racing fine horses. At the Gonzales County Fair in October 1875 Rebel's colts dominated the scene. A reporter noted that among the horses there to compete many were Thoroughbreds, although more than half were Rebel colts "and all beauties." In fact, at the spring races at Oleander Park in Galveston, Rebel offspring came in first in winnings with $3,100 total. Second place went to Planet, with $500 won by his colts. Other horses shown at the Gonzales County Fair were Old Billy colts San Jacinto and Lena Rivers. In addition, some of Keene Richards Thoroughbreds from Kentucky were in attendance. Brown brought Lone Star by Pilgrim and Alice May. Bill Fleming brought Little Blaze, Tom Gay, and Rover, all three by his stud, Old Billy. After leaving Gonzales, most of the horses would head for Galveston for the spring meet, although some would go to San Antonio or Victoria instead.[32]

Throughout the nineteenth century and into the twentieth, any connection to Steel Dust raised the price of a colt. Unless the seller was a reputable breeder, it was hard to know the authentic from the fake. One of the most unusual was a "fine blooded" two-year-old Steel Dust and Canadian roan pacing pony, the property of J. H. Murphy, that was raffled off at the Office Saloon in Fort Worth in October 1878. Those who wanted to take the chance could buy a ticket for $2.50, and it was noted that this was an "excellent opportunity to win a valuable horse for a mere pittance."[33]

Many of the breeding farms around Austin specialized in fine stock with Steel Dust lineage still in demand, especially those of Jim Brown's Rebel. W. A. Pitts' stable at the Capital Jockey Club grounds owned many Rebel offspring, including Coryell, a four-year-old filly by Rebel, dam by Steel Dust. Last Chance was by Regent, but his dam was the dam of Rebel. The famed Rebel and a host of others had "made a name for Texas horses even in Kentucky, the nursery of the world for fleet coursers." Another stable, that of T. A. Gay, occupied stalls in the northern portion of the fairgrounds. One stud was especially significant —Eglamore, an aged horse, was by War Dance, the famous Jeff Wells's stallion that had spent the Civil War years in Texas. He was a chestnut with white stockings and standing fifteen hands three inches. Gay also owned John Ireland, a three-year-old colt by Rebel, a dark bay at sixteen hands, and Fairy Belle, a two-year-old filly by Rebel. Fairy Belle was a blood bay standing fifteen hands two inches. F. M. Lilly also owned a War Dance colt, the gelding

Bob Ridle. Many of the same horses could be seen at county fairs and other places well into the 1880s. Other noted colts included T. K. Hawkins' bay Texian, his brown filly Fashion, and brown filly Tunie, all by Rebel. Batchler and Company showed a filly, Bessie Davis, by Rebel. S. O. Cloud exhibited the colt Roger Milles by Last Chance, dam by Steel Dust. These favored bloodlines appeared in many horses racing on Texas tracks.[34]

After the Civil War, as the nation healed its wounds and business prospered, there emerged a new type of turfman in the Lone Star State. Jim Brown was one of those as he gravitated from quarter mile scrub races to Thoroughbred tracks. His success brought him to the notice of those wealthy owners who wanted a trainer to run their horses at large professionally organized events with substantial purses. Men like Brown made a living following various circuits. Brown even created a syndicate for his own stable, and then took the next step of racing on out-of-state circuits from the Mississippi River valley to the East Coast. He might have made his money with Thoroughbreds, but he never forgot his Texas roots and continued to love and race quarter horses too.

Several factors made this possible. After the war the nation was united as it had never been before, and industrialization was rapidly bringing prosperity to many sections of the country. Transportation for horses was both safer and easier than before the war, and a stable could leave Texas and be at the tracks in New York state in a matter of days. Before the Civil War men headed west looking for a new start, bringing their horses bred in Kentucky and Tennessee. By the late 1870s, the direction reversed and often these same men, or their sons, headed east ready to show off what crossing those animals with stock in the Lone Star State produced.

One Texas facility that bred pure Thoroughbreds was the Elmonia Stud Farm of Dr. William Copeland Philips and John Hall Philips, two to three miles northwest of Austin. Dr. Philips moved to Texas in 1853 where he set up a medical practice in Austin. But as a strong Unionist and supporter of Sam Houston in the years before the Civil War, he fled to his home state of Missouri during the conflict and did not return to the Austin area until after the fighting ended.

In 1867, he became Texas Secretary of State and later chief clerk in the office of the state comptroller. As a graduate of Transylvania University in Lexington, Kentucky, he knew his Thoroughbreds and it was in 1875 that he bought the celebrated race horse Silent Friend. When in September 1875 Philips took his daughter to college in Kentucky, he returned to Texas with three yearling colts and the six-year-old Thoroughbred stallion. Silent Friend, a rich golden chestnut that stood sixteen hands high, was by imported Australian and his dam traced back to Lexington and American Eclipse. The local paper noted Dr. Philips could now boast of "one of the very finest studs in the United States." The stallion's reputation preceded him, and word quickly spread of his impressive victories at tracks from New Orleans to Chicago. Although his purchase price was not divulged, it was known to involve "considerable expense." Philips hoped his new stud would produce colts to rival those of Rebel.[35]

Silent Friend had been purchased for Dr. Philips by Sanders D. Bruce of the New York journal *Turf, Field, and Farm* from A. J. Alexander's celebrated Woodburn Stud Farm just outside of Lexington. It is possible that Philips and Bruce knew each other from their years at Transylvania University. Philips already owned some Thoroughbreds, and Silent Friend was an effort on his part to add quality to his stock. In November 1875 at the Capital State Fair, Silent Friend won first premium for the best Thoroughbred stallion four years and older. The following year he came in second in the Grand Sweepstakes, but in 1877 won Best Stallion, any age or breed. By 1879 his line dominated the winner's circle in many categories as well as on the turf. John Hall Philips, known as Hall, had a knack for training horses, and Elmonia had its own private track. As the decade ended the *Austin-American Statesman* reported of the Capital State Fair: "Never was there a more beautiful array of blood. There was the venerable and noted Rebel, the sire of so many noted horses and there, too, was his half brother, the scarcely less celebrated Last Chance. Here, too, was the beautiful and finished Silent Friend, whose colts are now beginning to make the reputation expected of this blood, and in the ring, too, was Incommode, an animal so beautiful that he should become the model of artists, and Eglamore, of most royal blood, and Jack Hardy and Tom McKinney, the everlasting grand son of Lexington, and a long line of bloods that years will develop into animals as notable probably as any upon the turf. . . . These horses show that the thoroughbred in Texas is in his element, that this genial clime, where air and water and the most delicious herbage combine, produces the best animals of the world. The sight of these horses proves beyond a doubt that Texas is unsurpassed for the production of fine stock, and before many years pass it will be so acknowledged by breeders throughout the world." Unfortunately, in July 1880 the two Philips announced plans to sell their Thoroughbred stock and quit the business. There was an auction on October 19 of twenty Thoroughbreds, including their prime racer General Philips and their stud Silent Friend. At some point Dr. Philips returned to his home of Boone County, Missouri, where he died in 1906. But Silent Friend and the many other Thoroughbreds would continue to dominate the Texas racing scene with their sons and daughters into the next decade and beyond.[36]

One of those studs associated with the Elmonia Stud Farm was a Texas born and raised colt that carried a well-known name. Tom McKinney, named for the late respected breeder, showed speed and bottom of the "highest class" during his early campaigns, and won a considerable amount of money for his owner A. P. Blocker, whose farm was three miles south of Austin. He was a grandson of Lexington, a bright bay with white hind ankles. He stood fifteen hands one inch high. But after swapping trainers and owners several times he was sold for $500 and put to stud. Horse thieves trying to nab the prized stallion annoyed one of his owners, L. S. Hughes, so much that he sent the stallion to Elmonia and placed him under the guidance of trainer Hall Philips, who brought out all the stallion's good qualities. He won the "grand free-for-all handicap, with 100 pounds up, against the 'crack' of Texas, and in the best time ever run over the Capital State Fair course," and Philips earned a share of the glory connected with that victory. Tom McKinney's name would appear in the pedigrees of many fine Texas racing stock in the decades to come.[37]

The 1870s were years of change for Thoroughbred racing in America. People wanting to start afresh moved west and in 1873 the Pacific Jockey Club announced races of four-mile heats for a purse of $20,000 in gold bullion. Racetracks appeared at Oakland, San Francisco, and Sacramento, but soon spread to almost any town of note. The pedigrees of the entries reflected the same bloodlines as those horses seen on the tracks in Texas: Australian, Planet, Glencoe, and Eclipse, among others. New names were popping up in the racing business—robber barons—men who made their fortunes in the boom time for the rich. Leland Stanford, president of the Central Pacific and Southern Pacific railroads and founder of Stanford University, became interested in racing trotters with Thoroughbred blood. Kentucky-born James Ben Ali Haggin moved to California and became one of the richest men in America with holdings in gold, silver, and copper. He eventually established the largest Thoroughbred stud farm in history at that time.[38]

In the East, New Yorkers discovered the pleasure of horse racing and a track at Brighton Beach in Brooklyn opened in the late 1870s, where it eventually became a site of racing year-round. In 1879, the Coney Island Jockey Club formed, led by James R. Keene, Leonard Jerome, and William Kissam Vanderbilt, with races held at the track at Sheepshead Bay, and it soon became the most popular in America after it opened in 1880. Other tracks in New York quickly followed. But the man who stood out was London-born James Robert Keene. Settling in San Francisco, his knowledge of mining stocks helped him turn $10,000 into $6 million in the stock market. At forty years of age, he bought his first race horse in 1878 and won the 1879 Belmont Stakes. Although his fortune would go up and down, each time he went broke he reinvented himself and came back strong. After relocating to Kentucky, he eventually owned a descendant of War Dance—the famous Domino—a horse destined to become a legend. Other names in the business at this time were brothers Pierre and George Lorillard who used family money amassed by their father Peter in the tobacco and snuff business to operate a breeding farm in New Jersey. George was part of a group of investors to buy the closed Monmouth Park, New Jersey, racecourse in 1878, which re-opened in 1882, and proved a popular destination for racegoers into the 1890s. In fact, in the final decades of the century almost every wealthy family in America had a relative involved in the business, whether breeding, training, racing, or just attending the races regularly.[39]

But racing was no longer just an enjoyable pastime. For many men it had become their occupation, a way to make a living. For the rich, owning winning horses was a status symbol. The big races attracted the wealthy. The Belmont Stakes, which crowned its first winner in 1867, was financed by European-born August Belmont and named in his honor. Held at the Jerome Park Racetrack located in Westchester County (now the Bronx), New York, from 1867 until 1889, and owned by Belmont's friend Leonard Jerome, it boasted of a lavish clubhouse that became the meeting place of the rich and famous. Jerome's daughter Jennie married Lord Randolph Churchill making Leonard the maternal grandfather of future British Prime Minister Winston Churchill. Both Belmont and Jerome were heavily invested in Thoroughbred racing, and Belmont served as president of the American (sometimes seen as National) Jockey Club from 1866 until 1877. Just as southern planters ruled the tracks in the antebellum days, the men of wealth in the North did the same after the war. The turf drew men of power together because, as August Belmont famously pointed out, Thoroughbred racing was "for the rich."[40]

Investors from the East Coast often bought cheap land in Texas. One of the most successful breeding establishments in the nation could be found in Gillespie and northeastern Kerr counties. New York broker Francis Morris bought 23,000 acres in 1856 for twenty-five cents an acre, later reduced to 16,000 acres. Morris, an avid Thoroughbred breeder, owned and bred Ruthless, the winner of the Belmont Stakes in 1867 and the Travers Stakes at Saratoga. Morris died without ever seeing his Lone Star holdings, but his son John Albert, born in 1836, continued his father's interest in Thoroughbreds and turned the family's Texas ranch into a prosperous breeding enterprise. As a young man, John traveled abroad with the legendary turfman Richard Ten Broeck where he experienced firsthand the workings of the sport in England. He spent an estimated half million dollars making his Texas spread one of the leading centers in the country. The complex included a track, housing for jockeys, a hotel for guests, a general store and post office, a school, a cotton gin, and a flour mill. At one point the ranch counted ten stallions and around 200 mares. But as racing laws tightened on the East Coast, the Texas ranch began to decline. By 1902, the horses had been sold and the area some eight miles southwest of Fredericksburg was divided into around seventy tenant farms growing cotton. Thoroughbred breeding in the Hill Country ceased to exist.[41]

The Morris family is an example of how wealthy northern entrepreneurs took over Thoroughbred breeding and racing in the last decades of the nineteenth century. Francis Morris's filly Ruthless was not only known for winning the first Belmont Stakes, but also for the fact she died one of the strangest deaths of any well-known Thoroughbred when a hunter wandering by the Morris Farm in Westchester County, New York, accidentally shot her. Morris's son John, who inherited his father's fortune, owned not only the breeding establishment in Texas but another in Europe, along with various properties from the East Coast to Texas, including real estate in New Orleans. In 1889, he and partner Leonard Jerome opened the Morris Park racecourse in what was then Westchester County. This track hosted the Belmont Stakes from 1890 through 1904, and also the Preakness Stakes in 1890. John Morris suffered a stroke while at his Texas ranch in 1895 and was fittingly buried at the former racecourse, the Metairie Cemetery in New Orleans, his worth valued at between $25 and $30 million. Fortunately, he did not live to see racing banned in New York state and the decline of his beloved sport.[42]

Texas would never be a center of Thoroughbred racing like New York state, nor would it even have the large tracks like those in New Orleans, Chicago, and Louisville, but it had its share of bloodstock that could be found on courses in the larger cities. Houston, Dallas, Fort Worth, Austin, and San Antonio advertised events not only for race horses, but offerings for trotters and pacers. As the 1870s drew to a close these hubs of racing, along with nearby small towns, created racing circuits that the dedicated turfmen could follow from week to week. Still, Texas was a small market compared to circuits outside the state, and Texas cities were not cities in the sense of Chicago or New Orleans. There was never an official body to oversee Texas racing but local communities, especially in North Texas, joined together to organize regional circuits. Turfmen in various towns met and agreed to host events in the spring and fall similar to the circuits seen elsewhere in the United States. This trend would continue through the end of the century.

As the decade ended, an incident in the late 1870s demonstrated that violence that began at the race often spread beyond the track. The episode occurred at a race near Giddings where Jim Brown entered one of his horses. A man named Sam Sparks also had a horse entered. Before the race Brown and Sparks quarreled over a petty matter, but it upset Brown enough to pick up a shotgun lying nearby. There was a scuffle, but friends stopped the fight. Brown tried to settle with Sparks, but Sparks refused, saying "I know your game, Jim Brown. You make up your quarrels, disarm suspicion and your victim is soon made away with by some of your desperate gang. I've got you for an enemy and I want the people to know it."[43]

Sparks knew he had angered a dangerous man, and after that he never went anywhere unarmed. Time passed, and in 1880 a friend persuaded Sparks to go for drinks one Saturday night and play pool. Before Sparks knew it, night had fallen. Sparks, who always tried to be home before dark, told his companion, John Carlisle, he should not have stayed so long, as "Brown's men have been waiting for a chance to kill me and now they have it. I am afraid to go to my horse, for they are sure to kill me." Carlisle told Sparks he was talking nonsense. Carlisle and another man, Ed Myers, walked Sparks toward his horse, but Myers decided to head back to the saloon. W. T. Sharmon, whose home was near the tavern, watched from his porch as Myers turned around and shot Sparks with a pistol, killing him instantly. A paper reported that since it was common to hear gunshots in the night, they did not attract attention and "the murder was unknown until the body was found the next morning." Not long after, "Brown and his gang threatened Sharman's life" if he told anyone what he had seen and warned him "to leave the country."[44]

This episode demonstrates how seriously competitors took disputes on frontier tracks and to the personality of one of Texas' best known turfmen. At the time of the murder, a paper reported that "there was no clue to the perpetrators," but with Sharmon's testimony, Myers was apprehended and sentenced to twenty years for murder. Carlisle disappeared, only to be arrested in Fort Worth where Brown and his friends posted his bond. For years the court postponed Carlisle's trial again and again. According to later evidence, Carlisle and Brown then hired Charles Luttrell to kill the only witness, Sharman, who had moved to Denison, almost 300 miles from Giddings, where the original murder occurred more than a decade before. In April 1892, a blast from a shotgun killed Sharman in his bed as he lay next to his wife and baby. Without the witness, when Carlisle showed up for trial at Giddings for the murder of Sparks, the judge dismissed the case. Unfortunately for Carlisle, he was quickly rearrested for the murder of Sharman. His trial, and that of Luttrell, was in Denison in 1892, where both were found guilty. Luttrell maintained his innocence to the end, saying "Jim Brown and a prominent attorney at Giddings killed Sparks." Nonetheless, both Carlisle and Luttrell were hanged in May 1893. While there was no evidence to implicate Brown directly in the murder of Sparks, the story followed Brown until his death. Part of the headline in the Austin paper following the 1893 executions read: "With Their Death the Murderous Jim Brown Gang of Assassins Loses Its Prestige." This headline and the stories that appeared in various newspapers kept the folklore surrounding Jim Brown alive.[45]

By the end of the 1870s Texas had changed dramatically. No longer did hostile Comanches and Kiowas roam the western plains. The last of the Comanches surrendered in 1875 when Quanah Parker led his small band into Indian Territory to settle on the reservation. The western part of the state, so long shunned because of the threat of hostile Indians, opened to settlers and investors alike. Existing ranches prospered and new ranches appeared. New towns emerged along the railroad lines connecting Texas not only with the Atlantic Coast but soon with the Pacific Coast. Texas turfmen could now ship their horses to tracks beyond the state borders. Moreover, no longer was it vital to import breeding stock to the Lone Star State. The quality of the Texas race horse had improved so much that the more confident owners were ready to test their colts on established tracks outside the state.

7 Into the Modern World

The 1880s

For Americans devoted to Thoroughbred racing it seemed that the sport was at the height of popularity in the 1880s. The center of racing shifted to the North and Midwest, and the distances run were similar to those seen at Thoroughbred tracks today. Serious turfmen could follow the Midwest racing circuit from Canada to the Gulf Coast. The southern end was the fairgrounds in New Orleans, which opened in 1872, and the northern end was Chicago. The cities with large tracks could be easily reached by rail or steamboat. Some of the most prominent were St. Louis on the Mississippi River, and Cincinnati and Louisville on the Ohio River. The facilities in Chicago rivaled the best tracks in New York state. Although Illinois counted numerous tracks, none touched the popularity of Washington Park in Chicago, where former Union Gen. Phil Sheridan once served as president. When it opened in 1884, it was a state-of-the-art complex, comparable to racecourses on the East Coast. Promoters bragged of a one and an eighth mile track with a smaller one sitting in the infield. The day of the American Derby the public turned out in droves and many businesses closed early. The purse was almost twice that of the Kentucky Derby. When Chicago hosted the World's Fair in 1893, Washington Park held the richest race in the nation. Wealthy Texans frequently journeyed to Chicago, just as their earlier counterparts sailed to the Metairie track in antebellum days. Improvements in transportation made the trip to Chicago as inviting as the earlier one to New Orleans. The 1880s were favorable for

Thoroughbred racing, and Washington Park held its preeminent position for about ten years, until Chicago finally had too many tracks to support public interest.[1]

For those who followed quarter mile racing the opportunities in Texas remained the same. It was still easy to see match races on any weekend, weather permitting, in many Texas counties. Hostile Indians no longer threatened settlements in the West. The buffalo was almost extinct, and the last of the Kiowas and Comanches lived on reservations in the Indian Territory. Texas cattlemen prospered by driving their livestock to railheads to the north, but by the middle of the decade cattle drives began to decline. In the interim the railroad expanded in Texas, and places like Abilene and Fort Worth on the Texas & Pacific line began to grow. Texas built its own stock pens for cattle shipped to the East. The cowboys who drove the cattle worked from horseback, rounding them up for branding and driving them to the railheads. Agile cowponies helped the cowboy rope and corral cattle on the ranches that dotted the western counties. These cowponies could often be seen at scrub races on the weekends, and many traced their ancestry to Steel Dust, Shiloh, Old Billy, or another bloodline well known to men at the time but whose names have been lost to history.

The cattle kingdom had come into its own. Both large and small ranches dotted the West Texas landscape. The King Ranch in southern Texas, which originated before the Civil War, would eventually be known for both the quarter horses and Thoroughbreds raised there—Assault won the Triple Crown in 1946, the only Texas-bred horse to do so. Soon other large ranches covered the Texas grasslands. Charles Goodnight started the JA Ranch in Palo Duro Canyon, and named it after his backer, wealthy Irishman James Adair. He became one of the first Texas cattle barons. The Four Sixes Ranch was the spread of Texan Samuel Burk Burnett, and the story goes its name came from a poker hand that won him the money to begin in the cattle business. Whether or not the stories about these early ranches are true, they persist in the folklore surrounding the mystique of the Texas cattle kingdom. Other ranches, too many to name, gave Texas the reputation as a wide-open wilderness that attracted many new settlers hoping to make their fortunes in the cattle business. A number of the well-known ranchers would also dabble in horse breeding and racing. Some eventually went into racing professionally.[2]

Horses and cattle went together and the two often made warm friends of the owners of large spreads. Two of those were Burk Burnett and William Thomas "Tom" Waggoner. Burk Burnett's family moved to Texas in the late 1850s, settling in Denton County when he was just a year old. Burnett went on his first trail drive at seventeen, and by the time he was nearly twenty he was a partner with his father in the cattle business. In 1871, he registered his own brand and began building the empire that became the Four Sixes Ranch. By the early 1880s he had established his name. His good friend, Tom Waggoner, was born in Hopkins County, Texas, in 1852. The Waggoners moved to Wise County where Tom became his father's partner in the cattle business in 1869. His father, Daniel Waggoner, founded the Three D Ranch before the Civil War, and by the 1880s ran both a horse and cattle empire. Tom Waggoner had a particular love of Thoroughbreds, and in 1929 opened Arlington Downs racetrack between Dallas and Fort Worth. When gambling on racing resurfaced in Texas in 1933, he was the man who led the campaign. The Three D Stock Farm and racing stable, adjacent to Arlington Downs, entered horses in several significant Thoroughbred races from the late 1920s through the 1930s. Strideaway, bred at the farm, carried the Three D colors in the 1933 Kentucky Derby.[3]

Newcomers to the state in the last quarter of the nineteenth century soon realized that Texans raced both quarter horses and Thoroughbreds, although most never saw a Thoroughbred in action since they ran almost exclusively in metropolitan areas. The last third of the nineteenth century saw rapid economic growth in the nation and, as businesses expanded, fortunes were made that allowed the wealthy to dabble in Thoroughbred breeding and racing. As in colonial days, raising expensive Thoroughbreds signified a status only attained by the wealthy. This separation would become even more pronounced by the end of the century, as Thoroughbred racing became the realm of the well-to-do and quarter horse racing remained the domain of the common man. Sheriff Jim Brown, whose shady reputation preceded him, was one of those who started with quarter horses but discovered the big money was in running Thoroughbreds. Brown made the move to Thoroughbred racing by using his skill as a trainer with an eye for a winner. He began racing full-time out-of-state in the 1880s, eventually taking his stable to places like St. Louis, Nashville, Louisville, and Chicago, as well as New Jersey and New York state, where he earned both loyal friends and bitter enemies. He was the first to carry the mystique of the "Wild West gunslinging" Texan to tracks in the Midwest and on the East Coast. The reputation he earned as a frontier lawman followed him as he took his Texas know-how outside the state. He could have been the main character in a dime novel, so true was his life to the fiction written about the lawless West. Americans from the Atlantic to the Pacific read about this native Texan and his exploits in Chicago in the early 1890s. His life story proved more spellbinding than any fiction could offer.

In the popular imagination, Texas in the days after the Civil War was characterized by outlaws and gunfighters, but by the 1880s one could see signs that a growing number of citizens wanted more law and order and the end of the violent culture that pervaded the state. Texas was advancing, but not overnight. It was slowly going from an agrarian state to one with metropolitan areas centered in the cities of Houston, Austin, San Antonio, Galveston, Dallas, and Fort Worth. It was still a state dominated by the menfolk, although the ratio of men to women was closing. Pastimes still reflected male tastes and in late 1880, turfmen in Dallas decided it was time to formalize local racing again. Apparently, the jockey club formed in 1869 had not survived. It is possible that the Panic of 1873, which caused a tightening of credit nationwide, had a negative, if brief, effect on racing in general and the Dallas club in particular. Whatever the cause of the demise of the original club, in November 1880 prominent horsemen proposed to organize a jockey club and sponsor yearly spring and fall races. It was not cheap though, as the club instituted a subscription of $600. In trying to attract members the promoters asked: "Why should Dallas be behind in this matter? There are a number of gentlemen in Texas devoting their attention to the breeding of thoroughbred horses, and we have in our state some as highly bred animals as can be found in the world." In trying to win over local citizens, the promoters pointed out that visitors to the city would spend money and thus help the economy. By December 1881, the *Dallas Daily Herald* could announce: "It is the object of the Jockey Club and the management to make Jockey Club racing popular, not only in Dallas, but throughout the State, that a new impetus may be given to the raising of fine and thoroughbred stock, and especially that Dallas may twice a year have sport so rare and pleasing that it will redound to her credit and honor abroad and attract thousands of visitors here on each occasion."[4]

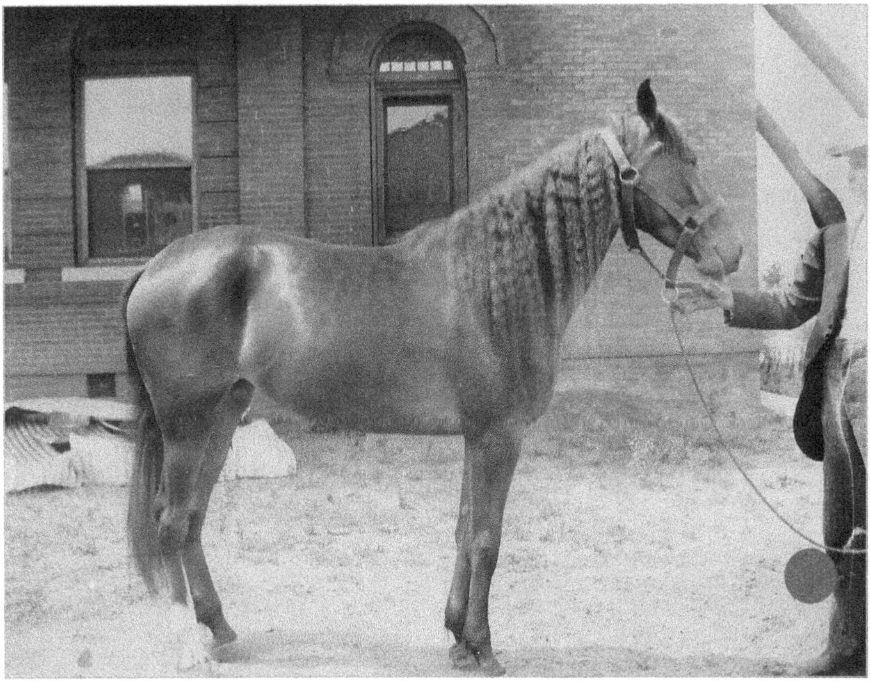

Image of a Texas race horse around the end of the century. Albumen Print, c. 1885–1890. Courtesy of Anne J. Bailey.

But it was Galveston that was the location of a memorable match race in July 1880. "I saw one horse-race I'll remember as long as I live," said one old timer as he brushed the cobwebs from his hat in 1886. "I saw more money lost before you could fairly look around than I ever saw lost on a race before or after." He happened to be on the island when the oleanders were in bloom and the roadways lined with red and white blossoms. There the firm of Levy Bros. owned a mare called St. Mary that "the whole town had just gone wild over." She was one of the dam unknown kind, "but as racy a-looking animal as you ever set your eyes on, standing about 15.1, and muscled all over. . . . She was a beauty, and no mistake, and for a little ways she could run so fast that even a deer would be ashamed of himself." The French-born Levys, who ran a livery stable, were so proud of her that they issued a challenge, offering to match her against any horse in Texas for $500 a side at a quarter of a mile. The ink was barely dry on the challenge before there appeared in Galveston a "little grange-looking chap" who said his name was Tom Harris and offered to accept the dare. After considerable beating about the bush and no end of talk, a date was set for July 3. After the money was put in responsible hands, the stranger refused to name his horse, and disappeared as quickly as he had come. A few days later a "lank, lean cow-boy" who gave his name as Joe Davis arrived. He said he hailed from Liberty County and he knew the unknown mare. He took wagers from those who backed St. Mary, and the papers "were full of talk about the match and excitement ran up to a fever heat. The whole town of Galveston was a backing St. Mary, and there was more rumors flying about than you could shake a stick at. Some said the unknown horse was Grey Eagle, who was being brought on from Colorado, and others were equally positive that it was Red Cross, a quarter-miler that had become famous over the Mexican border." Two days before the race St. Mary made a quarter mile in twenty-two seconds, and that was so impressive that every gambler in Galveston rushed to put money on her and the "granger-looking chap from Liberty county was bet to a standstill." A couple of days before the race the man called Tom Harris arrived with a party of cowboys, and the "way they bet their money on the unknown mare was a caution."[5]

On the day of the race, and long before the start at 2:00, nearly every business in Galveston shut its doors. Men, women, and children headed for the track, and it was estimated that at least $20,000 was staked on one of the two entries. "Upon the race opinions differ," the Galveston paper observed, and "it is a hard matter at the present time to pick out the winner. The Davis party claim that they will run to win, and will win if they can, but they are evidently not much in love with the prospect. Joe Levy, on the contrary, thinks that some of those Liberty county men will walk home after the race." No one had yet seen the challenger's horse, and when she was led on the track there was a general rush to get a glimpse of her. She was a light chestnut and stood about fifteen hands high with a "blood like head and legs like a deer's." The two started at the three-quarter pole and St. Mary shot ahead. She held the lead to within half a length of the finish and then the jockey on the unknown mare asked his mount for more, and she "shot to the front like a rocket and won by a half a length. In 21¾ seconds. It was the greatest race I ever saw, and more money was lost and won on it than any race of the kind, I guess, before or since."[6]

"Oh, you want to know who the parties were, do you," asked the old timer. "Well, the little chap who gave his name as Tom Harris was Jim Brown, the Sheriff of Giddings." The mare he raced was thought to trace back to Rebel, Brown's famous stallion by Steel Dust. What her dam was "the Lord only knows." Five years later the narrator of the story ran into Brown in New Orleans. Brown told him that Belle was a six-year-old mare ridden by a jockey named Aiken, who was a "great little jockey in his day." But, added Brown, like many other riders, "he rode one race too often and weighed in for the last time," when he was killed by a fall in Austin.[7]

For the most part the old timer's memory was excellent. When the Galveston paper wrote about the coming race two days prior to the event, it noted that the race was between the mare Belle belonging to Davis and the Levy Brothers

St. Mary for $500. It was also clear in the article that Jim Brown would be there, because he was on the program in a race scheduled between his black filly and "Galveston's crack half-miler Waco" for $100 a side. "This will be another rattling race from start to finish," continued the article, "and, as the Brown party say, 'Waco will be given a chance to show what he can do.'" Whether or not Brown masqueraded as Tom Harris in setting up the original challenge will never be known. But as folklore goes, never let the facts mess up a good story, and Jim Brown was becoming bigger than life in Texas racing circles by this time.[8]

A few months later, in November 1880, an article appeared in a Dallas paper embracing the virtues of racing at courses owned by jockey clubs run by prominent citizens. This contrasted with the kind of match racing seen at scrub tracks across the state. It read in part: "Jockey club racing for purses is a sport in itself innocent, and that meets with the hearty approval and endorsement of the better classes everywhere. The first gentlemen in every country engage in it, and by their encouragement, countenance and participation, elevate the sport to a genteel amusement, free from the tricks and frauds peculiar to mere gambling schemes where the unwary and uninitiated are at the mercy of the sharpers. This species of speed contests encourages, too, the improvement of horse stock, and leads to the breeding of pure, thoroughbred animals, and the development of the horse to the highest state of perfection." The writer concluded by saying that no matter how many races might come in the future, "there will be no better blood nor animals than those that will run next week."[9]

Racing in Dallas drew large crowds. At the Saturday races on May 12, 1881, a spectator could pay twenty-five cents to see a familiar name in local racing, Henry Batchler, the son of Jack Batchler from Ellis County, raced his horse Mate Chapman by Rebel Morgan. The races began at 2:00 p.m., and for twenty-five cents Siler's buses would transport fans to the track. Thursday, May 26, was the date of the first day's races of the Dallas Jockey Club, and spectators crowded the stands while a large number watched from their carriages and buggies. The big attraction was a half-mile dash for two year olds, but the "audience livened up smartly" to watch another race, a "bout for saddle horses" of a mile distance. There were only three starters, but one "stumbled and fell a fearful fall, sliding under the railing entirely outside of the track into the trotting track." The horse was not seriously injured, but the rider, a black teenager named Clarence, broke his arm and suffered a cut on the back of his head. In 1882, Batchler was running horses under the partnership of Batchler & Barkley. Henry would soon be known for importing Kentucky Thoroughbreds.[10]

Batchler continued to frequent the races in Dallas in the spring of 1882. When the Dallas Jockey Club announced its schedule, he arrived in the city "bringing his splendid stable, composed of a number of fine flyers." Breeders generally attended the same events each year, and in November 1883 the paper reported that the Dallas races were the finest ever witnessed. With city pride, it announced that racing like that had never been seen in the state before. Out-of-state visitors were surprised at the quality of the entries, "away down in Texas," making it sound as if Texas was at the end of the universe which, to many from the East Coast, it was. For those who followed the circuit, after Dallas they moved their stables to Gainesville, then Fort Worth. Those with ready cash could transport their horses by rail. The rest rode or led them to the next event, thus sometimes limiting the number of races they could attend. With such enthusiasm in North Texas, Galveston turfmen discussed organizing a "racing association" in October 1882 and joining the Texas racing circuit.[11]

Austin also attracted racing enthusiasts. In October 1881, the Seventh Annual Capital State Fair hosted a series of events. Turfman Jim Brown won second in the best stallion, two years old and under three, and second in best mare, one year old and under two. Men like Brown followed a racing circuit that not only included jockey club races, but also county and state fairs where both showing and racing their horses were part of the agenda.[12]

The Texas racing circuit attracted turfmen from all over. In March 1882, the Houston Jockey Club announced that the stables were rapidly filling with horses there for the spring meet at the fairgrounds. Twenty-five arrived from Dallas on one train. Two men came from Little Rock, Arkansas, with a "stable of six fine runners." A Mr. Atkins of Victoria also brought his racers, "a stable of noted horses—en route for Toledo, Ohio." The races included traditional distances for Thoroughbreds, but also a quarter mile dash between B. F. Keegan's Prince and a horse from Galveston named Brownie, with Prince the winner.[13]

In November of that year the Houston Jockey Club made the "grand old veteran of three wars, the Texas Revolution, Mexican war and Lost Cause," Dr. George A. Feris, an honorary member despite the fact that in February 1871 he had been involved in a "Bloody and Fatal Rencontre" in Richmond when a "difficulty" occurred between Feris and his son on one side and Henry Thompson on the other. Thompson, who was Feris's brother-in-law, fired two shots at the father and son, missing both. But the young Feris returned the fire, wounding Thompson who died two hours later. The newspaper account did not name which of Feris's sons fired the fatal shot, and concluded by saying the cause was an "old family grudge." Whether charges were filed is not known and Feris continued his work to improve the breeding of horses in the state. At age sixty-five "Uncle George" was still going strong. He professed that he did not feel his age, although he admitted that he forgot the name of a celebrated imported horse in running back the pedigree of a Thoroughbred "a short time since," and by that he knew he was "getting old." He believed he was a "monument of the Lord's mercy," and a Methodist friend added, "the devil's forgetfulness."[14]

Feris preferred breeding Thoroughbreds and Arabians, but Thoroughbred racing was changing nationally, and Texas turfmen generally followed the direction of the more established courses. In October 1883, M. Lewis Clark, president of the Louisville Jockey Club, called a meeting of the southern and western associations to be held at the jockey club offices on November 21. The purpose was to consider adopting a uniform scale of weights and rules, and to discuss how to promote the breeding and turf interests in these sections.

The intention was to consolidate various clubs throughout the South and West, including Texas. While this does not appear to have happened, the McKinney Jockey Club, which limited its July 1886 races to "Collin County owned horses," announced the event would be governed by the Louisville Jockey Club rules. Circuits such as the one that took horses from Austin to Gainesville then Fort Worth and Sherman and elsewhere often used different rule books, and serious horsemen wanted consistency. For example, just a few months after McKinney said it would use the Louisville Jockey Club rules, the Fort Worth Jockey Club announced it would follow the American Jockey Club rules in their fall races. The American Jockey Club, based in New York City, was considered the last word in turf matters. The weight of a jockey had always caused friction, as various clubs used different rule books regarding its requirements. This problem was only seen in events using a jockey club rulebook and was not an issue at scrub races where there were no written rules.[15]

Horse racing in Austin, however, struggled to survive. An editorial in the Austin paper in December 1884 noted: "The Capital State Fair Association is dead, and the inquest held on its remains" proved that fact. The writer noted that trying to "run a jockey club under the name Agricultural and Mechanical Fair association, and giving in [racing] purses the great bulk of the money taken in at the gate," left "all the essential features of an agricultural and mechanical fair association [to] scuffle along as best they could." The writer pointed out that the old jockey club "ceased to exist." When the Agricultural and Mechanical association took over the fair racing, it "failed to draw and pay and in the week just closed, with first-class performers at running, trotting and pacing, with celebrities and phenomenal performers, in the matter of attendance it was an ignominious failure." Interest in all kinds of horse racing was on a slow decline as Texans looked elsewhere for their amusements. Visitors to the fair skipped the racing and went to see the exhibits of various farm animals that were more family-friendly and free from the gamblers seen hanging around the track.[16]

In fact, life in general was experiencing challenges to the status quo. In a state still dominated by men, newspaper readers were astounded to read that a woman asked the Belgium Jockey Club for permission to ride her own horses in the "gentlemen's" races. Madame Stroobants, "for such is the fair Amazon's name," entered her horse for the Prix des Dames [Ladies' Prize] at Louvain in the Flemish region of Belgium about sixteen miles from Brussels. She threatened that, in the event her petition was rejected, she would go to the scales and insist on her right to be weighed as an ordinary jockey. "We may assume that it is her intention to don boots and breeches, after the fashion set by the professional horsemen of England, and she to ride upon a man's saddle." Without a doubt this resulted in heated discussions at the dinner table when men put forward their objections to such brazen behavior after this story appeared in local papers, even in Texas.[17]

Madame Stroobants's application was denied. A Scottish newspaper observed, "We are not informed whether it was the intention of the lady to mount en cavalier [in the style of a cavalryman], or to don the "habit, skirt, and cap." This Scottish viewpoint probably appealed to men across the Atlantic in the States, where proper ladies did not engage in such behavior. The paper went on the say that it was "hardly probable . . . and certain it is not desirable—that to the many professions opened of late years to women that of jockey should be added. Women are generally credited with bringing a refining influence to bear upon those sports and pastimes in which, together with the sterner sex, they take part. . . . But it is doubtful if the rough language of the turf, the maledictions of losers, the exuberant joy of winners, the vituperation of the weighing-room, or the ribaldry of the ring would be lessened one iota were [jockeys] Archer or Wood to find himself facing the starter with a number of the fair sex booted and breeched among his competitors for victory." While the author of the piece included a long list of objections, he concluded by saying "every right-minded man will hope that the time is yet far distant when women will be found in the ranks of a profession which, while it embraces a few honourable men, contains a very large number of knaves."[18]

Around the time that Madame Stroobants's story made the papers in Europe, Jim Brown was back in the news in Texas. As sheriff of Lee County, he was "known far and wide for his pluck and bravery, and his name has become a terror to desperadoes and violators of the law in his section." As a result, it was no surprise when in April 1884 there was an attempt to assassinate him. The story Brown told was that as he was returning home Saturday evening, he heard a noise in the stable where he kept a two-year-old colt. He went out to check, and when nearing the barn door someone fired from inside, the ball striking a book in his left-hand coat pocket. Although not hurt, the shot set his clothes on fire. The assassin, thinking he had mortally wounded Brown, pulled him inside the door so he could flee outside. "A desperate struggle ensued in which Sheriff Brown emptied the six chambers of his revolver, three shots taking effect." The would-be assassin fell dead, with a bullet in his head, one in his left arm, and a third through his right hand. The assassin, identified as John Owings, had been a convict guard at the Rusk penitentiary for four or five months, and had come to Giddings only two weeks prior to visit with his mother. During the coroner's hearing, Brown testified that he had "only a casual acquaintance with Owings," and did not believe that he was the victim for "personal motives," but was inclined to the theory that Owings "was acting as a tool of an element that would rest easier" if Brown was out of the way. The coroner's jury returned a verdict of justifiable homicide, and Brown immediately left for Arkansas on private business.[19]

He was in Fort Worth the following year, having moved to the growing city in 1885. It was there that he matched one of his horses against one owned by a son of Tom Haley, a prominent horseman in Johnson County before the Civil War. Tom Haley died as a result of a wound received in the war, but his son Charley bred and raised one of the prominent race horses of that decade —Rondo, a sorrel colt foaled in 1880, and later known as Lock's Rondo. He was by Whalebone, a stallion whose sire was a son of Old Billy by Shiloh and out of Paisana by Brown Dick. Rondo's dam was Mittie Stephens, a daughter of Shiloh Jr. by Shiloh. Rondo, although bred by Charley Haley, is known to

Charley Haley bred the AQHA foundation sire Rondo. He raised and raced both Thoroughbreds and quarter horses. Image courtesy of Mary Alice Christensen.

history by the name of the one of his later owners, W. W. Lock, after Haley lost him in a shady race in Fort Worth.[20]

The race was a match between a two-year-old filly owned by the Haley brothers and a filly of the same age owned by Brown. The match would be a quarter mile sprint for $1,000 a side. Before the appointed day Charley Haley, certain his colt was unbeatable, convinced his brothers to double the bet. Brown acted like he was concerned that he could lose and asked a friend, Tom Martin of Kyle, to come look over the two animals. Martin informed Brown he thought he had little chance of winning as the Haley mare appeared the better horse. But when Martin discovered that Haleys' jockey had ridden for him in the past (a fact that Brown probably already knew), Martin told the unfortunate rider if Brown did not win that he would be sorry.[21]

That a jockey would throw a race was not unusual, but this seemed to be a carefully orchestrated scam planned to make Haley think Brown was truly worried. Haley, who was unaware of the illicit arrangement with the jockey, remained convinced he owned the better horse and wagered all the money he and his brothers had on hand plus all they could borrow. Believing that nothing could best his entry, Charley even bet the stallion Rondo against $2,000 more.

There is no image of Charley Haley's Rondo, but he sired Texas Chief, seen here winning a race in Mangum, Oklahoma, in 1896. Robert Moorman Denhardt, *The Quarter Running Horse: America's Oldest Breed*, 1979.

This proved a disaster for the Haleys when his filly lost. After the race the Haleys were broke, and Rondo went home with a new owner who immediately shipped the stallion to another location. Following the race Brown gave Rondo and $1,000 to Martin, who stood him at stud for a couple of years before, in 1887, W. W. Lock of Kyle bought the stallion for $1,000. Lock eventually took Rondo to his ranch in Greer County, Oklahoma Territory, where he died at age seventeen in 1897, but not before siring many winning racers.[22]

The Haleys lost the best young prospect as well as their money, but losing to Jim Brown was not unusual for turfmen running on quarter mile tracks. Brown won more that day in bets than Rondo was worth at that time, so he probably did not regret parting with him as payment to Martin for his help. On the other side, the Haleys decided that it was time to move on and in 1887 sold the place on the Nolan River in Johnson County to John Wesley Smith for $12,000 in gold. After relocating to Sweetwater, Charley made raising and racing horses his main occupation.[23]

At his West Texas ranch Haley bred both Thoroughbreds and quarter horses. He was especially fond of breeding his mares to Silent Friend. In 1891, Haley had three colts, all by Silent Friend and out of "good mares." One colt boasted of Rondo blood too. Perhaps the most famous stallion Haley raised after Rondo was General Ross, foaled in 1888. General Ross, named for Gov. Lawrence Sullivan "Sul" Ross, who also served as a brigadier general in the Civil War, was by Havre, a stallion tracing back to Australian and Lexington. His dam was Mittie Stephens, the mare that produced several fine colts for the Haleys besides Rondo. Mittie Stephens also foaled Shelby in 1878. He was by Tom Driver by Steel Dust, and although bred by Charley Haley, he was owned by Shelby Stanfield of Thorp Spring and became one of Stanfield's better-known studs. Haley was still racing in 1901, when he brought six horses to the Abilene fairground to prepare for the fall meet. He died later that year at age fifty-four.[24]

By the time General Ross was foaled many Texans had decided the money to be made was found on the out-of-state circuits, and that was where the stallion made his name. Charley Haley sold him to Abilene resident Fred T. Wood when he was a colt. Wood added him to the stable of horses he took to Midwestern tracks after testing his merit at meets in the Lone Star State. In November 1892, he ran at Waco where he won two firsts and a second; then he headed for Dallas to try his luck. There General Ross proved able to race in any company, winning the four and a half furlongs against a field of fifteen other entries. The track was slow, and his performance was considered "remarkable." From Dallas he headed to Nashville. He was judged "one of the best horses, at his distance, ever bred in Texas. He has had more than ordinary success this season, and undoubtedly much of it is due to the careful fitting and training he has had from his owner, Fred Wood, who is one of the best in Texas with the gallopers. General Ross has, over different tracks, met and defeated some of the greatest half-mile horses in the southwest," and their "scalps are all dangling" at his belt. (Sul Ross was a noted Indian fighter in antebellum days.) In 1893, he was sixth in the inaugural stake at St. Louis. By then he had started sixteen times, and only failed to place twice. Early in June he won a "corking" good race at St. Louis at three quarters of a mile with the track very slow. The Texans who followed him from track to track "went away down in their trousers' pockets and hauled out a lot of money that hadn't been in circulation for several years to bet on General Ross." The General won "handily by four lengths." He was back in St. Louis in 1894 and entered in the Street Railway Stake for $2,000 in May. He won the "big race" in St. Louis; it was a six-furlongs handicap, and Ross "scampered home in front of a good field." It proved an exciting race that was "landed with ease by the Abilene horse." He had already run at New Orleans in March and Memphis in April, and it was "quite likely that the bookies paid a few Ross tickets to his owner, Fred T. Wood." In April 1895, Wood's stable was at Nashville.[25]

Texans interested in racing increasingly followed out-of-state circuits. Families often suffered when men left home since not all of them prospered and made enough money to cover their travel expenses. Fred Wood was an exception, as was turfman Jim Brown. Although Brown may not have made much money in his early days, at the height of his career he provided a comfortable living for his wife and children. His success meant he also received an unusual amount of attention, mainly because of his notoriety as a former sheriff, and his win-at-all-costs attitude on the track. He made news both on and off the track. One story that has passed down through the family involved his daughter Luna. Luna was born around 1868 when the family lived in Washington County. The story the family told was that when Luna was a teenager she enjoyed the attentions of two young men, Virge Woolley and John Owens. Her father preferred Woolley while she preferred Owens. After friends warned Owens that Brown would kill him before he would allow him to wed his daughter, the young man fled the town. But Brown found out where Owens was hiding and wrote him a note saying it was safe to come back, signing Luna's name. When Owens returned to the place he thought he would rendezvous with Luna, her father lay in wait and shot him dead. Luna, in a house nearby, heard the shot, ran outside, and soon realized what her father had done. This story, passed down through the family, cannot be verified, but it is known that Luna eventually married four times.[26]

In fact, the accuracy of this story is in question as the information comes from interviews with Brown's children in the twentieth century, but the only one living in Fort Worth at that time was William (Billy), who was only a small child when the murder occurred. What is known is that in 1886, after the Browns moved to Fort Worth, Luna Brown eloped to Gonzales with Hugh Adolph Testard on February 7, where they married two days later. The Fort Worth paper described the bride as the daughter of "J. M. Brown, the well-known race-horse man." Brown objected to the attention of Testard, not because of any personal aversion, but apparently because he disliked the young man's father. Hugh's father was Adrian Testard whose parents were French immigrants to Brenham in Washington County where both he and Jim Brown lived in 1870. At one point Adrian Testard ran a livery stable where he boarded horses and apparently tried his hand at racing. At a Brenham Jockey Club meet Testard raced a sorrel, winning one race, where "considerable money changed hands, some being happy and others disconsolate." It was well known that Brown made many enemies at tracks across Texas and Testard apparently was among those. The couple had been engaged for three years, and during that time Brown warned Testard not to visit his daughter. But when Brown left for the races in New Orleans in early 1886 the couple took advantage of his absence. Brown learned by telegram what his daughter had done. Brown's new son-in-law was in business in Gonzales and was said to be well respected. Later that year a daughter, May or Mae, was born. The child and her mother would make national headlines in the early 1890s.[27]

Brown frequently raced in New Orleans. His daughter Luna was just a teenager when her family moved to Fort Worth and her father left to try his luck racing outside the state. Among the horses he took was a filly named for his daughter. The mare Luna Brown was probably the one in the 1898 edition of

The American Stud Book. That entry has her foaled in 1882 and by the British import Hyder Ali. Her dam was Plenty by Plantagent. Brown's two older sons, Ed and Gaylon often accompanied him. Eventually there would be a well-known horse named Galen Brown for Brown's son Gaylon.[28]

Brown probably chose Fort Worth as his home because of the lively racing circuit within easy distance of the growing city, and a local paper noted that it was "only a question of a few years until Tarrant county will take position among the older counties in the state in raising as fine horses as can be found." Still, Fort Worth could hardly be called a city, the population in 1880 was less than 7,000. But electric lights would soon arrive as would a telephone exchange. Brown frequented a part of downtown, later known as "Hell's Half Acre," where law and order were often absent and gambling, drinking, and ladies of the night could be found. It was also where he made friends with bar owner Luke Short. Brown's partner in the horse business, gambler Jake Johnson, was Short's associate in the notorious White Elephant Saloon. The saloon is known in Fort Worth's folklore as the site of the last gunfight between Short and Timothy Courtright, known locally as "Long-Hair Jim," in February 1887, a story that became part of the city's Wild West history.[29]

Fort Worth boasted of a lively racing scene that Brown undoubtably enjoyed when at home, which became less and less frequent. There were men who wanted to bring law and order to the track, thus attracting families to come and enjoy the sport. Although there had been a racecourse near downtown, it was replaced in 1883 with one built by the Fort Worth Driving Park Association, with the new site being about a mile from the courthouse. Driving Park Associations were popular in Texas, and the Gainesville Driving Park and Blooded Stock Association's success may have influenced the decision of Fort Worth horsemen to start their own. These associations did not limit events to Thoroughbred racing as did jockey clubs, but also included pacing and trotting. The Fort Worth association received a charter from the secretary of state as a domestic for-profit corporation in March 1883, and immediately set out to build a course before the races in the fall. The capital stock was guaranteed by incorporators Jake Johnson, G. H. Day, C. W. Baradall, and J. T. Wilkes. Robert McCart, a prominent lawyer who moved to Fort Worth in 1877, became president. McCart was also instrumental in arranging for Fort Worth to join the racing circuit for the fall. Nine years later, McCart would be a partner in Jim Brown & Co., when the stable competed in Chicago. Jake Johnson, formerly Brown's partner, was also a "noted character" at the Chicago track. These Texans certainly lived up to their "Wild West" reputation when in Illinois.[30]

The Driving Park's track exceeded expectations. Completed in record time, a high wooden fence extended entirely around the grounds preventing anyone from watching who failed to pay. Some 200 yards from the gate was a grandstand that could seat 1,500 people, 500 more could stand in the space underneath. There was a separate reporters' stand with a telegraph wire so that results could be "flashed promptly." A boarded fence went the entire length of the grandstand, "a very wise precaution against danger from horses that feel inclined to jump the course." There were two tracks, the running track, about a mile in length, being the outer one. Inside of this was the track used for trotting and pacing. A rail fence four feet high surrounded both. At the north end could be found the stables that accommodated 150 horses. Just a day before the November races, "Everybody in Fort Worth possessing a carriage or able to hire one seemed to be there driving around, possibly on the lookout for pointers." But they would be disappointed, since most of the horses had not arrived from the Gainesville track where they raced just a few days before. The large purses offered by the North Texas circuit attracted entries from across the South and West.[31]

Fort Worth advertised the coming fall races throughout the region. Under a headline "HO! FOR THE RACES" the local paper bragged, "No city in Texas can show a better list of attractions. . . . We have a beautiful opera house, splendid drives," and the best racecourse in the state. What they lacked was hotels, and the paper pleaded with citizens to open their homes to visitors. One of the most extraordinary events planned was one involving female riders: "Not the least of the attractions of the week will be the long distance races between two of the most daring and accomplished equestriennes of the country. There will be two races, a two and a ten-mile ride. The ladies who have engaged in these contests have earned a national reputation for daring and endurance." If this was a blow to a male-dominated sport, the paper did not mention it. Perhaps it was a way to attract a wider audience, because a section of the grandstand was set aside for ladies and families. A "committee of reception" would be there to see that seats were provided for them.[32]

The inaugural races proved a huge success. More than 2,000 spectators watched the second day of racing with an estimated $15,000 in bets placed. Local authorities rarely interfered with gambling at tracks, and it was a popular draw for those inclined to test their knowledge of the entries and place a wager. The local paper noted: "In order that all the clerks may get to take their sweet-hearts to the races, the business houses will close to-day at noon. The banks will close at 11, so that parties wishing to try their chances should gauge themselves accordingly." The races began promptly at one o'clock, and "Everybody should go, the ladies especially. . . . Special attention will be paid to their comfort. . . . Those of the public who do not go will regret it." Some complained about the price of admission, which was one dollar, but the paper reminded them that the cost of races was higher on the East Coast and at eastern tracks spectators paid an additional fifty cents extra for entrance to the grandstands. Carriages were also taxed. "The association spent $25,000 in buying the grounds and preparing them and are giving away about $9,000 in premiums. They cannot afford to run the track and keep it in condition for nothing." Unfortunately, newspaper accounts only list the names of the winning horses and not the owners or the animal's breeding, making it impossible to know what bloodlines were popular in the 1880s.[33]

In January 1885, the Fort Worth Driving Park Association voted to change its name to the Fort Worth Jockey Club. Dick Harrold was elected president; Jake Johnson, vice-president, J. D. Reed took over as general manager, and

A. J. Roe became the secretary and treasurer. They immediately made plans for spring races, to begin in April. Later in the month they voted to make Jim Brown the track manager, saying "Mr. Brown is an experienced horseman and has a number of race horses at the park." After the April races, in May 1885, Brown shipped his horse Luke Short from Fort Worth to Covington, Kentucky, where the Latonia Jockey Club began their spring races on May 27. Latonia opened in 1883 and was considered one of the finest in the nation, drawing 100,000 spectators annually. The Fort Worth paper noted: "Texas proposes to show those bluegrass fellows what she can do in the matter of horse flesh."[34]

Those Texas turfmen who did not race beyond state boundaries could follow the Texas racing circuit. Many of the larger towns laid out permanent tracks that allowed them to schedule meets during the year. The Denton County Fair and Blooded Stock Association held its fair in 1885 with two days of running and trotting horse competition on its forty-acre venue. By 1895, they had a half-mile horse race, and in September 1896 three races of running, trotting, and pacing with winners qualifying for the Dallas State Fair. The 1897 event saw crowds gather for a three-eighths mile free-for-all dash for a prize of $75 and a four-and-a-half-furlongs race that paid $100.[35]

These events were for white persons only, as laws prohibited black people from attending. That did not mean that African Americans did not also enjoy similar festivities, however. In October 1887, around the time of the State Fair in Dallas, Fort Worth was the site of a three-day Colored State Fair, although the exact location is unknown. On the third day, the weather was fine, and a large crowd attended to see the various events. The Galveston Cadet Cornet band furnished the music, and the day began with the local black baseball club the Young Strikers losing to the Galveston Fly-a-ways by a score of twenty-two to two. But the main attractions were the races. The first was a sprint of five-eighths of a mile with four entries, which resulted in a dead heat between Germania owned by R. E. Maddox and True Blue owned by Adams & Thomas, with a runoff scheduled for later in the day. After that race the announcer declared a quarter mile dash had just been agreed upon between four police force horses for a pot of $20. Those entries were Sheriff Jim Maddox and officers J. W. Coker, Ben C. Evans, and Dick Kitts. The sheriff's horse won. The second scheduled race of the day was for seven-eighths of a mile, and included Maddox's Luke Short, Eva Britton owned by William Sandford, and Susie S owned by William Lambert. In this case Luke Short was distanced, with Susie S declared the winner. The final race was the runoff between Germania and True Blue, with Germania taking the lead at the half-mile post and never relinquishing it. Once the racing ended there was a series of balls in the evenings at the pavilion, and the local newspaper recorded, "colored people are having a continuous round of pleasure this week." Even though more than twenty years had passed since freeing the slaves, the fact this fair made the paper is remarkable. Moreover, the Denton fair in 1900 designated the second day as "Negro Day," and "about 500 of their own race, and a good-sized crowd of white people" attended. There was no mention of racing at that event.[36]

Tarrant County was the home of the Maddoxia Stock Farm. Located two and a half miles south of Fort Worth, it was established in 1889 by R. E. Maddox. Known for importing both fine blooded horses and cattle, his stables included draft horses, trotters, and runners. Maddox counted 110 brood mares, many of them chosen from the best in the nation, and several stallions that he "selected and bred with the greatest possible care." A reporter who saw the twenty-four he displayed in a parade in Fort Worth in 1887 observed that it was a "sight well worth watching." Stock breeders from Kansas, Missouri, and Kentucky pronounced the animals "equal to any they had ever seen." Hospodor, a nine-year-old bay stallion, carried a value of $10,000. He also owned the well-known stallion Luke Short. A four years old chestnut, Luke Short had previously raced in Jim Brown's stable. But by 1887 Brown spent part of the year racing outside the state and it is likely Luke Short did not accompany him. Ownership is difficult to follow at this time, but it is possible Maddox had bought the stallion, as he was valued at only $1,500. Maddox also owned a four-year-old chestnut Doctor V, sired by Wild Bill, and dam a Steel Dust mare, valued at $500.[37]

Scrub racing also remained a popular pastime. One such match was between a black horse and sorrel at the old fairground in Dallas in 1886, and the headline in the paper simply read "Scrub Race." Although one jockey used a saddle, the other rider rode bareback. The reporter, watching from a streetcar, noted: "Whether the mules attached to the street car went too fast for the race horses, or the race horses stopped to blow before getting around, is a problem the reporter is unable to solve. It is a fact, however, they lacked a good deal of getting to the home stretch when last seen from the car." Unlike regular racing, only about twenty-five people witnessed the event. Another scrub race at the Galveston fairgrounds was between Modoc and Wonder, with Wonder winning in the third heat. The race was for $100 a side, half-mile heats. The winning horse was owned by a man known only as "Frenchy" and the loser belonged to William J. Williams. Those present pronounced it "very exciting." The town of Wharton, around 100 miles west of Galveston, aspired to rise above scrub racing, however, and organized a jockey club. Such things, a year previously, would have been unheard of in Wharton where "a scrub race or a dog-fight would have been considered a big thing. Verily we grow." Despite the town's plans to improve culture, at the Wharton County Jockey Club races in April 1886, a Tom Callaway offered his two pet bears and a pet deer as prizes in a shooting match held on the second day.[38]

Where Wharton was just starting a jockey club, racing in Galveston, so popular in antebellum days, had declined. In June 1886 two men from Waco, who represented a syndicate of horsemen, visited the city in the hope of persuading local turfmen to join a Texas circuit. They proposed to promote four days of racing, running, and trotting, or sixteen races, four each day at no expense to local citizens. They even offered to rent the track for $100 per day. But they met with no encouragement and dropped the idea. No one could adequately explain what happened. Horsemen described the Galveston course as "nearly as speedy as the track at Chicago, equal to Cleveland and better than many of the courses in America." There was not anywhere on the continent "equal to this island for wintering their stock, and that if the facilities and fair treatment could be had, there is no reason why every horse making the Texas, Arkansas, Missouri and Louisiana circuit should not winter on the island, that the circuit could begin and end on this course." The argument continued that the city "has a population of 6000 adult men" and if each contributed a little the grandstand could be repaired, a new fence erected, and there would be some left over for the purse. To fail would mean that "all work and no play makes Galveston a dull place." Racing was needed for the retailer, the mechanic, and tradespeople generally. Support was not forthcoming, and Galveston never regained the prominence it enjoyed before the war when its racecourse drew entries from all around, including New Orleans.[39]

Another city to experience a decline in interest in racing was Dallas. In February 1884, a paper reported that there would be no spring race meeting, "that thing is settled—and it is doubtful if she has a meeting next fall." The North Texas circuit for April would be Sherman, Gainesville, and Fort Worth, Sherman being substituted for Dallas. This was a blow for Dallas turfmen as the city was once known as "one of the great race meeting centers of the country, and ranked second in the South only to New Orleans." The cause was laid at the door of those opposed to gambling. Race horse men would not bring their stock and their money to a town "where sporting is treated as severely as it has been in Dallas." Local breeders engaged in raising Thoroughbreds also became discouraged and "abandoned the idea." It was estimated the city would lose many thousands of dollars from the revenue brought to businesses and other enterprises in the community from a good race meet.[40]

Part of the objection to gambling was the violence associated with such wagers. Newspapers frequently carried stories of shootings at the tracks or fights that broke out because of backing a loser. While this had always been a problem at scrub races, the ever-growing population made such occurrences even more common. In Baird, twenty miles east of Abilene, a race took place in late August 1884 that drew sporting men from across the region. It was between Maggie May, owned by a Mr. Weller, and a brown mare that belonged to Jim Jackson, for $500 a side. Maggie May was a known winner, but to the surprise of all the brown mare crossed the finish line first. "After the race a large portion of the crowd took freely of kill 'em straight, the natural consequence followed, [and] black eyes and bruised noses were in order." A report concluded that "several wear these ornaments" following the incident.[41]

Almost on the same day in late August there was "A Shooting Affray" at Burneyville, some thirty miles north of Gainesville in the Indian Territory where Texas horsemen gathered for a race meet. A Mr. Robinson and a Mr. Greenwood agreed on a wager that resulted in Robinson winning $15 from Greenwood. The day after the race a dispute arose between the two men. Greenwood went for his Winchester rifle and Robinson brandished a shotgun. When Greenwood fired he hit Robinson in the left hand, grazing his side. The latter returned fire with both barrels of his shotgun, killing Greenwood instantly. The public blamed these violent episodes on gambling and drinking, and local papers did not fail to sensationalize such happenings. In Arlington just a month later, William Vernon was shot and killed by J. E. Wetherington regarding a "difficulty" that occurred after a race. The murder of Vernon, a father and grandfather, by Wetherington, a "respectable citizen of this community," could only mean that racing was becoming too violent for average people to support.[42]

Despite these indications that gambling at the races was becoming a public nuisance, turfmen still tried to revive the endangered sport. The year 1886 was an important one for lovers of the turf. On January 30, a group of businessmen chartered the Dallas State Fair and Exposition as a private corporation. But the directors differed on the site for the new fairgrounds and Dallas ended up with two fairs that year. One site, in East Dallas, was within the boundaries of the modern State Fair of Texas. A second site proposed was north of the town and would be the Texas State Fair & Exposition. The latter announced it would open one day before the Dallas State Fair. Both sites built a racetrack and both sites attracted large crowds. But the competition for patrons meant that neither showed a profit so the following year the two merged to become the Texas State Fair and Dallas Exposition. As would be expected, the main source of income was from wagering on the races, and as gambling came under increased fire from various religious and civic groups, the races in Dallas would not survive much longer before the city put a stop to them, with the state not far behind in passing anti-gambling legislation aimed specifically at horse racing.[43]

The first annual Dallas State Fair and Exposition opened its gates "to the eager public exactly at 8 o'clock" on October 26, 1886. The headline in the local paper read" "150 RACE HORSES." The grounds were a source of pride, and the racecourse was a spectator-friendly facility. The grandstand, overlooking the track, could seat an estimated 8,000 spectators and there was a lunch counter and saloon on the ground floor where another 5,000 could be crowded if necessary.[44]

The fair was a huge success. Electricity was a sign of the times and lights lit up the exhibition halls and some of the walkways. Comanche Chief Quanah Parker took in the sights by electric light. Still, racing highlighted the entertainment. There would be trotting, pacing, and running daily by the "Finest Stable of Horses in America." A reporter noted, "we learned there were in all 400 stalls and every stall taken." Moreover, there were no "'wheel within wheels,' no put up jobs," or in other words, parties were not allowed to arrange the outcome of races to suit themselves and win money. An official informed the reporter that "such a thing would not be tolerated for a moment." Turfman Jim Brown was more than willing to introduce the horses he brought to a local reporter touring the facilities. An estimated 5,000 spectators saw Brown's Kensington win the mile dash.[45]

Racing had numerous critics though, and many of the criticisms came from the horsemen themselves. Dallas was back on a circuit, and when the horses left the city after the fair some of them departed for the Fort Worth races, some to the Shreveport races, and many to the New Orleans track to compete there. Others scattered to various places to go into winter quarters. A few remained in Dallas to await the opening of the spring circuit. Many of those who raced in Dallas came from other states and were unhappy with the management of the races. Some shipped horses from as far away as Chicago on the assurance certain races would be run. The cost of transport varied from $100 to $150 per horse. One man sent three of his best Thoroughbreds by express to be in Dallas on time only to find the race he entered did not fill and was not run. Turfmen also complained that the men in charge failed to follow racing rules to the letter. There was a closing date for any contest, but the Dallas directors did not always adhere to that rule. Many turfmen felt that the Dallas administrators were ignorant of racing rules and methods rather than purposely being unfair. But it was widely believed that changes needed to happen if Dallas was to be saved from a "serious decline in the very near future." One solution was to establish a jockey club in connection with the fair association, and allow only horsemen to manage racing matters, eliminating much of the dissatisfaction seen in the recent races. Therefore, in June 1887 Dallas horsemen organized a jockey club with the intention of cooperating with the Texas State Fair and Dallas Exposition to take over control of the racecourse and the racing at the next fair.[46]

But racing in Dallas still could not match the appeal of New Orleans. In March 1886, Jim Brown was there at the same time the locals celebrated Mardi Gras, so turfmen took a day off to enjoy the festivities. Unfortunately for Brown, when his mare Luna Brown exercised down the track's backstretch beside the horse Governor Roberts, the jockey collided with another mare, Miss Brewster, coming from the opposite direction. Luna Brown was not seriously injured, but Miss Brewster was badly hurt, and the two jockeys bruised. Whatever her injuries, Luna Brown was competing in Brooklyn, New York, in late May where the Texas entry took on some of the Northeast's finest. It was at this time that Brown began taking his stable out of state with more frequency because of concern about the future of racing in Texas.[47]

That trend could be seen when the races opened in Fort Worth in early November 1886 with low attendance, a mere 400 spectators. The weather was perfect and the track, having received rain earlier in the week, was in good condition. Unfortunately, there were only four entries in the quarter mile dash after one withdrew. Kensington took the lead at the start, Sam Harper, the favorite, did everything in his power to catch him, urged on by a skilled jockey. The field of four—Kensington, Idle Pat, Sam Harper, and Nat Kramer—were bunched together until the home stretch when Kensington came under the wire head and neck in front of Harper. While the outcome was legitimate, it could not be overlooked that meetings in Fort Worth earlier in the year had been plagued with "jockeying, hippodroming [manipulating], and 'fixing' the races" to benefit a select group.[48]

The Fort Worth judges, including well-respected lawyer Robert McCart, did their best to avoid this illegal behavior. In the three-quarter dash there were three starters, Germania, Hindoo Rose, and Myrtle Johnson. Myrtle Johnson was not in race condition, so it was clear the race was really between the other two horses. The trio got off to a good start with Germania in the lead, but at the end of the first quarter the rider of Hindoo Rose pulled or jerked her, causing Rose to lose a considerable distance and Germania came in under the wire first. The time of the race was slow, and the judges called the rider of Hindoo Rose to their stand. They wanted to know why the jockey did not ride to win. The nervous jockey answered that he only pulled his horse to straighten her out and that, in any case, she was coughing before the race. Even though the owner verified the mare had been coughing, that did not satisfy the judges. In their opinion they thought Hindoo Rose could have won the race and deferred a decision on the outcome until later in the day. Adding to questions of irregularities surrounding racing, the paper noted that there was a race on the track a few months before where "people were robbed. This instance had become notorious."[49]

There were other indications that racing was coming under fierce scrutiny. A Dallas city ordinance in 1887 prohibited both baseball and horse racing within the corporation limits of East Dallas on Sundays between the hours of 2 a.m. and 10 p.m. A violation would cost no less than $5 nor more than $50. There was also an occupation tax for racing and baseball of $5 per day, along with various taxes on the sale of liquor. Racing had always been immune to such laws, and even when passed locally lawmen rarely enforced them. As reform-minded Americans pushed for more regulation, Texas began to fall in line.[50]

But that did not stop racing enthusiasts. Both gambling and horse racing were popular southwest of Dallas in Johnson County where well-bred horses could be found at many farms and sprint races happened weekly. Mark Kennard and Miles "Pid" Hart owned a stable of fine race horses. One report claimed a mare that the two men owned won $125,000 in one year.[51]

Pid Hart's "famed stock farm" was one mile south of the village of Parker, fourteen miles southeast of Cleburne. The partnership of Kennard and Hart (that included Hart marrying Kennard's sister) marketed from forty to fifty head of horses annually. The stud that Shelby Stanfield of Thorp Spring raised carried his friend's name, Pid Hart. A chestnut foaled around 1887, he was sired by Shelby, a son of Tom Driver, a stallion that traced back to Steel Dust. His dam, Jenny Capps, went back to Shiloh. He became one of the best-known race horses of his day. Rocky Mountain Tom, foaled in May 1890, was Pid Hart's first colt, and a man who raced him in the early 1890s said he sported the "biggest jaws I ever saw," which was a characteristic of many Steel Dust prodigy and a trait much admired in the quarter horse. Rocky Mountain Tom was a "beautiful black with star in forehead." He was still alive in 1914, and a broadside advertised his services for $15 west of Newark, Texas. Rocky Mountain Tom was a popular name for race horses apparently, as one with that name competed in the 1886 races in Fort Worth, but if 1890 is correct for Stanfield's horse, this must have been an earlier one.[52]

Even as late as 1886 Texas horses fascinated Northerners. A headline in the Galveston paper read "Mustangs in Yankee Land" in September of that year. Farmers in eastern Connecticut wanted mustangs, and "a galaxy of cowboy horse-traders" traveled about the state with a "big herd of wild western ranch steeds." Even "staid deacons and clergymen have yielded to the popular craze." Horse fanciers thought that the western mustangs were "tougher, more wiry and gamier than eastern horses, and they enjoy seeing them, after they are hitched up, prance and snort and fling gravel as they forge through country villages." The cowboys selling the mustangs advertised them in local papers, and then drove the herd to the village park or county fairgrounds and turned them loose. "The whooping of the cowboys, their long locks, and picturesque attire, blown by the wind, as they ride recklessly about the park, stir the blood of the farmers, who subsequently purchase the mustangs at auction at good round figures." The cowboys did a thriving business even though few of the horses were broken and none ever tasted grain before going East. "All have deep-rooted prejudice against it, and would much rather eat Canada thistles or full-grown nettles than oats; neither do they fancy eastern customs and Connecticut barns, never having been inside a wooden structure until their trip East. The farmers have got their hands full taking care of them, and their daily encounters with them are more stirring than pleasing." This kind of publicity meant that when turfmen like Jim Brown headed to the East Coast to race, he met with the belief that anyone from Texas was a cowboy. He enjoyed promoting that image by carrying a .44 caliber, pearl-handled pistol.[53]

While the antics of the Texas mustangs alarmed many Connecticut farmers, those who followed Thoroughbred racing knew that there were problems brewing caused by gambling at tracks on the East Coast. At the Brighton Beach course in Brooklyn, founded by the Brighton Beach Racing Association in 1879, there was "interference" with the betting that concerned many owners. Jim Brown took his horse Luna Brown to Brighton Beach in May 1886, the same week that many owners removed their horses to other tracks when racing was suspended there. The fear was that betting might not return, and if it did not the owners of the large stables would be forced to take their horses further west to Chicago and St. Louis. In this case the problem was not just a moral objection to gambling but, as one newspaper writer who was apparently pro-gambling complained, it was "merely because a sufficiently large 'boodie' was not supplied to the hungry crew of legislators at Albany," the state capital. After Brown moved on to Chicago the issue was apparently settled at Brighton Beach where gambling continued until 1908 when the New York legislature passed a law that again brought gambling into question. Gambling was a serious moral issue by this time and reformers wanted it to end. Amendments to this law finally shutdown all New York tracks by 1911 forcing Thoroughbred owners to ship their horses to Canada or Europe to run. But for Brown, the best-known race horse man in Texas since the end of the Civil War, he spent the rest of his career at Midwestern tracks.[54]

As a sign of the times, the famous old Union Course in New York, which from 1821 until around 1866 was the center for horse racing on Long Island, was sold. This was where the northern horse American Eclipse beat the southern entry Henry for $20,000 in 1823 in front of a crowd of 60,000. Thoroughbred racing had fallen into disfavor in the Northeast in the years after the war with trotters taking over as the main attraction. According to *The Abilene Reporter* in 1888, the Association that owned the fifty acres sold it to real estate dealer Benjamin W. Hitchcock, who planned to convert it into building lots for new housing. Nothing remains to remind New Yorkers of the track today except the Union Turnpike, named for the course that was once a popular attraction. Little could followers of horse racing at organized tracks know that as the 1890s opened, they were witnessing the final decade of the sport they loved.[55]

8 The Gay Nineties

The 1890s

Texas racing would undergo significant changes in the last decade of the nineteenth century. Even before gambling on horses became illegal in 1903, there were signs that the popularity of the sport was on the decline among the public. While some newspapers still carried racing results, those stories competed with other sports that were gaining a devoted following. In addition, reformers never missed an opportunity to point out the evils seen at various racetracks. Gambling and drinking had always been part of the sport, but by the 1890s critics could add fixed races, crooked promoters, devious owners, and unscrupulous jockeys among their criticisms. Increasingly, judges watched each race carefully in case a jockey made a move to prevent his mount from winning, and disqualification usually followed any infractions. Most average Americans never visited a racecourse, nor had they ever heard anything but how horrible and profane horsemen were. Violence at tracks remained a problem, although it was not seen on Thoroughbred courses as often as at scrub tracks. Still, little by little, many state legislatures across the nation began to ban gambling on racing, and by the end of the century Texas lawmakers decided to pacify reformers by doing the same.

But for those devoted to the sport, racing was still king. In San Antonio in November 1894, some 3,500 people attended the third day's meet of the Jockey Club's fall races where money changed hands freely. In a special race Dandy Jim triumphed against Ryland T., "which nearly broke the hearts of the bookmakers." Transportation was improving too, and "One Hundred and forty-two Yoakumites took passage on the excursion train for San Antonio to witness the races." A trip from the small town of Yoakum, around 100 miles east of San Antonio, would have been an exciting adventure for both fans of racing and those who just wanted to see what drew so many people to the track.[1]

Texas was also earning respect outside the state. One historian of Thoroughbred racing was Massachusetts-born Lyman Horace Weeks. In 1898, he published *The American Turf.* While focusing mainly on racing at the well-known tracks across the nation, he admitted that "Texas, too, has come into the ranks of racing States, the meetings at Houston, Dallas, Victoria, Denton, and other centres of population having attained to a character that entitles them to more than passing notice." Texas was the home of some of the best known and respected leading American turfmen. The horse interests, both Thoroughbred and "otherwise," developed strong riders and trainers, "men who have been familiar with horses from their earliest youth, and who have a complete and accurate understanding of the equine nature. Some of them have been the outgrowth of cowboy experience and it is interesting to note in passing that, among cowboys of the Southwest, the old-fashioned quarter racing that was so much practiced in the colonies, a century or more ago, has continued much in vogue even in the present time."[2]

Texas horses gained notice by breaking national records in Thoroughbred racing, and Weeks included some of these speedy times in his book. In Dallas on November 2, 1887, Kittie Pease, a four-year-old by Jack Hardy carrying eighty-two pounds won the five-eighths of a mile, best two in three heats, in 1:00 and 1:00. A local paper described this as a "great race in which the world's record was beaten." There were nine entries but five were distanced in the first heat. The horses got off to a good start with Kittie Pease and Susie S in front. Coming down the stretch the riders "were using the whip and spur, and it was a race for blood." Susie S pushed Kittie for all she had, but Kittie came in under the string the winner by a nose. In the second heat Kittie won easily. In this race Kittie lowered the world's record at the distance. Another record fell in Dallas on November 1, 1890, when Eclipse Jr. won the best two in three heats at one-half mile with times of 0:48 and 0:48, and finally one more world record was bested in Lampasas on August 15, 1891, when Fashion, a four-year-old, won the three-eighths mile dash with a record time of 0:34. Texas had come a long way since those early days of racing along the Gulf Coast decades before.[3]

In the early days of racing, wealthy turfmen argued about the excellence of their Thoroughbred's breeding down to "Brothers, Sisters, Uncles, Aunts, Nephews, Nieces, & Cousins to the fourth Degree!" By the 1890s, turfmen could be from any social class, although Thoroughbred racing continued to attract those with money. Noted trainer Sam Hildreth observed that he looked at the world from the back of a race horse. He rated humans he met by comparing them with Thoroughbreds he knew much better. The town with the best track was his idea of the center of civilization, and the man with the best racing stable was the nation's leading citizen. "I was looking at the world through the back of a race-horse. . . . If there was anything of any consequence in this world besides breeding horses and racing them," he observed, "it had cantered right past me in the first furlong of my life, without even raising a cloud of dust." If anyone asked him what book learning he had, it would go like this:

> ***Question***—What important event marked the last year of the eighteenth century?
>
> ***Answer***—They brought the English Derby winner Diomed to Virginia in 1799 [1798], and all the best horses we've got can be traced back to Diomed.
>
> ***Question***—What was the most important battle ever fought in this country?
>
> ***Answer***—The battle of Union Course, May 27, 1823, when Sir Henry, the four-year-old from the South, lost to American Eclipse, the nine-year-old of the North.

> ***Question***—Give the date of the battle of Lexington.
>
> ***Answer***—April 24, 1855. Lexington, owned by Richard Ten Broeck, beat Lecompte [*sic*], from the stable of T. J. Wells, in their second match on the Metairie Course, New Orleans.[4]

If Hildreth had been from the Lone Star State (he had been born in Missouri, although he later raced in Texas), a question would have been added that asked: "What event led to a minor civil war in Texas?" The answer would have been: "When the owner of Monmouth from north of Dallas challenged the owner of Steel Dust from south of Dallas to a match race, won by Steel Dust and thus sealing his fame." Forty-some years after this race, little had changed regarding Texans' fascination with Steel Dust. In 1891, Young Steel Dust advertisements hit the newspaper in Brenham. A "beautiful chestnut sorrel," he was bred by George J. Dunlap and was from the "very best race stock in the country." His sire was Red Cross by Pat, the "noted Jim Brown Race Stallion." Young Steel Dust's dam was a Rebel mare that locals claimed was a "noted race mare." Rebel, of course, also belonged to Brown and was sired by Steel Dust. It is believed that Brown owned Steel Dust at his death. Young Steel Dust's pedigree was described as "ultra fashionable" and, that as a sire, he would prove all that his "rare breeding indicates," especially that he was a grandson of Pat, the "King of race Stallions of the South-West." But in West Texas in Abilene a reporter warned novice breeders to beware of breeding a mare to "one of the thirty million decendants [*sic*] of Rondo and Steel Dust to be found all over Texas." Everyone, it seemed, claimed their animals went back to one of these famous stallions.[5]

Brown's notoriety extended far beyond his success racing quarter horses and Thoroughbreds. One of the most sensational stories of the 1890s, maybe even the entire nineteenth century, involved him in a way that was fitting for a Texan of his time. While horsemen knew his name since he raced his stable across the state, in 1878 he made headlines by hanging noted outlaw William P. Longley when sheriff in Giddings. Rumors claimed he killed several men before he retired from office and turned his full attention to racing. In the 1880s he moved to Fort Worth where he formed partnerships with cattleman and speculator Jake Johnson and local lawyer Robert McCart to buy and race Thoroughbreds. He frequently took his stable east of the Mississippi River. While it is impossible to know all the places where Brown raced, there is a sample trail of his circuit in extant newspapers. During the mid-1880s he raced the filly Luna Brown as well as a chestnut colt, Luke Short, named after his former partner. The circuit was grueling and hard on both man and horse. The railroad, of course, made this schedule possible and the racecourses Brown headed for were well known. Newspapers in the larger Texas cities carried the results of the out-of-state circuits regularly and sporting men subscribed to one of the many racing magazines available. A sample of those out-of-state cities where Brown raced into the 1890s include New Orleans, Chicago, Eatontown (New Jersey), Covington (Kentucky), Buffalo, Brooklyn, and Niagara Falls in New York. At Niagara Falls in September 1887, however, the "judges were not satisfied with Luna Brown's running, and declared all bets off." Regan, her jockey, was suspended.[6]

While it is impossible to track Brown's entire schedule, what is known is that he won enough that he often made the results published in newspapers. He raced most often on the Western circuit and based his operations in Chicago for part of the year. He was a frequent winner at both the Hawthorne and Garfield Park tracks in that city. He was frequently identified as Jim Brown "who never lost a match" or Captain Jim Brown of the "famous Texas racing firm." But he never forgot where he came from and how he started with quarter running horses. In October 1891 while in Chicago, Brown tried to work out a match race with some Westerners who owned the quarter horse Bob Wade. Brown wanted to test his quarter horse Addie against Bob Wade for $1,000 a side but the Westerners, who certainly knew Brown's record, thought $500 a side enough and declined. Brown was a winner, and everyone knew it. Still, trying to get up a match race in Illinois in October took him back to his Texas roots.[7]

By 1890, J. M. Brown and Co.'s stable numbered more than thirty horses. He wintered that year at Memphis where he weeded out the poorer ones at a sale and kept the stake horses and two-year olds. He sent the others to New Orleans for the spring meets. Brown was very particular about his jockeys, only hiring the very best. A reporter for a Chicago paper noted that "Jim Brown is a man accustomed to get a ride for his money," and anyone who rode for him knew that. The star in his stable at this time was a horse called Bobby Beach. He was a "grand looking" steed and was considered the best animals in the West. Bobby Beach did so well at Sheepshead Bay in September that one reporter commented that "Eastern turf followers are suspicious that Jim Brown had other rods in pickle." Expressed in modern terms, that obsolete phrase may well mean he had payback in mind if his horse lost. Brown brought controversy wherever he raced, while at the same time his Texas style of preparing his colts gained him many admirers. He earned the "reputation of being a trainer who never hurries his horses, and this lot of yearlings bears evidence of the correctness of his methods of training."[8]

One of those to see Bobby Beach run was Sam Hildreth. It had been twenty years since as a child Hildreth first met "Sheriff Jim" when his mare Gray Alice had beaten Vince Hildreth's Red Morocco in the quarter mile race on the Texas prairie. Both Hildreth and Brown had moved up in the racing world since then, and they ran across each other from time to time at both Eastern and Western tracks. Hildreth knew the success Brown enjoyed with various horses but Bobby Beach was a particular favorite, a "sprinter with a great flight of speed," recalled Hildreth. Bobby won his first race on futurity day at the fall meeting at Sheepshead Bay in 1890, "romping away from the seven to ten favorite, Meridan." Bobby went to the post at six to one odds and Brown and his Texas bunch "cleaned up a fortune." Bobby lost his second race but in the third he again returned a winner, and the "Texas betting crowd walked off with another huge killing." That year Bobby Beach won fifteen firsts out of eighteen starts. In 1891, Brown owned Addie M, a winner of twelve races that he sold for $9,000 to the wealthy tobacco manufacturer and Thoroughbred racing enthusiast Pierre Lorillard IV. In 1892, he owned the best two-year-old colt and best two-year-old filly in the West, G. W. Johnson and Red Banner.[9]

In the years between Hildreth's first meeting with Brown when he was a child and their encounters as an adult, Brown made a name for himself and appears in almost all the historical accounts of Thoroughbred racing in the early 1890s because of his consistent winners. But he had also become known as a man who "was either your good friend or your bitter enemy. There was no half-way business with him," wrote Hildreth. "He might be for you to-day, but if he had any reason to suspect you weren't playing on the square he'd be against you to-morrow." Hildred often saw him with "Big Ed" Corrigan, the owner of the Hawthorne racetrack and one of the most prominent turfmen in the West. They made a strange pair, "the sheriff a small bundle of nerves who barely reached up to the shoulder of the stolid Corrigan," reminding Hildreth of a "snappy little terrier snarling at a great Dane." But they were both competitors and friends of a sort.

"Panther face, panther face," Brown would cry to Corrigan. "I'll shoot you full of holes if you ain't careful, panther face."

"Easy, Jim, easy," Corrigan would respond. "From his expression I think he had it in mind that the sheriff was right handy with a gun," recalled Hildreth.[10]

The Texas crowd that followed Brown's personal circuit varied. J. M. Brown and Co. consisted at different times of his Fort Worth friends Jake Johnson and Robert McCart as partners, but the entire entourage was much larger, including grooms, stable hands, jockeys, and just hangers-on. The stable was considered one of the finest on the Western Circuit. In July 1891, when racing at Garfield Park, the "Texas gentlemen who form the 'Co.' to J. M. Brown's stable" left the track with "all kinds of money." But at the same time Brown and McCart were heard "discoursing to some friends on the uncertainty of horse racing." Those men who made racing a profession understood that the current attitude toward gambling threatened their livelihood.[11]

Besides worrying about the future of racing, other problems occupied Brown's mind. In 1892 he was at Garfield Park when the governor of Texas sent a requisition to Illinois for him to be returned to Texas to stand trial for the murder of Sam Sparks that occurred more than a decade before in Lee County and for his part in the murder of W. T. Sharman in Denison earlier that year. But Joseph Fifer, the Illinois governor, refused to honor the request. The governor was friends with Brown's sometime partner Robert McCart, who was working as Brown's attorney at that time. A Texas sheriff even went to Chicago to return him to the state, but accomplished nothing as Brown's immense wealth and powerful friends protected him. Brown filed an affidavit with the Illinois governor saying it was a political matter, and if sent back to Texas he would be assassinated.[12]

But on September 6, 1892, he was caught in the middle of a dispute between rival tracks in the Windy City. Armed with warrants to close down Garfield, the police raided on that fateful Tuesday when seven wagonloads of lawmen rolled down the track to the grandstand. The police quickly surrounded the betting ring and placed any race judges and officials they found under arrest. Another detachment of officers headed for the stables to gather grooms and jockeys, although most had already fled. Brown, standing on the roof of one of the barns, watched the police pursuit, but when sighted quickly jumped to the ground and began to walk rapidly away. When told to stop and throw up his hands, he refused. According to one account, when a policeman started shooting at his feet, Brown returned fire, killing the officer instantly. As Brown fled, chased by a second lawman, he turned and mortally wounded his pursuer before being gunned down himself. This was not the first police raid on the track and Brown previously warned that "he would allow no man to arrest him as long as he was not violating the law," and if any policeman attempted to, Brown vowed "he would kill or be killed before he was dragged to the police station." The Austin paper's headline read: "James Brown Killed While Resisting Arrest on the Garfield Park Race Track: Two Officers Fell Before the Noted Turfman's Revolver—Surrounded by Officers He Refused to Surrender and Was Riddled With Bullets." In his hometown, the Fort Worth paper ran a similar headline: "Jim Brown of Texas, Killed on Garfield Race Track, Chicago, by Officers. HE WAS VIOLATING NO LAW. He was a Square Man and Rich."[13]

Many Texas papers were quick to jump to Brown's defense when they heard of the shootout, as he was widely known in local racing circles. *The Galveston Daily News* carried a lengthy story under the headline: "JIM BROWN IS DONE FOR. A NOTED TEXAS TURFMAN KILLED AT GARFIELD PARK. His Unerring Revolver Sends Two Policemen Into Eternity." An introduction to the story included a brief biography reprinted from Brown's hometown paper of the previous day that in part read: "He has been known as a prominent horseman for many years, beginning his career as an owner and trainer of racing stock in 1865." Several years before he moved to Fort Worth and until "this season he had been a partner of Jake Johnson of Fort Worth, and is now acknowledged to be the owner of the best string of racing horses in the east. Mr. Brown was for eight years sheriff of Lee county and during his official career had an enviable reputation as a brave and efficient public servant. It is said that he, during the time he was sheriff, captured and secured the conviction of more desperate criminals than any sheriff in the state. He owns property in Williamson, San Saba, Lee and Tarrant counties, and his estate is said to be worth in the neighborhood of $100,000." The Galveston paper was more specific, writing: "For ten years the deceased was sheriff of Lee county. It is said that at different times while sheriff he killed twelve men. . . . Mr. Brown has been a racing man for twenty-five years commencing in Texas with a quarter horse. In 1886 he came to Washington park [in Chicago] with a small stable, his partners being Robert McCart and Jake Johnson. Among the well known horses owned by J. M. Brown & Co. were Bobby Beach, Arundel, Borealis, Little Billy [Billie] and Tom Elliott. This year he had in G. W. Johnson and Red Banner, the best 2-year-olds in the west and great things were expected of them next season. He had priced G. W. Johnson at $35,000."[14]

Brown's name certainly stirred controversy in Texas, for he was not liked by everyone. In Brenham, some thirty-five miles east of Giddings, the paper

Texan Jim Brown's entries in the 1892 Tennessee Derby and Arkansas Derby. Tom Elliott proved the better of the two in Tennessee, while Little Billie came in second. In Arkansas a week before, Little Billie won, and Tom Elliott was second. *The Memphis Appeal-Avalanche* (Tennessee), April 11, 1892.

published: "He was ten years sheriff of Lee county and it's said all the killing he ever did was in his official capacity. . . . His long residence in Lee, the adjoining county, and the fact that he was well known here made the tragedy of such unusual local significance here. In this city he had some warm friends and some bitter enemies and the comments on the affair were varied. His enemies say that he terorized [*sic*] Lee county while there and that though he was not justifiable in all his fourteen killings, he could not be convicted on account of the fear in which he was held." His estate was estimated at nearly $1,000,000, a much-exaggerated amount, but such were the legends growing around Jim Brown.[15]

Whatever Texans thought of Brown's actions in the shootout, not all of the events that led to his death were his fault. When he arrived in Chicago, he stepped into a political situation not uncommon for large cities. By the early 1890s there were rival tracks in competition for business. In this case it was the Hawthorne and the Garfield tracks. Canadian born "Big Ed" Corrigan, who

Those men supporting one of Brown's two entries celebrated as their picks came in first and second in both the Arkansas Derby and Tennessee Derby in 1892. *The Memphis Appeal-Avalanche* (Tennessee), April 12, 1892.

was the owner of Hawthorne, opened it in Cicero, Illinois, in 1891. He persuaded the Chicago mayor that because Garfield sat within the city limits to help put his rival out of business. It was this conflict that led to the police raid on Garfield on that September day. In fact, the raid that saw Brown die was the fourth in five days, including one on a Sunday. It probably did not help that Brown raced some of his string at Corrigan's Hawthorne track where he took home money. The public saw Brown and Corrigan as personal enemies. But after Brown's death, Corrigan issued a statement that read: "Jim Brown and myself were on friendly terms and no one regrets his death more than I. Brown and I had hot words one day some years ago when I was running what is now Garfield Park. There were no blows struck, no pistols drawn, and the affair blew over quickly. Not three days thereafter I loaned Jim Brown $1,000, which of course he returned as per agreement. Since then we have raced horses on many courses, and never has an unkind word passed between us. Two days before his death he was at Hawthorne, and I believe intended to bring his entire stable there to race." But as a result of Corrigan's desire to shut down Garfield there were "two dead men, one of them a millionaire, and the third fatally wounded." Ironically, Corrigan, once described as "the man who at one time controlled more racing property and owned a greater stable of horses than any other turfman of his time," including the 1890 Kentucky Derby winner, eventually went bankrupt and sold Hawthorne for a mere $2,000. The early nineties saw Hawthorne, Garfield Park, and a track at Harlem compete for spectators and the overabundance of racing, along with falling public interest in the sport, eventually forced the popular Washington Park to close. There was a brief resurgence but the competition between the tracks, along with continued political intrigue, soon led to a suppression of the sport. The consensus was that the "trouble in racing circles in Chicago has given the sport a blow from the effects of which it will take a long time to recover. The better element always refuse to countenance any sport where bloodshed and rioting rule and as a result horsemen here incline to the opinion that racing in Chicago has seen its best days for some time to come."[16]

Brown and Johnson managed a "string of fine horses," but after their business association ended Brown became one of the largest horse owners in the United States, and his stable was "only excelled by one or two" on the west side of the Mississippi. A friend remembered Brown as being "small of stature, but active and wiry, and did not look to weigh much more than his jockeys." Moreover, "he did not look the desperate man," although he was well-armed the day of the police raid. It was reported he carried a .44 caliber, pearl-handled pistol "of the kind that helped to fill the earlier graveyards of Texas." His body was brought back to Fort Worth, where he was buried in Oakwood Cemetery. In an odd turn of fate, Sam Hildreth was at the Garfield track on his honeymoon and witnessed the police raid that resulted in Brown's death. Two of Brown's sons, Gaylon and Ed, were also in the city, and Gaylon became administrator of the estate, consisting mainly of horses and valued at $25,000. Ed accompanied his father's body back to Fort Worth while Gaylon stayed in Chicago in charge of the stable.[17]

Brown's legacy could also be seen in the young men who rode for him. "Jockeys are born, not made," wrote one authority on Thoroughbred racing and Jim Brown hired the best. Jockeys were evolving along with the sport. In

Gaylon Brown followed in his father's footsteps as a successful trainer. He eventually took his talent to France where he could be found at the famous Chantilly Race Course. Although his name was John Gaylon, newspapers generally published it as Galen, and he rarely corrected the mistake. *Courtesy of Anne J. Bailey.*

the old days they rode horses bareback or "with long stirrups and wore sharp spurs and carried big whips and came down the stretch slashing their horses unmercifully. The blood ran out of their sides," wrote jockey Max Hirsch. "Then along came Tod Sloan," who got his start with Jim Brown. James F. "Tod" Sloan rode for the Texas trainer for two years at Garfield Park where Brown "afforded him the opportunity for rapid advancement in his work." Born in Indiana in 1874, Sloan also rode for trainer Sam Hildreth at one point, and in 1955 was elected to the National Museum of Racing and Hall of Fame. He was known as the "gayest figure on the American racing scene during the Gay Nineties," and what he lacked in size he made up in "grandiose behavior." He was as famous off the track as he was on, both in the United States and England, being friends with Diamond Jim Brady and Lillian Russell in America and the Prince of Wales in England. Not only were the Thoroughbreds and their rich owners followed in the news, but increasingly jockeys were also becoming superstars and their every move watched by an adoring public. Moreover, Sloan was revolutionary, he rode with short stirrups and did not abuse his mount. Other jockeys soon followed his example, and their horses began to "run kinder for jockeys than they did in olden days." Fellow jockey Max Hirsch described Sloan as the "first jockey to baby his horse, cluck softly in his ear —that's why he leaned forward the way he did—and the horse responded to kindness. . . . It wasn't long until he was a sensation both here and in Europe."[18]

Brown also employed Dallas native Henry Shields to ride for him. Born in 1875, Shields began his racing experience at fourteen as an exercise boy for Brown. He eventually rose to the saddle and rode for Brown for several years with his first win coming on Giveaway. On October 8, 1890, Giveaway came in second in the seven-eighths mile dash in San Antonio, but on September 24, 1891, in Bonham, Giveaway came in first in the three-quarter of a mile

Jockeys were superstars in the late 19th century. Two who rode for turfman Jim Brown were James F. "Tod" Sloan, the "gayest figure on the American racing scene during the Gay Nineties" (second from left, back row), and Dallas native Henry Shields (center, front row) with the pistol pointed at his head. In 1955, Sloan was elected to the National Museum of Racing and Hall of Fame. Samuel C. Hildreth and James R. Crowell, *The Spell of the Turf: The Story of American Racing* (Philadelphia: J. B. Lippincott, 1926).

dash setting a state record of 1:15. It is possible that Shields was aboard. After Brown's death, Shields continued to work for Brown's stable, then under the direction of Brown's son Gaylon. He rode at all the noted tracks of the day in New York as well as Louisville, New Orleans, Memphis, Nashville, Cincinnati, St. Louis, Chicago, and in California, sometimes riding horses trained by Hildreth. In April 1898, Shields "rode a grand race" in Oakland, California, when aboard a colt belonging to Gaylon Brown, but the following year judges at the track ruled he was guilty of "certain suspicious riding," and declared he could no longer accept mounts other than those belonging to his employer. "Shields can steal for Brown if he chooses," declared the judges, "but he cannot steal for any other owner." A Chicago paper noted the Texas jockey "had not made any kind of a hit" with some of the judges in California. After a number of state legislatures banned gambling, Shields, like many other jockeys, went to Canada and then Europe to work. But he eventually came home to Dallas, where in 1910 he recorded his occupation as an out-of-work jockey, a casualty of Texas' decision to end gambling at the racetrack.[19]

In an interview in 1898, Dallas native Henry Shields said that he began riding when he was ten, and rode in his first race when he was twelve. He worked for three Browns—Jim Brown and his sons, Ed and Gaylon. *The San Francisco Examiner* (San Francisco, CA), April 10, 1898.

Perhaps the most famous jockey to come from Texas was Maximilian Justice "Max" Hirsch. Born in 1880 in Fredericksburg, he also became one of the most successful trainers in the history of Thoroughbred racing. He was unusual in that his parents were part of the migration of German immigrants to the Texas Hill Country—his father Jacob Hirsh was a carpenter and native of Hanover, Germany, and his mother was Mary Neffendorf. He began his career at ten years old, racing down the Main Street of his hometown, and spent his early years as a jockey at county fairs in Texas onboard quarter horses. He caught the eye of Thoroughbred breeder and racer John A. Morris, who later employed him as a groom and jockey at the Morris Ranch in Gillespie County. When he was twelve, he stowed away with a shipment of horses bound for the Morris facility in Baltimore. He later recalled that while helping to load the horses, "It was a hot day, and I was barefooted" when "Suddenly, the urge hit me. I had to go with the horses. So, clad in blue jeans and without a word to my parents, I climbed aboard a freight car with the horses and was off to Baltimore." Once he arrived, Morris gave him a job as a "full-fledged jockey." Being a Texan, he described himself as a "whoop-dee-do-rider" and could "beat the gate like hell." The object, he said, was to go "to the front as fast as I could" and "stay there as long as I could." Like Hildreth, when he became too heavy to race, he turned to training and at age twenty was one of the youngest licensed trainers in the United States. Before he died his principal client was Robert J. Kleberg Jr. of the King Ranch. Prior to that Hirsch trained for a variety of owners and won his first of four Belmont Stakes in 1928. In 1936, he won the Kentucky Derby and Preakness Stakes with Bold Venture and in 1946 captured the Triple Crown with Bold Venture's son Assault (foaled on the King Ranch). In 1950, he won his third Kentucky Derby with another of Bold Venture's sons, Middleground, that also was the winner of the Belmont Stakes. Hirsch was inducted into the National Museum of Racing and Hall of Fame in 1959. Even more notable, his daughter Mary was a pioneer for her sex when in 1935 she became the first female trainer licensed by The Jockey Club (which then held that authority for the state of New York). His sons, William J. "Buddy" and Max Jr. also became noted trainers.[20]

Another jockey who gained fame was John Huggins. He started his career in Fort Bend County racing at Churchill Fulshear Jr.'s track known as Churchill Downs. Born in 1848, in 1886 he won the Preakness Stakes with The Bard. He also enjoyed success racing in England after he became a trainer. His win of the Epsom Derby was the first ever by an American trainer. When abroad he worked for Pierre Lorillard at a salary said to be around $50,000 a year. At his death in 1917 the *Daily Racing Form* wrote "He had a load of friends among the horsemen and was successful in his chosen profession. He was reputed to be a wealthy man and retired from active participation in racing several years ago." He spent his last days in Fulshear in Fort Bend County where he is buried.[21]

Jockeys were becoming celebrities, although one reporter wrote: "Jockeys are inscrutable institutions. The best of them ride like artists on Monday and like farmers on Tuesday. On Wednesday they are suspended and on Thursday we find them reinstated. On Friday they are generally drunk, in consequence of which on Saturday they ride without vigor, being weak from 'reducing' [to keep their weight down]. What jockeys do on Sunday the Lord only knows." Their antics often made the local papers. Jim Brown retired his jockey Tommy Magee in November 1890 because, judged one reporter, "his lack of ability has cost his employers thousands of dollars." Brown replaced him with a jockey named Fox, who was known as "one of the best of Western jockeys, but has long lived under suspicion." Fox promised Brown he would "mend his ways," because he wanted a chance to ride good horses and "always go to the front."[22]

Brown was an exceptional trainer, and his Texas roots taught him how to win. Although he began on scrub tracks before the Civil War, he made his name with the Steel Dust colt Rebel in the postwar years. By the time he died he managed one of the most successful stables in the West. Dubbed a "Texas gun fighter," at the end of the 1892 racing season in Chicago, just a few months after his death, J. M. Brown and Co. came in third in winnings out of the 500 or more stables whose horses competed around the city. Ed Corrigan led with $50,213, roughly $1,700,000 today; the Kendall Stable was second with $41,722, or almost $1,500,000, and Brown's Texas stable followed with $37,259, around $1,300,000 today. That was without the guiding hand of Jim Brown for the last months of the calendar year. Although he was respected in racing circles, his deadly gunfight with the police left his legacy tarnished. His former partner, Jake Johnson, maintained that "Brown never went with desperate men. He was cordially displeased by desperadoes. He was regarded as one of the most effective and fearless officers Texas ever had. . . . He was cool and never quarrelsome, and when he made a man bite the dust it was in the discharge of his duties. He never picked personal quarrels, and he was thoroughly respected in Texas." Unfortunately, not all Texans would have agreed with Johnson's assessment of his friend. Still, that does not detract from his skill as a trainer, and one of the most successful turfmen that nineteenth century Texas produced.[23]

Gaylon and Ed Brown, both Texas natives, continued to race their father's stable but could not escape his shadow. Gaylon, the elder brother, had been born in 1862 while Ed came along six years later. They traveled with their father on the racing circuit as soon as they were old enough to leave home. Gaylon managed the horses that were kept at the Hawthorne track and took over the stable at Garfield after his father's death. Described as tall and slender with dark hair and a reddish mustache, he was "unusually quiet and polite, but a Texan whom men avoid having any trouble with." After his father died, many thought Gaylon would "kill the man who killed his father before he slept." Instead, he focused on racing and led the Brown stable to many impressive wins.[24]

Gaylon did not have the reputation of a Texas gunfighter like his father but, like his father, he was well-known in racing circles running under the name J. G. Brown and Co. He and his brother Ed seemed to have divided working the circuits between them. At one point Gaylon was on the West

Coast, running his string at Oakland. In 1898, Gaylon announced he was retiring his racer Libertine to stud. At that time Libertine held the mile record on a circular track, traveling the distance over the Harlem racetrack in Chicago on October 24, 1894, in 1:38¾. But tragedy struck the family again in 1900 when in December Ed was killed in a railroad accident in Kentucky, while possibly transporting horses from Cincinnati to Lexington. Gaylon continued in the business alone, but in 1904 was accused of using $25,000 of his father's estate while acting as administrator and making G. M. Noyes, who was said to be a bondsman of Jim Brown's, responsible for the money, sending the dispute to court for the next two years. But the hand of fate was not yet done with the Brown family. Gaylon's sister Annie was murdered by a spurned suitor just blocks from the Fort Worth courthouse in May 1905. Despite family tragedies, Gaylon went on to a distinguished career. When racing fell into disfavor in the United States he headed for Europe. His father's estate was finally settled in 1906, and he was awarded $7,500, an amount equivalent to around $280,000 today. With this money he left for Europe, racing near Paris, France, from April 1907 until February 1914, and in Berlin, Germany, from February 1914 until November 1914. In February 1914, he listed his occupation as horse trainer on an application at the Consular General of the United States in Berlin. He returned to the States at the outbreak of World War I, but went back to France in 1919, after the war ended. One of his daughters had married and remained near Chantilly on the outskirts of Paris, where Gaylon trained race horses, and he and his wife Norma joined her there. He had already accepted a position as horse trainer in France before leaving the States. Chantilly Race Course was the home of some of France's most prestigious races, and the largest training facilities in the country could be found in the surrounding communities. As a Texas-born trainer, Gaylon did well for himself, and he must have seemed quite exotic to the French. Returning to the States in 1925, he took a position as manager of Shandon Farm in Lexington, Kentucky, not long after, staying there into the 1930s. The owner was entrepreneur and sportsman Gifford A.

Cochran (winner of the Kentucky Derby and Preakness in 1925 with two different horses.) When Gaylon passed away in Naperville, Illinois, in May 1938, still listing his occupation as race horse trainer, he was buried in Lexington beside his wife. This ended the Brown family's connection to horse racing which began with Jim Brown and his quarter running horses in Texas in the late 1850s.[25]

Brown's daughter Luna, for whom he named a race horse, also attracted almost as much notice as her father, and newspapers never failed to point out she was Jim Brown's daughter. When her father was killed by police in 1892, Luna was still living with husband Hugh Testard and daughter May in Dallas. A year after her father's death, in April 1893, Hugh went home to San Antonio for his father's funeral. When he returned to his family, he found his house closed and his wife and child gone. After searching for Luna in Chicago where brothers Gaylon and Ed kept their stable of horses, he located her in New Orleans where he claimed she had "fallen from virtue," and was living in a "place of easy morals." Their young daughter May was in a Dominican Convent. Luna declared that she was safe and living with her brother Gaylon who had his racing string in New Orleans at that time. J. G. Brown and Co. moved to the Crescent City Jockey Club track after rumors circulated that the Hawthorne track was about to close. During the confusing events of the next few days, Hugh took the little girl at knife point from the convent and quickly returned to Texas. The Associated Press spread the kidnapping story from coast-to-coast and it was read nationwide. While Luna claimed spousal abuse, the newspapers generally sided with her husband. One headline from the Austin paper read: "Trail of the Serpent. Sequel to the Murderous Career of Jim Brown, His Married Daughter Gone Astray and her Child Abducted from a New Orleans Convent by its Distressed Father, a Well Known Texan."

The couple reconciled briefly, and the Fort Worth paper noted on November 23, 1893, that husband and wife were at Sherman as witnesses in the trial, the *State v. John Poe*, who was charged with being an accomplice to the murder of W. T. Sharman in Denison in 1892, the crime for which John Carlisle and Charles Luttrell had been recently hanged (and also the case in which the Texas governor tried to have Jim Brown extradited from Chicago). With controversy surrounding the couple, the Testards' reconciliation did not last, and Luna eventually filed for divorce. In April 1895, the judge granted her divorce on the grounds of cruel treatment, and she was given custody of their daughter. Luna later remarried and lived in Fort Worth before divorcing and remarrying. Luna and her third husband later moved to California where they also divorced and she married for a fourth and last time. The story of Jim Brown, his horses, and his family became part of local lore.[26]

While large cities began to prohibit racing inside their boundaries, small towns continued to support the sport. In Cleburne, a town of around 7,000 residents thirty miles south of Fort Worth, racing prospered. To the delight of the temperance advocates, the Johnson County Fair and Driving Park Association races were dry, as the organization prohibited the sale of whiskey. Probably to teetotalers' dismay, however, the local paper observed that did "not mean that everybody goes dry, for the number of little empty flasks would indicate what can be seen on the grounds," and there was an "immense amount of 'kicking' Friday at the racetrack—we regret to report, [but it] is a matter of fact." Still, the paper noted that many churchgoers were in attendance, as almost all the churches counted members on the grounds.[27]

Some familiar names turned up at the Johnson County Fair. In October 1890 former Johnson County resident Charley Haley brought his stable from West Texas. Once the owner of Governor Roberts, "one of the fastest three quarter mile horse in the world," his current crop looked just as able to win. A reporter noted that if Haley started a horse on the track "it will mean something." One of his horses, Uncle Frank, was named for well-known Johnson County resident Frank Menefee, "one of the smartest men in Texas." Another horse trainer in attendance was Pid Hart, whose stock farm was near Parker. This was an exciting occasion, as it was the first county fair in twelve years, although there had been races at local tracks during that time. The Driving Park Association owned 130 acres, all neatly fenced, and a stable for seventy horses, which had been constructed in the summer of 1890. The Stubblefield Band, composed of "handsomely uniformed well-behaved" young men, furnished the music. The following year Marion Martin, who served as lieutenant governor in the early 1880s, brought a stable of "fine race horses" to the track in August. Even though he was a well-known prohibitionist, and the Prohibition party nominated him for governor in 1888 where he earned almost 100,000 votes, he supported horse racing. Johnson County must have suited him, since the county fair was dry.[28]

Texas was modernizing as the new century approached and reformers grew more vocal. In southern Texas, Houston was rapidly growing into a city. In the early 1880s Houston installed its first telephone exchange followed soon by an electric power plant. In the 1890s it boasted of the first electric streetcar and automobiles appeared on its streets by the end of the decade. By 1901, Spindletop changed Texas forever when oil was discovered. But before the nineteenth century ended, some of the men who pioneered fine horses in Texas still maintained an interest and kept racing alive while also trying to police the sport. In Houston in the mid-1890s there was a meeting of the Texas Racing Circuit management at the Hutchins Hotel, the largest hotel in the state when it was built in 1861. In attendance were George Feris of Richmond, Wiley Jones, who owned a hotel in Waco, and David P. Shepherd of Houston. They selected Judge Gustave Cook (Cooke) as one of the judges to fill the vacancy created by Josiah Crosby. The first choice, F. A. Ryan, declined because he was secretary of the Texas Racing Circuit. Feris, associated with racing since the early years, was described as a "member of the Committee of Judges and is another distinguished citizen of Texas, and is high up in the seventies. His fame as a turfman and lover of horseflesh extends all over the South, being probably the best informed man on the subject anywhere. He drew up the first constitution and by-laws of the Houston Jockey Club, more than thirty-five years ago. He distinguished himself in the late war, and was surgeon-general of the trans-Mississippi department on the Confederate side.

He has been closely connected with the history of Texas from the time of the earliest settlers."[29]

His love of horses was well-known and endured throughout his life. In March 1892, when Feris was standing in front of the post office in Richmond, a "big burley" man "came riding up on a poor little old stack of bones that could hardly stand up under so great a burden." When Feris saw the state of the animal he gave the rider a "tongue lashing in the true Kentucky style, such as he will not soon forget for his cruelty to the animal." Feris then turned to the poor animal and gave it a "few kind strokes on the head and a word or two of sympathy and then walked off." When he stopped in front of a store, he noticed several men pointing and laughing, and saying something about the latest "Feris importation." The doctor turned around to see the little horse following him. Feris answered the jeers by saying this was "one of the highest compliments he ever received from a dumb animal, although he has imported from Arabia as well as other foreign and home countries some of the finest specimens of horse flesh that ever came to Texas, and was one of the prime movers and the first president of a state fair in Texas." He remained prominent in jockey club affairs until he died in April 1898 at age eighty-one, one of the most respected and best-known horsemen of his time.[30]

The Houston races were always a festive occasion. In preparation for the event the local merchants planned to "close their stores at 1 o'clock" on Thursday, and on Friday "Galvestonians will be hauled by the railroads at two third rates." Also, the night before there was "pool selling" or a form of gambling on the horses at the Hutchins House Exchange room, and the "faces of many well-known turf men" were there during the evening. Besides the auction there was plenty of liquor flowing to entertain the bidders. There was also something for the ladies when it was announced "Miss Williams and Miss Raebor will ride mile heats on thoroughbred horses. This will be in addition to the races. They will ride the latter part of the week." One can only imagine the parties and gala events associated with race week. The golden age of horse racing with elegant balls and elaborate festivities was fading, just as the nineteenth century was passing into history. Automobiles would soon take over the roads, and elegant long dresses for the ladies would soon give way to the short dress of the 1920s flapper.[31]

Still, Dallas fans continued to enjoy the races and a local paper called those most devoted to the sport "turfites." In October 1894, the paper observed that the "races this year at the state fair and under its auspices will be better than ever before." That was the result of Texans having given a "great deal of attention to horse breeding, and today magnificent stock farms dot the state from Denison to Laredo and from the borderland of New Mexico to Colorado. Texas bred horses are coming to the front and Texas is acknowledged by even the horsemen of Kentucky, Tennessee, Missouri and Ohio to possess superior advantages for breeding purposes." There was something in the climate particularly suitable for raising horses, and in the "years to come Texas will distance Kentucky, and this favored section of the Lord's vineyard will be the home of the thoroughbred." John N. Simpson, the managing director of the racing division for the fair, said there would be from 400 to 600 horses stabled on the grounds. "If Texans want good racing they should attend and lend their influence and patronage." W. J. Scott, manager of the races, who had just returned from a tour of the Midwestern racing circuit, noted that they are "afraid of Texas up north, for they realize that Texas is to be the home of racing in the future."[32]

The promoters were not disappointed, as there was scarcely a vacant seat over the thirteen days of racing with five events scheduled each day. One horse stood out above the rest, a four-year-old called Sallie McMillan. She was a bay mare by Havre that went back to both Lexington and imported Australian. Her dam Lula Brown, foaled in 1886, carried the blood of Lexington and Boston (not to be confused with the race horse Luna Brown). It is possible Sallie McMillan was from Johnson County, south of Fort Worth. No longer did the owner or breeder have their names in the papers. Racing was all about gambling, so generally

Texan Jim Brown's entries in the major races in Tennessee and Arkansas. Tom Elliott is shown crossing the finish line first in the Tennessee Derby, while Little Billie came in second. In the Arkansas Derby a week before, Little Billie won, and Tom Elliott was second. *The Memphis Appeal-Avalanche* (Tennessee), April 12, 1892.

only the horse's name appeared, along with the odds. The sire and dam were rarely listed as seen in earlier days.[33]

On a cool, crisp day, October 30, 1894, people "carried their overcoats and cloaks and marched into the grand stand and the betting ring and the club house." Reports estimated 8,000 to 10,000 in attendance at the fair. Many came to see the six-furlongs dash (three quarters of a mile). There were twelve starters, but only three were favored—Stella M., George Miller, and Sallie McMillan. "After three or four saddles had gone to pieces at the post and one boy had fallen off," the starter "got them bunched and gave them the flag." Stella M. leaped to an early lead with Sallie right at her saddle skirts, and George Miller was keeping his place on the outside. The others were all behind the leaders. The three horses came around the turn as "quick as a man can say scat and were in sight of the wire," nose-to-nose, too close to call. "They rushed like an avalanche for an eighth of a mile and then Stella M. faltered and dropped back just a little. Not so with George Miller. He was never a coward nor a quitter." Just as victory was in his grasp, Sallie's jockey Slaughter, "with one of those marvelous finishes," landed his mare just a nose in front. The time—1:14—was the best ever made in Texas for the distance, and was therefore a state record. This record would last to the day gambling ended in Texas in 1903.[34]

While Sallie McMillan's history remains something of a mystery, she was no mystery to racing fans in 1894. What is known is that she raced a half-mile in Waco in May, coming in second. In Cleburne in August she won the three-quarter mile dash, listed under the headline the "Cleburne Flyers" and leading to the speculation that she was stabled in the area. At Belton in September, she came in first in the one-half mile dash, and also won at three-quarters of a mile. At the Dallas races on October 22 Sallie won the five and a half furlongs race. On that day the track was in almost perfect condition even though it was black waxy soil. Around 2,000 spectators watched, equally divided between men and women. Betting was heavy and thousands of dollars changed hands. On October 27, Sallie won again, with eight to five odds. On November 1 the wind was blowing almost a gale, but the attendance was still "exceedingly large." Sallie McMillan was a favorite in the second race for five and a half furlongs. She won easily. Leading from start to finish Sallie again defeated Stella M.[35]

Sallie McMillan had a grueling schedule in October, winning most of her starts, but she was not given time to rest. November 22 found her in Houston racing before an audience of 2,500 to 3,000 spectators, many of them women. She ran under the colors of Turner and Stansbury. The Houston Driving Park Association organized the races, and it urged places of business to close from noon until 5:00 p.m. to allow fans to attend the races. To make the day pleasant for visitors, the management hired Herb's Light Guard Band to take an early train to Galveston and escort Galvestonians to the races as well as to give the island visitors a serenade. Sallie brought many admirers with her to the event, and when she came in second, they claimed that she was still the fastest, and said that the "fact that she was too heavily weighted" was responsible for her failing to take first money. Her jockey, Masterson, weighed in at 119 lbs. Of interest is that third place went to a horse named Galen Brown, for Jim Brown's son, Gaylon, since newspapers often used the wrong spelling of his name. Two days later, Stella M. finally had her revenge, beating Sallie at five furlongs, Sallie coming in second. When the spring races opened in 1895, Sallie could be found in New Orleans, although how she placed is unknown. She was back in Cleburne in October racing at the Cleburne Jockey Club. In late October she was in Dallas, winning at five and a half furlongs. But just as she mysteriously appeared in 1894, she disappeared in 1895. It is likely she became a brood mare, but even that is speculation. She remains one of the finest racers Texas produced in the last decade of the nineteenth century.[36]

As racing became more a question of morality than sport, defenders of the industry fought back. "It is true," wrote one racing advocate, that the turfman "had drawn around him men who are anxious to bet, but that is not the fault of the industry. . . . The race horse man is ambitious in his business and proud of his success." Supporters were convinced that racing would continue at Texas state fairs. They argued that turfmen worked hard to achieve success, a success that advocates believed they deserved. Despite numerous devotees arguing that gambling was not the main reason horsemen bred and raced their animals, the fact was that betting at the tracks was now a business, and it was a business many Americans condemned. More and more cities and states limited racing within their boundaries. While racing remained a popular attraction for horse lovers, the numbers attending the races continued to decline. There would never again be the huge attendance seen in the antebellum days. The first sign of trouble was when Thoroughbred racing began to wane.[37]

Thoroughbred racing still existed in the Lone Star State in the last years of the nineteenth century, but it increasingly attracted a more specialized audience, and most owners were men with money. Quarter racing, however, was picking up in popularity. An Abilene newspaper gave detailed instructions for laying out a half-mile track. The distance to the fences on both sides was measured carefully. It is unlikely many Texans engaged an engineer to run the curve as suggested, but instead just found ground level enough to clear a straight path of around half a mile, suitable for races of a quarter mile and longer. Moreover, times were changing. At the second annual spring stallion show held in Abilene in 1892 a reporter noted that the event "was really remarkable for one thing—there was not a 'Morgan or Steel Dust,' or a 'Steel Dust and Rondo' horse on the ground." The writer continued that he understood the value of the horses just mentioned but pointed out that locally he had seen so many stallions "without breeding, scrubs in appearance, for which the owners claim the blood of the great Steel Dust, from which Texas has attained a national reputation for fast short distance runners." Moreover, "Steel Dust horses were in the hands of the old quarter horse men, who in the early days were as shrewd in their methods of breeding as are the breeders of to-day. The quarter horses, or Steel Dusts, were valued very highly and were being developed as race horses all over the state and were in great demand."[38]

By the beginning of the twentieth century, Thoroughbred racing in the United States was no longer run as informal events. Before the 1890s many tracks operated independently, although some belonged to a circuit and there was an exchange of information about men who violated the rules or cheated. Individual jockey clubs scheduled their own racing dates, often with meets overlapping nearby tracks. Names of horses proved confusing too, since so many carried the name of one of the famous race horses of previous decades. Thoroughbred racing associations had been unsuccessful at centralizing the sport. In metropolitan New York the clubs operated under the rules of the American Jockey Club, but it did not control decisions of the various groups outside its realm. Interested turfmen understood they needed more centralization, and in 1891 they established a Board of Control in New York City, which was the first step towards a general government for Thoroughbred racing throughout the nation. Reciprocal arrangements with the western clubs soon followed. By 1894, The Jockey Club superseded the Board of Control. With headquarters in New York City, its goal was "not only to encourage the development of the thoroughbred horse, but to establish racing on such a footing that it may command the interests as well as the confidence and favorable opinion of the public." The club wrote the rules of racing, licensed jockeys and trainers, appointed officials, set racing dates, and in 1896 took over publishing *The American Stud Book* making registering Thoroughbreds at one central location official. It was not unusual for someone selling a horse to allege he was "registered" without any evidence to prove his animal's pedigree. This new organization ended fraudulent claims of breeding, and any track refusing to accept the new governing body was deemed an "outlaw." Horses that ran at one of those tracks could not compete at recognized tracks until reinstated.[39]

At the same time racing made dramatic changes in the way horses started. Throughout the history of racing the most important man on the track was often the starter and many a dispute or court case occurred when the starter failed to perform his duties to the satisfaction of everyone. Even Gaylon Brown came under criticism when substituting for the regular starter at the Hawthorne track in October 1893. "Mr. Brown," wrote a sympathetic reporter, "did fairly well as starter," but he was not likely to drive the regular starter out of business because with only two horses to get away he gave one horse a two lengths advantage. In 1894, the first automated contraption to start a race in Chicago appeared. Pioneered in Australia, it was a single strand barrier consisting of wire about the height of the horse's head that was attached to a spring at either end. When activated the device sprang up and away from the horses, and they were off. When used in New Orleans in 1896, Gaylon Brown observed, "I never saw a thing so simple and yet so perfect." Another turfman noted, "I've got nothing but praise for it. I wish it had been invented years ago. I think I have paid $20,000 in fines for the want of something like that, to give all the boys an equal chance."[40]

The Gay Nineties brought some of the most colorful people in American history to the forefront in racing. Those men and women who engaged in the sport might see their horses appear in the *Daily Racing Form*, a tabloid newspaper founded in Chicago in 1894. Although its main goal was to publish information about past performances of horses as a service to bettors, it also published stories about owners. No longer was racing confined to men. Women also showed an interest and one of those was Lillian Russell, who was a nationally known singer and actress. She had a long-term relationship with Diamond Jim Brady, a New Yorker known for his "penchant for diamonds and modish clothes." His activities in "racing and theatrical circles made him a national figure," and inspired Russell to participate in the sport firsthand. Brady owned a winning string of Thoroughbreds. In the next decade Russell bought eight colts by a New Zealand stallion and competed under the stable name of "Mr. Clinton" (the name coming from her hometown of Clinton, Iowa). Gone were the days when women limited their participation to attending the balls during race week or sitting in separate stands as they had in the past. Women like Russell could now be seen in the winner's circle.[41]

The Gay Nineties also brought the birth of one of the most celebrated horses of the century. Domino, foaled in 1891 in Lexington, Kentucky, was bought as a yearling by British born James R. Keene, a major figure in Thoroughbred breeding and racing as well as the founding of The Jockey Club in New York City. Not to be confused with A. Keene Richards, James Robert Keene was born in London in 1838, and came with his family to the United States in 1852. By the mid-1870s he had made his fortune and determined to join

Advertisement for the "Texas State Fair and Dallas Exposition in 1895." *The Southern Mercury* (Dallas, Texas), October 3, 1895.

the ranks of Thoroughbred owners. Despite a brief financial setback, by the 1890s his stable in Kentucky was one of the most prosperous in the nation. Domino, one of his most successful runners, was by Himyar but his dam was out of Lizzie G by War Dance. Old-timers around Austin remembered when War Dance came to Texas during the Civil War to prevent his confiscation by Union or Confederate forces. No doubt many Texans remembered his brief stay in the state because he later belonged to Keene Richards, whose Texas connection to George Feris was well-known among turfmen. In turn, knowing of Domino's tie to Texas, they perhaps followed his career with interest. A number of the most famous Thoroughbreds of the twentieth century went back to Domino, including Secretariat, War Admiral, Seattle Slew, Native Dancer, and Affirmed. His tombstone reads: "Here lies the fleetest runner the American Turf has ever known, and one of the gamest and most generous of horses."[42]

Just a few years before the beginning of the twentieth century, the *Fort Worth Gazette* reported that John N. Simpson, managing director of the racing department of the Texas State Fair, said: "Texans love fine horses, and there will be more and finer horses at the state fair than ever were assembled at any one place in the south." But the critics mounted a challenge. After the fair ended in November 1894, an article appeared in the local paper criticizing the widespread profanity and gambling and asking the management to make the fair, a family friendly atmosphere again. While "the racing pleased the devotees of the turf immensely," reformers wanted to see the day when all forms of gambling would be excluded altogether. Despite the objections to gambling, the fair in 1895 promised premiums of $75,000 and a program of races with the largest purses ever offered in the South.[43]

By the time the century ended, quarter horses had become the dominant breed in the state. Of those found in Texas, Traveler was probably the most mysterious. Foaled sometime in the 1890s, his breeding is unknown, and any speculation about it is just guesswork. He was first discovered pulling a wagon along the right-of-way for the Texas and Pacific Railroad in Eastland

Of those foundation sires of the American Quarter Horse, Traveler was probably the most mysterious. His age and breeding were unknown, but he became the sire of many outstanding race horses. Public domain.

County. At that time, he was probably around eight to ten years old and had never been ridden. No one knows for sure who bought him from the railroad contractor, but one of the first races he won was against a mare named Mayflower ridden by Will Crutchfield. A friend of the mare's jockey later said that "Crutchfield could not have thrown a rock off of Mayflower and touched Traveler's dust." One story has him bought by John Cooper and Brown Seay, who may have owned a saloon in Granbury where they first harnessed him to a buggy. When tapped with the whip he "stepped out" prompting Seay to observe, "He sure is some traveler." Thereafter they called him Traveler. After his racing days ended, he stood stud for many years, having several different owners; he probably died in Alfred, near Corpus Christi, around 1912.[44]

The death blow to Texas horse racing had come some years before, in 1903, with a law passed in Austin by the Twenty-Eighth Legislature. It made betting on horse racing illegal. For those taking or accepting any bet the punishment was a fine of not less than $200 nor more than $500, and imprisonment in the county jail for not less than thirty nor more than ninety days. Anyone who made a wager of anything of value could be fined $25 to $100. The owner of the land where the track was located could be fined $200 to $500, and jailed for thirty to ninety days if there was gambling on the premises. Each day of violations was considered a separate offense. Lawmakers approved the bill on March 23 to go into effect ninety days after adjournment. Amendments to the law in 1905 eased the restrictions a little, but the reformers had won. Racing ended in Texas for three decades.[45]

The amendment was probably the result of the almost impossible job of stopping gambling on scrub races across the state where policing the sport was difficult. The ones hurt by the legislation were organized jockey club events, and various state fairs that were widely publicized and carefully watched. One man who tried to test the constitutionality of the statute was Mike Herman at the San Antonio State Fair in November 1903, when he proceeded to operate the races "wide open." But he found that the law was "as sound as a gold dollar, and that in addition to paying the penalty required by the law, he will have to get beyond the State limits [line] if he desires to continue the business of racing horses for money." At the same time many cities also enacted laws against racing in the streets.[46]

The 1903 law was far reaching. The Dallas papers noted in July that the Texas State Fair scheduled for the fall would have "absolutely nothing doing in the way of horse racing or gambling, still there will be no lack of track and grand stand attractions of the most absorbing character." The following month it was reported in Waco that many sporting men "had already left the place, and others were going . . . and that the gambling which is being done is in a quiet way and that those engaged in it were forced to keep a sharp lookout in order that they might not be caught."[47]

The Golden Age of Racing in Texas was winding down. Still, there were many men who contributed to horse racing during the century, far too many to name. A few stand out. Before the Civil War, Tom McKinney did much for organized racing from Galveston to Austin. His love of Thoroughbreds brought many fine bloodlines to Texas in the early years. George Feris added to the mix by importing Arabians and promoting Thoroughbreds from his home near the Gulf Coast. His influence lasted long after the Civil War ended. Mid Perry, Jones Greene, Jack Batchler, and Bill Fleming are associated with the legendary quarter horse foundation sires of Steel Dust, Shiloh, and Old Billy, and would be surprised to learn that they made history by raising animals that would one day make the American quarter horse registry. But after the Civil War ended, racing became more specialized, breeders focused on bloodlines that could win and no longer rode those horses for pleasure. Charley Haley, who followed in his father Tom Haley's footsteps, took his breeding operation from Johnson County south of Fort Worth to Sweetwater in western Texas and continued his success in raising fine stock, including both Thoroughbreds and quarter running horses. But without a doubt the most notorious, and successful, turfman after the war was Sheriff Jim Brown, who also crossed the divide, racing both quarter horses and Thoroughbreds. He was, most certainly, the man who epitomized

Peter McCue, foaled 1895, one of the foundation sires of the American Quarter Horse. Public domain.

DIED WITH BOOTS ON

Nemesis of the Old Garfield Race Track's Projectors.

DREAD END OF SEVEN

Captain Brown the First and Colonel Clark the Last.

CAPTAIN "JIM" BROWN.

ABOVE LEFT: An extract from "Died With Boots On." "Seven of the men who formerly owned or were intimately connected with the management of the old Garfield park race track have in as many years died sudden or violent deaths." *The Inter Ocean* (Chicago), April 30, 1899. **RIGHT:** Captain James Madison "Jim" Brown as seen in an article "Died With Boots On" published years after his death. *The Inter Ocean* (Chicago), April 30, 1899.

the unique nature of the frontier state. He knew his horses, but he was also a typical Texan of the nineteenth century—armed and often dangerous, he was rough around the edges but an expert judge of horseflesh.

Perhaps Sam Hildreth said it best when he summed up the history of Texas racing by saying, "I can't help thinking of how different it all was a few years back in the West. Gone are the old quarter-horses that fought in their way for the same things their pampered descendants of to-day struggle for in theirs, gone are the quarter-mile tracks out on the prairie, so utterly different from the great plants of luxury and comfort that have come to take their place, and gone are the Sheriff Jim Browns who gave to the game a thrill and a touch of color that will never return." As for Brown, a paper noted: "He died as he probably would have elected to die if given the choice—with his boots on."[48]

A 1902 newspaper clipping says more about the importance of Texas horses than any amount of writing can. The headline on the front page read: "Noted Mare Dead: Sallie McMillin Who Held the Dallas Track Record, Dies in Cleburne Last Friday." She was only twelve years old. Although her name was actually spelled McMillan, the praise is sincere:

> Sallie McMillin is dead.
>
> Sallie was a race mare of the purest thoroughbred strain and had proved not only her breeding but her speed and bottom on many a hotly contested track.
>
> She will be remembered by race horse men and admirers of fast horseflesh as the 4-year-old who in 1894 took the Dallas fair track record by going around the three-quarter mile elipse [*sic*] in 1:14, a figure which stands today unbeaten in the State. . . . Sallie McMillin was the fastest 4-year-old ever known in Texas and on many occasions put money in her owner's pockets. She had not been on the track in some time, but was cared for at the Cleburne Jockey Club track stables where her death occurred. Sallie was owned by Col. S. E. Moss for many years, but was the property of Mr. Chas. Ferguson when she died.[49]

A fitting tribute to a Texas horse, and one of many in the racing history of the Lone Star State. As the nineteenth century drew to a close, the days when the death of a race horse could make the front page would also come to an end. Horse racing was in a slow decline, and stories about it no longer made the local papers. No longer could jockey clubs be found in all the major cities, nor did Thoroughbred tracks draw large crowds as they had in earlier years. The nineteenth century closed the door on the glory days of racing in Texas.

Epilogue

The Race has been Run

The death blow to Texas horse racing came in 1903 when the Legislature declared gambling at the track illegal. In January, the Houston paper reported that the Grand Jury returned 125 indictments for gambling and that the "law and order league is starting a crusade." In Dallas, the Grand Jury returned 210 indictments. While these were not charged against racing, the message was clear. Reform-minded citizens wanted an end to gambling in Texas. Rev. George C. Rankin was on a mission. He was one of the leaders of the movement in Dallas and did "not hesitate to state that he desires to see all gamblers prosecuted."[1]

The state legislature could not help but notice, and by February a bill was in the House. Outrage was growing. In Houston, the paper reported on February 20 that "during the last few weeks there has been an outbreak of gambling, especially on turf events, which has swept over the entire country." By mid-March, the Senate conducted its third reading of a bill to prohibit betting at the races. The bill had already passed the House. One man reported: "To wager one's earnings upon a horse race . . . is about as sane and profitable a business as going against a game of stacked cards or loaded dice." Legislators agreed and approved the law on March 23 to take effect ninety days after adjournment.[2]

Gambling did not end, of course, but for the next thirty years betting was done behind closed doors and in private. Reformers struck at alcohol and gambling, resulting in many tracks suffering financial difficulties. In 1897, there were 314 Thoroughbred tracks in the United States. By 1908, the number dropped to only thirty-one. By the 1920s only three states allowed betting at the track, one of which was Kentucky. Owners of Thoroughbreds, their trainers and jockeys, headed for Europe to enjoy the sport they loved. In Texas, this opened the door for quarter horse racing on scrub tracks. Local racetracks dotted the landscape and gambling continued, but participants wagered in places out of sight of local law enforcement.[3]

Other sports grew in popularity. Eventually the radio allowed Americans to listen to baseball and boxing and even college football. George Herman "Babe" Ruth Jr. became a household name as a player for the New York Yankees. William Harrison "Jack" Dempsey thrilled radio listeners with his boxing skills and became a cultural icon in the 1920s. Football drew spectators. The Texas-Oklahoma football game began in 1929, and in 1930 a 46,000-seat stadium that would become the Cotton Bowl replaced the track at the Texas State Fair as a new venue for the latest source of entertainment. With the invention of television in the 1930s, racing took a backseat to sports that appealed to the public. The races attracted a much smaller audience. Texans' enjoyment shifted to rodeos, and in 1929 organizations began forming to standardize the rules of this truly western sport.[4]

It was also in 1929 that Thoroughbred racing returned to Texas, albeit without gambling. At Arlington, a small town between Dallas and Fort Worth, the Texas Jockey Club and William Thomas "Tom" Waggoner teamed up to bring racing back to the Lone Star State. Waggoner, who made a fortune in oil, built Arlington Downs, which opened that year. He also owned the adjacent Three D Stables. Since all but the Maryland tracks closed by late October, owners from coast-to-coast could ship their horses to the new "splendid racing plant" for the November meet. The Three D Stables accommodated 400 horses, and the barns were full of Thoroughbreds ready to compete for the $70,000 in prize money. The stands could hold 15,000 spectators with seats for 11,000, and plenty of standing room. Fashionable ladies in their finest frocks sat in the box seats, and the average fan could make the round trip from Fort Worth to Arlington Downs, including bus fare, for just $1.00 with the Northern Texas Traction Company. General admission, including the grandstands, was $1.50. Clubhouse admission for ladies was $2.50 and for gentlemen it was $5.50. Before the first meet, William Dondas, who served as secretary, noted there would be no illegal wagering on the horses since betting was "not necessary for racing."[5]

But Waggoner knew that was not true. Thoroughbred racing needed betting to succeed long-term and he worked hard to see that happen. Waggoner spearheaded the return of parimutuel betting in 1933, a legislation that gave the sport new life in Texas. The governor, Miriam "Ma" Ferguson, thought gambling might help the financial problems brought on by the Great Depression, and favored the change when she took office in 1933. As soon as parimutuel passed, new tracks appeared. It is no surprise that the largest were in the cities associated with Thoroughbred racing in the nineteenth century. Besides Arlington Downs, there were tracks at Epsom Downs in Houston, which began on Thanksgiving Day (November 1933), Galveston Downs on New Year's Day (January 1934), San Antonio's Alamo Downs (April 1934), and the State Fair of Texas track in Dallas (April 1934).

As expected, Waggoner's track continued to prosper when parimutuel returned. According to a local paper it was "America's Playground Midway Between Dallas and Fort Worth" where spectators could "Thrill to This Sport of Kings" for "21 Glorious Days." Hall of Fame trainer Charlie Whittingham remembered it in 1937 as "first-class, and racing in Texas was good. Very good." Waggoner built a track to rival any in the United States, and a brick clubhouse became the home of the Texas Jockey Club, a prestigious group whose headquarters was in the Adolphus Hotel in Dallas. Arlington built two tracks, one was one and one-eighth mile (although some said one and a quarter mile) and a second was a one-mile inner track. The infield included a large duck pond where workers fished after their day was done. When completed it was called the South's greatest racetrack. Governor Ferguson attended its grand opening, along with Vice President James Garner, Postmaster General James

Farley, and comedian Will Rogers. Shortly after it opened, Waggoner turned it over to the American Legion for a day, which sponsored Armistice Day races for charity. There was a free barbecue, and a reported forty beeves were slaughtered to provide the food. Nearly 15,000 attended. Until the track closed, it sponsored two meets each year, a twenty-one-day season in the spring and a thirty-day season in the fall. Local businesses prospered as it was a boon for them during the Depression, and the races put a smile on the faces of "hotel keepers, merchants and restaurant men."[6]

Epsom Downs, located a few miles from Houston, took its name from the famous track in England. Owned and operated by the Texas Breeders and Racing Association, the $600,000 racing plant was completed in the record time of eight weeks. An estimated 30,000 spectators flocked to the opening. The first president was local businessman E. J. Hussion and managing director was Lou Smith. The grandstand could seat nearly 8,000 people and an additional 10,000 could be accommodated in the lawn and floor areas. The parking lot held 10,000 cars and the clubhouse 5,000 people. There were stalls for 800 horses but that was increased to 1,000 by 1934. The inaugural races drew almost 30,000 spectators, and Governor Ferguson was in the winner's circle to greet the jockey and owner of the horse that won the race run in her honor. The *Houston Chronicle* declared it "an artistic triumph and a financial success." Moreover, the "parimutuel booths underneath the grandstand did a rushing business as South Texas walked up and laid bets on the ponies, a privilege denied them" for years.[7]

The birth of Galveston Downs came when Bassett Blakely, Houston financier and cattleman, announced he had leased the abandoned dog racing plant near Sixty-first Street and Broadway west of the city and would build a modern horse racing facility there. The already present grandstand, not in use since dog racing ended in 1927, would be sufficient, but Blakely planned a new track and stables. He intended to hold his season immediately following the close of the one in Houston. Although smaller than Epsom or Arlington Downs, Blakely noted "it will be right up-to-the-minute and I believe it will prove a credit to Galveston." The general manager, J. M. Sheppard, admitted that "we are not going to have a second Arlington Downs here, but we are going to have a good little race meet. We will specialize in Texas bred horses, and will run for the full 30 days of January." Twenty betting windows could be found under the grandstands. Fans listened to the call of the race through four loudspeakers. It seems fitting that Galveston, which opened its first track in the 1830s, would see it return a century later.[8]

San Antonio enjoyed racing even before settlers arrived from the United States, but not like that seen at Alamo Downs, which opened in 1933. At a cost of $400,000 it boasted of grandstands that could accommodate 5,000 spectators. The first day saw Governor Ferguson attend as guest of honor. The *Fort Worth Star Telegram* reported that, "Thousands of car[s] kept traffic in a jam all afternoon, and possibly 15,000 people visited the new arrangement, including the stables for a look at the ponies." The track advertised a $15,000 starting gate, stables, and a one-mile oval track that was expected to be "one of the fastest in the nation." Like the other tracks, parimutuel drew big crowds.[9]

In Dallas, racing at the State Fair dated back to the late nineteenth century when it was a popular sport during the festivities. The first track had long disappeared, so by April 1934 there was a new one under construction. Promoters scheduled elaborate ceremonies to open what they claimed was a $250,000 racing plant, although one expert estimated it cost only $150,000 for a grandstand, bleachers, clubhouse, barns, and track. A downtown parade sponsored by local businessmen preceded the opening. Horsemen on the scene proclaimed the track "among the best in the country," and the barns stabled more than 500 Thoroughbreds waiting for the bugle's call that would send them to the post. Speakers planned for the opening included Governor Ferguson; Rosser J. Coke, president of the Texas State Fair; businessman R. B. George of the racing committee; and Mayor Charles T. Turner. Coke and George entered a partnership to build the facility, and the profit from the operation would be shared between George and the Fair on a 60:40 basis for the next ten years. General admission to enjoy a day at the races that ran from April 28 until May 22 was only $1.00. Thoroughbred racing returned to Dallas after a lapse of a quarter of a century.[10]

The first year of legalized racing saw the recently created Texas Racing Commission (TRC) issue an annual report to Governor Ferguson in 1934. Chairman of the TRC was Guy L. Waggoner. From 1922 until 1928 he had been married to Anne Burnett, who inherited the Four Sixes Ranch. Waggoner, a renowned breeder of quarter horses, later helped found the American Quarter Horse Association (AQHA). The TRC maintained offices in the Austin Hotel in the state capital through the courtesy of the hotel management until it moved to the Littlefield Building. In a letter to the governor, Waggoner pointed out that Texas was one of eighteen states to legalize parimutuel betting on racing. "Having no precedent for the organization and conduct of this department," he wrote, "and appreciating the value of experience, we have looked to and received valuable assistance from other States in the framing of our rules, etc. Texas, as is the case with most other States, has patterned its rules largely after those of Kentucky where legalized racing has been in force for more than a quarter of a century." He went on to point out that the "cooperation of Kentucky's State Racing Commission, as well as that of others, including the New York Jockey Club, through its very courteous secretary . . . has been invaluable to our Commission in its formation and operation."[11]

Waggoner went on to discuss why the TRC would succeed: "Much has been done towards placing racing on a high plane and we feel that racing in Texas has been conducted in a clean manner." Most importantly, with the help of the State Live Stock Sanitary Commission, the TRC "has been able to combat the doping evil. Persons found guilty of the violation of our rule 237, which prohibits the possession or use of stimulants on horses, are promptly suspended from the track and their cases referred to the Commission for their action." He reported there had been a minimum of cases in the state.[12]

During 1934 the National Association of State Racing commissioners organized with the purpose to "discuss and study problems of State supervision of racing; to encourage the adoption of uniform rules and regulations as are conducive to the elevation of the sport, and to do generally whatever may be necessary to achieve and maintain public confidence in racing." The TRC was a member of this organization, as were nearly all state racing commissions in the United States.[13]

The TRC also wanted to encourage the breeding of horses so at the beginning of the spring racing season it adopted a "rule permitting unregistered horses to race at County Fair meets and as a result a number of horses which were not subject to registration with the New York Jockey Club have been permitted to race at small meets." These horses, many a Thoroughbred-quarter horse cross, would eventually join the AQHA.[14]

The TRC hoped to stop wagers placed with bookmakers instead of at the track, where the state could realize some revenue. So it added a rule that read: "All race tracks in the State of Texas licensed by the Racing Commission shall on and after this date exclude from their enclosures all telephone, telegraph wires, radio or other means of transporting or disseminating any information to any person, poolroom, barroom, saloon, restaurant, gambling house or other place outtside [*sic*] of the racing enclosure where bets on the horse races are made and accepted, nor shall they lease or sell to any person or persons, firm or corporation whatsoever any privilege or license for the purpose of disseminating such information." A violation meant revoking the license of the track involved. The TRC also recommended that the state suppress bookmaking.[15]

The control of the TRC was far-reaching, including licensing tracks, jockeys, and trainers. During the year it licensed almost 600 trainers, more than 200 jockeys, and 100 plus apprentice jockeys. It registered colors for owners, authorized agents, and recorded partnerships. Some of the money collected from fees went into the Jockey Fund, which was "used in defraying the expenses of hospitalization of jockeys injured while in the discharge of their duties upon tracks under the supervision" of the TRC. Moreover, with the increased number of licensed tracks and county fairs, the TRC had to expand its number of supervisors to oversee that parimutuel betting followed the rules and the state received its fair share of the bounty. While the TRC operated with a budget of $20,000 in its first year, the Commission asked for an increase to $30,000 for the coming year.[16]

The report also listed official race meets—those that were considered major as well as county fairs and other small meets. The major sites were the previously mentioned tracks in Arlington, Houston, Dallas, and San Antonio. Galveston was not large enough to be listed with the big four but fell somewhere between the big four and the approved minor tracks. Those county fairs and other small meets sanctioned by the TRC occurred in Brady, Haskell, Hondo, Georgetown, Fort Bend, Seguin, Kingsville, Marfa, Amarillo, and Victoria. Many of these were traditional locations of racing in the nineteenth century.[17]

The TRC also printed its own *Rules of Racing*. Adopted in 1934, it contained 110 pages (compared to the twelve pages of the Webber's Prairie Jockey Club rule book of 1849 described earlier), and covered every imaginable infraction, including prohibiting "profane or indecent language, carrying or exhibiting a deadly weapon, or otherwise disturbing the peace on any race track enclosure." Anyone violating this rule would be either fined, suspended, or ruled off. That one rule alone would have been a bane to many nineteenth century Texas horsemen. Also, any person found to "break, train or race, any horse or horses belonging to or under the supervision, management or control of any person or persons who stand suspended from the turf may, themselves, be fined or suspended."[18]

Other rules included a variety of topics. One prohibited no more than two meets per racecourse per year, and applicants must file with the commission. In a town with no more than 3,000 inhabitants the fee was $100. For a town of less than 10,000 the fee was $200, progressing up to a city of more than 100,000 where the fee was $2,000. Jockeys of the nineteenth century, who often rode bareback, would be surprised at rule number sixty-eight, which required jockeys to wear helmets. Additionally, a jockey had to fill out an application accompanied by a $5 fee and two written statements by reliable witnesses that he was personally known to them, and that he was a person of good reputation and a capable rider and at least sixteen years of age. Any boy under sixteen could apprentice for three years to learn the trade. Most importantly, horses must be registered with The Jockey Club in New York City.[19]

Governor Ferguson left office in 1935 and her successor James Allred was a staunch opponent of gambling, saying "People are more inte[re]sted in pensions than horses." He campaigned on a promise to "rid Texas of the vile practice of betting on horse racing." By March 1937, legislators hotly debated a bill to repeal betting on races. Speaking against repeal, William C. Repass, managing editor of the *Houston Chronicle*, pointed out that "Repeal of the race track betting law will not end race track gambling. Like prohibition, it will bring on a greater evil. The gambling instinct is universal, and I would rather my son gamble at a well regulated track than in the back room of a cheap dive." Among others speaking about saving racing was Robert J. Kleberg of the King Ranch. But the opposition was strong. Churches came out firmly against gambling and Rev. E. D. Head of the First Baptist Church in Houston said that forty-two Baptist churches in his city wanted repeal. By June, the House voted ninety-four to thirteen to lower the curtain on horse racing. When Governor Allred put his signature on the parimutuel repeal bill, and the State Racing Commission refused permits at the major tracks, Epsom Downs in Houston saw its last official race on March 27. In June, the TRC denied racing permits for Epsom Downs, Arlington Downs, and Fair Park past September 1 of that year. The last of Waggoner's racing stock at the Three D Stock Farm was sold in the fall of 1937. Mexican President Lázaro Cárdenas del Rio purchased the two imported English stallions, Phalaros and Stamford.

While trying to develop a Kentucky Derby winner, Waggoner paid $60,000 for Phalaros and $50,000 for Stamford. After only four years, Thoroughbred racing disappeared from Texas again.[20]

It was also during the 1930s that supporters of quarter horses began to discuss an official registry for the breed. Horsemen could easily recognize a quarter horse by its conformation, but it was not until around 1900 that an Englishman, William Anson, living in Christoval near San Angelo began tracing the origin of western quarter horses from colonial times. Still, it would be more than three decades before Robert M. Denhardt spearheaded the effort to put a story to their past that they became a true breed. Denhardt, born in California in 1912, received a master's degree from the University of California at Berkeley, and accepted a job teaching history at what would become Texas A&M University in 1937. Soon after moving to Texas, he began researching the background of horses that claimed to trace back to Steel Dust. In 1939, he met with breeders in Fort Worth at the Southwestern Exposition and Stock Show and proposed a "Western Quarter Horse Breeders" association. By 1940, Denhardt had enough support to advocate for a breed registry and stud book similar to what The Jockey Club had for Thoroughbreds. As a result, the first meeting of the newly formed American Quarter Horse Association convened in Fort Worth in March 1940. The by-laws declared: "The registration of all horses by this Association shall be based on these qualities, namely, Quarter Horse bloodlines, Quarter Horse conformation, and Quarter Horse performance. All horses applying for registration must satisfy the Association that they have these three qualities." The ideal quarter horse must meet these specifications, and breeds that fell short included spotted, pinto, appaloosa, and albino horses. One concern of the early organizers was that the bulldog type horses were being destroyed by the blood of too many Thoroughbreds in their pedigrees.[21]

The early years were not without controversy. Many of those who raced quarter horses could not register their animals. They failed both in conformation and bloodlines since they often had Thoroughbreds in their lineage. So in

1945 a rival organization formed in Tucson, Arizona—the American Quarter Racing Association. The purpose was "to promote Quarter racing as a sport and to provide a means of standardizing rules and regulations and insuring clean racing on a national basis." Others, unsatisfied with the AQHA for various reasons, formed the National Quarter Horse Breeders Association in Alice, Texas, in 1945. It was not until four years later, in 1949, that the three associations worked out their differences and merged. *The Quarter Horse Journal*, founded the year before, announced in December 1949: "Historians of the Quarter Horse world will record 1949 as one of the breed's greatest. Not since the foundation of the 'Stud Book' and the beginning of an organization, the American Quarter Horse Association, has the future of the Quarter Horse seemed so secure. Amalgamation has brought with it the promise that the breed will reach the heights which the three associations originally pledged to attain. Through the individual efforts of the three, one association was born. Through unification, the improvement in breeding and performance of the Quarter Horse is sure to be found. . . . The American Quarter Horse will be synonymous with the best—on the track and the range, in the rodeo arena and in riding pleasure everywhere."[22]

As with Thoroughbreds, those who supported the organization of the AQHA enjoyed the means and money. Names such as Bob Kleberg of King Ranch fame, who raced both Thoroughbreds and quarter horses, gave the organization validity. Kleberg believed that Thoroughbred blood enhanced the performance of pure quarter horses. Another, James Goodwin Hall, was married to Anne Burnett, daughter of Tom Burnett and granddaughter of Samuel Burk Burnett of the Four Sixes Ranch (Anne's first marriage to Guy Waggoner and his role in the TRC has been previously mentioned). Officers for the first few years of the AQHA were men of wealth and prestige: President W. B. Warren; Vice President Jack Hutchins; Second Vice President Lee Underwood; Treasurer Jim Hall; and Secretary Bob Denhardt. All were Texans, except Denhardt. Hutchins, who later served as president, once remarked, "We have seen the beginning of the end of the bulldogs." He owned and raced

Thoroughbred-quarter horse crosses, and when asked why he raced half-breeds, he answered "to win, but you will not find my racing string mixed with my Quarter Horses, nor will you find my cowboys riding racehorses." Yet many turfmen understood that a quarter horse with some Thoroughbred blood could prove superior, as had breeders in nineteenth century Texas. With the formation of the AQHA and the founding of its permanent headquarters in Amarillo, the quarter horse became official. While jockey clubs typically published rule books for racing, quarter-racers had never printed rules before. Times were changing.[23]

Gone were the days when racing, both Thoroughbred and quarter-distance horses, reigned supreme and gambling was a popular pastime and any man who owned a horse could race anywhere. Never again would there be racing as seen in the nineteenth century. Texans who enjoyed the sport in the previous century did not have to deal with state regulations. What rules they used were those of the local jockey clubs or traditions that were respected on small tracks or agreements at scrub races between individual participants. There would never be another Sheriff Jim Brown in a shoot-out at the racetrack nor young boys riding bareback in a neck-to-neck sprint to the finish line. There would never be another George Feris importing Arabians to a state with tens of thousands of feral horses or a Tom McKinney promoting Thoroughbreds in a frontier environment that was still home to hostile Kiowas and Comanches. No longer was horse racing the main equine attraction. Rodeo eventually became the official sport of the state, and rodeo was the domain of the quarter horse, leaving the nineteenth century as the true "Golden Age" for those who loved to see a good horse race.[24]

Notes

PREFACE

1 Robert Moorman Denhardt, *Quarter Horses: A Story of Two Centuries* (1967; rpt., Norman: University of Oklahoma Press, 1980), 134–38, 159–67. While Denhardt is the better known of the early historians of the quarter horse, William Anson (1872–1926) was the first to define the quarter horse as a breed. Anson, the son of the second Earl of Litchfield and his wife, the oldest daughter of the first Duke of Abercorn, was born in England. He arrived in Texas in 1889 where his two older brothers, Claude and Frank, had purchased cattle ranches. He was one of the first to urge the founding of a quarter horse registry but died before that became a reality.

2 Edward L. Bowen, *Masters of the Turf: Ten Trainers Who Dominated Horse Racing's Golden Age* (Lexington, KY: Blood-Horse Publications, 2007), 135.

CHAPTER 1

1 *American Turf Register and Sporting Magazine* (1838), 52; *Spirit of the Times* (1839), 282; Ashbel Smith to "My dear Will," December 20, 1838, Ashbel Smith Papers, Dolph Briscoe Center for American History, University of Texas, Austin. All quotes from William Ransom Hogan, *The Texas Republic: A Social and Economic History* (1946; rpt., Austin: University of Texas Press, 1969), 131–32.

2 John Ferdinand Dalziel Smyth, *A Tour of the United States of America* (London: G. Robinson, J. Robson, and J. Sewell, 1784), 139, 361; Robert Moorman Denhardt, *The Quarter Running Horse: America's Oldest Breed* (Norman: University of Oklahoma Press, 1979), 5. Full text of Smyth's original book can be found at https://openlibrary.org/books/OL24592986M/A_tour_in_the_United_States_of_America [Accessed July 15, 2021].

3 John Hervey *Racing in America, 1665-1865*, 2 vols. (New York: Privately Printed, The Jockey Club, 1944), 1:17; William H. P. Robertson, *The History of Thoroughbred Racing in America* (New York: Bonanza Books, 1964), 8. See also, Katherine C. Mooney,

Race Horse Men: How Slavery and Freedom Were Made at the Racetrack (Cambridge: Harvard University Press, 2014), 5.

4 Smyth, *A Tour of the United States of America*, 20–22.

5 Lyman Horace Weeks, *The American Turf: An Historical Account of Racing in the United States with Biographical Sketches of Turf Celebrities* (New York: The Historical Company, 1898), 34; Mooney, *Race Horse Men*, 125. Race times were recorded in minutes and seconds with a colon between. A full text of *The American Turf* can be found at https://archive.org/details/americanturfhist01week/page/n7/mode/2up [Accessed July 9, 2022].

6 Hervey, *Racing in America, 1665–1865*, 1:21–23, 131. There is a dispute regarding when course racing came to the South. Some authorities believe it was not until 1730 when the first blooded horse, Bulle Rock, was imported into Virginia. Others argue that it started around 1691 when the royal governor of Virginia awarded prizes for horses running long distances rather than a quarter mile.

7 Hervey, *Racing in America, 1665–1865*, 1:24; Robertson, *The History of Thoroughbred Racing in America*, 15. See also, Denhardt, *The Quarter Running Horse* for a discussion of the distinction between Thoroughbreds and quarter horses.

8 Hervey, *Racing in America, 1665–1865*, 1:83.

9 John Rogers Williams, ed., *Philip Vickers Fithian: Journal and Letter, 1767–1774* (Princeton, NJ: The Princeton University Library, 1900), 148–49, 236, located at https://www.loc.gov/resource/lhbtn.30673/?sp=1 [Accessed February 11, 2022]; J. Frank Dobie, Mody C. Boatright, Harry H. Ransom, eds., *Mustangs and Cow Horses* (1940; rpt., Denton: University of North Texas Press, 2000), ix.

10 Smyth, *A Tour of the United States of America*, 22–23; Denhardt, *The Quarter Running Horse*, 50, 286; Wayne Gard, *Fabulous Quarter Horse: Steel Dust—The True Account of the Most Celebrated Texas Stallion* (New York: Duell, Sloan and Pearce, 1958), 21–22. Smyth was one of the first to mention short-distance horses in the colonies.

11 Robertson, *The History of Thoroughbred Racing in America*, 16; Hervey, *Racing in America, 1665–1865*, 1:71–79, 111.

12 To obtain the height, a horse is measured in inches from the ground to the highest point of the withers—the base of the neck above the shoulders. The total number of inches is divided by four, which translates into the number of hands—four inches equals one hand. The Godolphin Arabian (c. 1724–1753), named for his best-known owner, Francis Godolphin, Second Earl of Godolphin, was foaled in Yemen but eventually ended up in the possession of Louis XV of France and from there came to England. He is buried in Cambridgeshire, England. Also known as the Godolphin Barb, he was an Arabian stallion that was one of three studs crediting with founding the modern Thoroughbred, the other two being the Darley Arabian and the Byerley Turk. See Kent Hollingsworth, *The Kentucky Thoroughbred* (Lexington: University Press of Kentucky, 1976), 33, and Don Worcester, "Quarter Horses, Mustangs, and Longhorns," Unpublished Manuscript, Chapter 2, p. 3, Donald Emmet Worcester Papers, Southwest Collection, Special Collection Library, Texas Tech University, Lubbock, for the quote about height.

For more on Janus, see Walter Osborne, "Mighty Janus," *The Quarter Horse Journal* (November 1967), 28–29, 138–39; Helen Michaelis, "The Sons of Janus," *The Quarter Horse Journal* (July 1971), 62, 66, 68, 70 184–88; Helen Michaelis, "Janus Family," in M. H. Lindeman, *The Quarter Horse Breeder* (Wichita Falls, TX: Humphrey Printing Co., 1959), 106.

13 *The Texas Gazette*, San Felipe de Austin, August 14, 1830. A copy of the advertisement is in Malcolm D. McLean, *Fine Texas Horses: Their Pedigrees and Performance, 1830–1845* (Fort Worth: Texas Christian University Press, 1966), xiv, 8. See also, "Stout, Owen H.," *Handbook of Texas Online*, accessed March 16, 2025, https://www.tshaonline.org/handbook/entries/stout-owen-h; "Roberts, Andrew," *Handbook of Texas Online*, accessed March 16, 2025, https://www.tshaonline.org/handbook/entries/roberts-andrew; Merle Weir, "Bell, Josiah Hughes," *Handbook of Texas Online*, accessed March 16, 2025, https://www.tshaonline.org/handbook/entries/bell-josiah-hughes.

14 Hervey, *Racing in America, 1665–1865*, 1:78; McLean, *Fine Texas Horses*, 42, 102–103.

15 May Wilson McBee, *The Life and Times of David Smith, Patriot, Pioneer and Indian Fighter* (Kansas City, MO: E. L. Mendenhall, Inc., 1959), 26, 34; Hervey, *Racing in America, 1665–1865*, 2:58.

16 McBee, *The Life and Times of David Smith*, 30–32.

17 Ibid., 39–40, 48–49, 52; McLean, *Fine Texas Horses*, 27, 38–40, 42, 44, 59–60, 63, 73, 80–82, 135.

18 Reuben Gold Thwaites, ed., *Early Western Travels, 1748–1846*, 32 vols. (Cleveland, OH: Arthur H. Clark Company, 1904), 3:243. Full text of Thwaites's original book can be found at https://books.google.com/books?id=BFjItLAoYJcC&printsec=frontcover&source=gbs_ge_summary_r&cad=0#v=onepage&q&f=false [Accessed July 15, 2021]. A note at the beginning reads that *Travels West of the Alleghanies* is "a separate publication from 'Early Western Travels: 1748–1846,' in which series this appeared as Volume III." For the "Minutes of the Transylvania House of Delegates, May 23, 1775, to May 27, 1775," see Documenting the American South, University of North Carolina, Chapel Hill.

19 Twaites, ed., *Early Western Travels, 1748–1846*, 3:244–45; Keith Thomas, *Man and the Natural World: A History of the Modern Sensibility* (New York: Pantheon Books, 1983), 117.

20 John L. O'Connor, comp., *Notes on the Thoroughbred from Kentucky Newspapers* (Lexington, KY: Transylvania Printing Company, n.d.), 1–2, 4.

21 Hollingsworth, *The Kentucky Thoroughbred*, 14; Hervey, *Racing in America, 1665–1865*, 1:228; Foster Ockerman, Jr., *Hidden History of Horse Racing in Kentucky* (Charleston, SC: The History Press, 2019), 48. The Lexington Jockey Club lasted until 1823. In 1826, the Kentucky Association replaced it. Shares cost $50 each and entitled the man to enter a private clubroom at a local hotel and later a clubhouse for members only.

22 Hervey, *Racing in America, 1665–1865*, 1:233; Robertson, *The History of Thoroughbred Racing in America*, 66.

23 Robertson, *The History of Thoroughbred Racing in America*, 41–46; Hervey, *Racing in America, 1665–1865*, 2:57–61.

24 McLean, *Fine Texas Horses*, 23.

25 *Rules and Regulations of the Metairie Jockey Club* (Published for the Club, 1860), 7–9, original in the Texas State Archives, Austin. The Metairie Race Track was located at the present site of the Metairie Cemetery on Metairie Road in New Orleans. The oldest copy of a Texas rulebook in the author's possession is that of Webber's Prairie in 1849, and it contains only nine pages of rules as compared with Metairie a decade later in 1860, which contains twenty-five pages of rules. See *Rules and Regulations of the Webber's Prairie Jockey Club* (Austin: William H. Cushnew, printer, 1849), 6, original in the Texas State Archives. Webber's Prairie was a village in Travis County, Texas. There had been settlements there as early as 1827 and it was formally organized in 1839. It was later renamed Webberville.

26 Robertson, *The History of Thoroughbred Racing in America*, 37–38; Wikipedia, "Diomed," last updated August 24, 2007, https://en.wikipedia.org/wiki/Diomed [Accessed May 3, 2021]. See also, McLean, *Fine Texas Horses*, for more information on Texas horses with Diomed blood.

27 Robertson, *The History of Thoroughbred Racing in America*, 47–48; Denhardt, *The Quarter Running Horse*, 95–98. See also, Elizabeth Amis Cameron Blanchard and Manly Wade Wellman, *The Life and Times of Sir Archie: The Story of America's Greatest Thoroughbred, 1805–1833* (Chapel Hill: University of North Carolina Press, 1958).

28 McLean, *Fine Texas Horses*, 82–83; Denhardt, *The Quarter Running Horse*, 146.

29 O'Connor, *Notes on the Thoroughbred from Kentucky Newspapers*, 92–93, 96; Denhardt, *The Quarter Running Horse*, 91–95, 111–12. His two names came from the men who owned him: William B. Cook and E. M. Blackburn.

30 "Early Times in Texas, or the Adventures of John Dobell" in John C. Duval, *Early Times in Texas* (Dallas: H. P. N. Gammel & Co., 1892), 27.

31 J. Frank Dobie, et al., *Mustangs and Cow Horses*, 3–17. See also, Robert M. Denhardt, *The Horse of the Americas* (1947; rpt., Norman: University of Oklahoma Press, 1975) and T. R. Fehrenbach, *Comanches: The Destruction of a People* (1974; rpt., New York: Da Capo Press, 1994), 298–99.

32 "Concerning Philip Nolan," *The Quarterly of the Texas State Historical Association*, Vol. 7, No. 4 (April 1904), 308, 311–12. These letters were copied from the library of the Department of State and there is no editor. For more information see, Dobie, Boatright, and Ransom, eds., *Mustangs and Cow Horses*; Maurine T. Wilson and Jack Jackson, *Philip Nolan and Texas Expeditions to the Unknown Land, 1791–1801* (Waco: Texian Press, 1988); Denhardt, *Horse of the Americas*, 143–45. Nolan River in Johnson and Hill counties is named for him, and a historical marker in Hill County marks the place thought to be near where Nolan died.

33 Don Worcester, "The Ghost of the Llano Estacado," in Don Worcester, ed., *Western Horse Tales* (Plano: Wordware Publishing, Inc., 1994), 3–4.

34 Andrew Forest Muir, ed., *Texas in 1837: An Anonymous, Contemporary Narrative* (Austin: University of Texas Press, 1958), 108. The anonymous visitor who wrote *Texas in 1837* was from Ohio and provides a look at the first year of the Republic. See also, A. A. Parker, *Trip to the West and Texas* (1835; rpt., Concord, NH: William

White and Boston: Benjamin B. White, 1836), 174. Full text at https://archive.org/details/triptowesttexas00park/page/12/mode/2up [Accessed September 9, 2020].

35 Muir, ed., *Texas in 1837*, 108, 125.

36 Don Hedgpeth, *They Rode Good Horses: The First Fifty Years of the American Quarter Horse Association* (Amarillo: Trafton and Autry Printers, Inc., 1990), vi.

37 Abner J. Strobel, *The Old Plantations and their Owners of Brazoria County Texas* (Houston: The Union National Bank, 1930), 10–11; Mary Nixon Rogers and Abner J. Strobel, *A History of Brazoria County Texas; The Old Plantations and Their Owners of Brazoria County, Texas; Steamboats on the Brazos* (1958; rpt., Literary Licensing, LLC, 2012); 25–26. This is a reprint of Strobel's 1930 book on Brazoria County plantations with an addition on early steamboats. See also, René Harris, "Ellersly Plantation," *Handbook of Texas Online*, accessed March 16, 2025, https://www.tshaonline.org/handbook/entries/ellersly-plantation; and "McNeel, John Greenville," *Handbook of Texas Online*, accessed March 16, 2025, https://www.tshaonline.org/handbook/entries/mcneel-john-greenville.

38 Rogers and Strobel, *A History of Brazoria County Texas*, 36–37, 42, 54; Brett J. Derbes, "Bingham, Francis," *Handbook of Texas Online*, accessed March 16, 2025, https://www.tshaonline.org/handbook/entries/bingham-francis; Marilyn M. Sibley, "Jackson, Abner," *Handbook of Texas Online*, accessed March 16, 2025, https://www.tshaonline.org/handbook/entries/jackson-abner; and Andrew F. Muir, revised by Randolph B. "Mike" Campbell, "Herndon, John Hunter," *Handbook of Texas Online*, accessed March 16, 2025, https://www.tshaonline.org/handbook/entries/herndon-john-hunter.

39 Parker, *Trip to the West and Texas*, 150; McLean, *Fine Texas Horses*, 8–9. The earliest known American-style races were at San Augustine, Nacogdoches, and then San Felipe. Soon there were races in Columbia, Brazoria, Washington-on-the-Brazos, and Quintana, all before 1834. But there were probably many races not reported in the newspapers long before these dates. Boston, known as Old Boston today, was founded in the early 1830s. Cecil Harper Jr., "Old Boston, TX," *Handbook of Texas Online*, accessed March 16, 2025, https://www.tshaonline.org/handbook/entries/old-boston-tx.

40 Hervey, *Racing in America, 1665–1865*, 1:247–48; Robertson, *The History of Thoroughbred Racing in America*, 33.

41 See Denhardt, *The Quarter Running Horse*, 16–18, for a brief discussion of the history of the American Quarter Horse.

42 *The Morning Star* (Houston), January 4, 1840.

43 Grady McWhiney, *Cracker Culture: Celtic Ways in the Old South* (Tuscaloosa: University of Alabama Press, 1988), 136.

44 Hervey, *Racing in America, 1665–1865*, 1:242, 253–71; Weeks, *The American Turf*, 35, 79; Robertson, *The History of Thoroughbred Racing in America*, 52–55; James Douglas Anderson, *Making the American Thoroughbred* (Norwood, MA: The Plimpton Press, 1916), 151–63. See also, John Eisenberg, *The Great Match Race: When North Met South in America's First Sports Spectacle* (Boston and New York: Houghton Mifflin Co., 2006).

45 Madam Tonson is also sometimes seen as Madame Tonson. Hervey, *Racing in America, 1665–1865*, 2:35–37; Robertson, *The History of Thoroughbred Racing in America*, 44–45.

See also, Pedigree Online: Thoroughbred Database, "Monsieur Tonson," online database, https://www.pedigreequery.com/monsieur+tonson [Accessed January 22, 2021].

CHAPTER 2

1 McWhiney, *Cracker Culture*, 137.

2 *American Turf Register and Sporting Magazine* (1838), 51–52.

3 McLean, *Fine Texas* Horses, 129–34; O'Connor, *Notes on the Thoroughbred from Kentucky Newspapers*, 81, 240–41; Hervey, *Racing in America, 1665–1865*, 2:107; Robertson, *The History of Thoroughbred Racing in America*, 45; Wikipedia, "Leviathan (horse)," last updated March 3, 2024, https://en.wikipedia.org/wiki/Leviathan_(horse) [Accessed June 22, 2021].

4 *Austin City Gazette*, August 12, 1840, quoted in McLean, *Fine Texas Horses*, 92–93; Willis W. Pratt, ed., *Galveston Island or a Few Months Off the Coast of Texas: The Journal of Francis C. Sheridan 1839–1840* (Austin: University of Texas Press, 1954), 104.

5 Feris refers to Richards as his cousin, but cousin is a loose term in the South, and often meant distant relations. Although they were probably related, George Achille Feris and Alexander Keene Richards do not appear to be first cousins. Feris's father was Dr. Maise Alexander Feris, a native of France, and his mother, Elizabeth Frazer, a native of Scotland. Richards's parents were Dr. William Lawrence Richards and Eleonora Elizabeth Keene Richards. Both Richards and Feris grew up in Georgetown, Kentucky. See Hervey, *Racing in America, 1665–1865*, 2:262–63; L. E. Daniell, *Types of Successful Men in Texas* (Austin: Eugene Von Boeckmann, 1890), 429; Weeks, *The American Turf*, 82; Robertson, *The History of Thoroughbred Racing in America*, 45; Thornton Chard, "Arabian Horses in Texas Over Eighty Years Ago: Dr. George A. Feris' Stud at Fort Bend and Richmond," *The Cattleman* (September 1944), 22, 32–33. See also, "Alexander Keene Richards," Find a Grave website, https://www.findagrave.com/memorial/24843093/alexander-keene-richards [Accessed May 24, 2021].

6 Daniell, *Types of Successful Men of Texas*, 429–32; Chard, "Arabian Horses in Texas Over Eighty Years Ago," 22, 32–33; "Dr. George Achille Feris," Find a Grave website, https://www.findagrave.com/memorial/45401639/george-achille-feris [Accessed January 1, 2021]. Feris was in Texas during the Revolution, later fought Indians, was in the Mexican–American War, and the American Civil War.

7 "West Main Street Historic District, Georgetown, Kentucky" National Register of Historic Places Inventory—Nomination Form, National Park Service website, https://npgallery.nps.gov/GetAsset/7c6f477c-53bf-4c15-b379-f5353bc8c007 [Accessed August 18, 2021].

8 *Rules and Regulations of the Metairie Jockey Club*, 7.

9 Mary Austin Holley to Mrs. William M. Brand, December 19, 1837, quoted in Hogan, *The Texas Republic*, 7–8.

10 Rosa Groce Bertleth, "Jared Ellison Groce," *The Southwestern Historical Quarterly*, Vol. 20, No. 4 (April 1917), 358–59; Charles Christopher Jackson, "Groce, Jared

Ellison," *Handbook of Texas Online*, accessed March 17, 2025, https://www.tshaonline.org/handbook/entries/groce-jared-ellison.

11 *Rules and Regulations of the Webber's Prairie Jockey Club*, 6. Times might vary with different jockey clubs.

12 Ibid, 7. Distances might vary at different jockey clubs.

13 Hogan, *The Texas Republic*, 130–31.

14 McLean, *Fine Texas Horses*, 11–13. Splane is seen spelled both with and without the "e" and as "P. R. or R. R." See also, *The Morning Star* (Houston), January 4, 1840.

15 Malcolm D. McLean, compiler and editor., *Papers Concerning Robertson's Colony in Texas: Those Eleven League Grants, December 6, 1831, through October, 1833*, Vol. 7 (Arlington: University of Texas at Arlington Press, 1980), 392–93; McLean, *Papers Concerning Robertson's Colony in Texas: Robertson's Colony, November, 1833, through September, 1834*, Vol. 8 (Arlington: University of Texas at Arlington Press, 1981), 103; McLean, *Fine Texas Horses*, 32–36. An early stallion in Texas became a celebrity after the revolution ended. It was said that following the Battle of San Jacinto, Mexican Gen. Antonio López de Santa Anna tried to escape on Allen Vince's "fine black horse." Vince, who was from Georgia and had been one of Austin's original settlers, had moved into the San Jacinto area in 1822, and his stallion, known as "Old Whip," may have been a Thoroughbred. The well-known animal was spotted after the battle being ridden by one of Santa Anna's servants, captured, and returned to Vince. By this time it was "carrying a common saddle," and not the owner's fine one. Vince eventually moved to Fort Bend County where he operated a stock ranch until he died in 1849. The lack of records makes it impossible to know if he bred his stallion to local mares, but it is likely he did. "Reminiscences of Mrs. Dilue Harris," Pt. 3, *The Quarterly of the Texas State Historical Association*, Vol. 7, No. 3 (January 1904), 217–18; Frank X. Tolbert, *The Day of San Jacinto* (New York: McGraw-Hill Book Company, 1959), 165–85; Diana J. Kleiner, "Vince, Allen," *Handbook of Texas Online*, accessed March 17, 2025, https://www.tshaonline.org/handbook/entries/vince-allen. See also, "'Old Whip' The Horse that Santa Anna Rode at San Jacinto," Texas Genealogy website, http://www.texasgenealogy.org/fortbend/oldwhip.htm [Accessed July 7, 2021].

16 McLean, *Fine Texas Horses*, 19, 32–33; McLean, *Papers Concerning Robertson's Colony in Texas: Robertson's Colony, November, 1833, through September, 1834*, 103.

17 Pratt, ed., *Galveston Island*, 18–19. New Market or Newmarket was a popular name for racecourses. There was a well-known one at Petersburg, Virginia, but the first was in Suffolk, England, that had been around since Charles I. The original Newmarket was founded in the early seventeenth century in England. See also, *The Weekly Picayune* (New Orleans), April 16, 1838, quoted in Joseph William Schmitz, *Thus They Lived: Social Life in the Republic of Texas* (San Antonio: The Naylor Company, 1936), 123.

18 McLean, *Fine Texas Horses*, 21–22. See also, *Velasco in Texas History* (1936; rpt., Velasco United Methodist Church Historical Museum, 1992) for more on the background of Velasco.

19 Strobel, *The Old Plantations and their Owners of Brazoria County, Texas*, 23; Rogers and Strobel, *A History of Brazoria County Texas*, 37–42; Hogan, *The Texas Republic*, 28.

20 Pratt, ed., *Galveston Island*, 14, 19, 22; Wharton J. Green, *Recollections and Reflections: An Auto of Half a Century and More* (Raleigh, NC: Edwards and Broughton Printing Co., 1906), 30–44, discusses the life of Thomas Jefferson Green. See also, the Thomas Jefferson Green Papers, Southern Historical Collection, University of North Carolina Library, Chapel Hill; Mattie Austin Hatcher, ed., *Letters of an Early American Traveller, Mary Austin Holley: Her Life and Her Works, 1784–1846* (Dallas: Southwest Press, 1933), 73; *History of Brazoria County* (Brazoria County Federation of Women's Clubs, 1940), 58.

21 Thos. J. Green to Ashbel Smith, February 17, 1839, and B. T. Archer to Ashbel Smith, February 19, 1839, Ashbel Smith Papers.

22 Clarence R. Wharton, *Wharton's History of Fort Bend County* (San Antonio: The Naylor Co., 1939), 144, 165; Revised by Randolph B. "Mike" Campbell, "Randon, David," *Handbook of Texas Online*, accessed March 16, 2025, https://www.tshaonline.org/handbook/entries/randon-david; McLean, *Fine Texas Horses*, 27–29, 39–40; United States Eighth Census, Slave Schedule (1860), Fort Bend County, Texas; United States Eighth Census (1860), Fort Bend County, Texas. In 1860, Randon reported $178,000 in real estate and $119,300 in personal estate. See McLean, *Fine Texas Horses* for more on the horses Randon raced.

23 Some consider Pittsville a ghost town. It is located three miles north of the town of Fulshear in Fort Bend County. Wharton, *Wharton's History of Fort Bend County*, 146, 154; United States Seventh Census (1850), Fort Bend County, Texas; Terry Crockett, "Churchill Fulshear Jr.: His Land, His Family, His Home and His Legacy," *Explore Fulshear*, magazine article, May 4, 2020, https://issuu.com/realpropertymg/docs/explorefulshear_pages2020 [Accessed May 4, 2021]; "Churchhill, Fulshear, Jr.," *Handbook of Texas Online*, accessed March 16, 2025, https://www.tshaonline.org/handbook/entries/fulshear-churchill-jr.

24 McLean, *Fine Texas Horses*, xxii, 65–66, 80; E. B. Settle to T. J. Green, July 10, 1839, Thomas Jefferson Green Papers.

25 *Spirit of the Times* (1840), 138; (1842), 103, 183; McWhiney, *Cracker Culture*, 136.

26 R. W. Withers to T. J. Green, August 7, 1839, Thomas Jefferson Green Papers; McLean, *Fine Texas Horses*, 29; "Dr. Robert Walker Withers," Find a Grave website, https://www.findagrave.com/memorial/86226455/robert-walker-withers/photo [Accessed May 21, 2021]; Pratt, ed., *Galveston Island*, 29.

27 For the life of Thomas McKinney, see Margaret Swett Henson, *McKinney Falls: The Ranch Home of Thomas F. McKinney, Pioneer Texas Entrepreneur* (Austin: Texas State Historical Association, 1999). See also, the Thomas F. and James P. McKinney Papers, Dolph Briscoe Center for American History.

28 Charles W. Hayes, *History of the Island and the City of Galveston: From the Discovery of the Island in 1526, From the Founding of the City in 1837, Down to the Year 1879*, 2 vols. (1879; rpt., Austin: Jenkins Garrett Press, 1974), 2:816; Pratt, ed., *Galveston Island*, 30; Henson, *McKinney Falls: The Ranch Home of Thomas F. McKinney*, 7; James Perry Bryan, ed., *Mary Austin Holley: The Texas Diary, 1835–1838* (Austin: University of Texas Press, 1965), 78–79.

29 Undated item, Samuel May and Austin May Williams Papers, Dolph Briscoe Center for American History; Pratt, ed., *Galveston Island,* 29, 49–50; *Telegraph and Texas Register* (Houston), April 22, 1840.

30 Henson, *McKinney Falls: The Ranch Home of Thomas F. McKinney,* 6–8.

31 Matilda Charlotte Houston, *Texas and the Gulf of Mexico; or Yachting in the New World* (1844; rpt., Philadelphia: G. B. Zieber & Co, 1845), 291–92; Hayes, *History of the Island and the City of Galveston,* 1:307; Margaret Swett Henson, *Samuel May Williams: Early Texas Entrepreneur* (College Station: Texas A&M University Press, 1976), 108–109. It would be interesting to know how much of a role Cary McKinney played in Thomas McKinney's horse business. But as a free black man, finding any information for him and his family is difficult. He was one of two slaves manumitted during the Republic, partially for service "during the Revolution" Cary was "of much service in carrying expresses, &c." Thomas F. McKinney to Cary, November 11, 1839, Williams Papers, Rosenberg Library, Galveston, Texas. Cary later bought his wife and child too. Harold Schoen, "The Free Negro in the Republic of Texas," Pt. 2, *The Southwestern Historical Quarterly,* Vol. 40, No. 1 (July 1936), 32. McKinney never owned a large number of slaves; the most recorded was twenty-one persons in 1860 but seven of those were under the age of ten. He seems to have housed them in family groups as there were five cabins for slaves on his ranch at that time. The adults served as house servants, general handymen, and horse handlers. Henson, *McKinney Falls: The Ranch Home of Thomas F. McKinney,* 8–9.

32 Henson, *McKinney Falls: The Ranch Home of Thomas F. McKinney,* 15–16. The 1860 census shows Nancy McKinney as head of household in Brazoria County. Living with her were two nieces and two boarders. She died in 1869 and with no relatives in the county, she gave her property to her neighbor on her deathbed. United States Eighth Census (1860), Brazoria County, Texas.

33 Henson, *McKinney Falls: The Ranch Home of Thomas F. McKinney,* 16; McLean, *Fine Texas Horses,* 27–29, 80.

34 McBee, *The Life and Times of David Smith,* 68; Andrew Forest Muir, ed., "Diary of a Young Man in Houston, 1838," *The Southwestern Historical Quarterly,* Vol. 53, No. 3 (January 1950), 284; B. H. Carroll, ed., *Standard History of Houston, Texas from a Study of the Original Sources* (Knoxville, TN: H. W. Crew & Co., 1912), 42; McLean, *Fine Texas Horses,* 80. Andrew Jackson Smith died in Galveston on April 15, 1861.

35 Pratt, ed., *Galveston Island,* 100, 112.

36 *Brazos Courier* (Brazoria), April 21, 1840; *The Austin City Gazette,* May 6, 1840; Max Freund, ed., *Gustav Dresel's Houston Journal: Adventures in North American and Texas, 1837–1841* (Austin: University of Texas Press, 1954), 37–38.

37 *Telegraph and Texas Register* (Houston), May 11, 1842.

38 Freund, ed., *Gustav Dresel's Houston Journal,* 99.

39 Carroll, ed., *Standard History of Houston,* 46. Since many of the officers of the Houston Jockey Club and Houston City Jockey Club are the same, it is safe to assume that they are the same organization. Quotation from the New Orleans *Daily Picayune,* June 1, 1845, quoted in Hogan, *The Texas Republic,* 118.

40 Denhardt, *The Quarter Running Horse*, 146.

41 Hervey, *Racing in America, 1665–1865*, 1:252; McLean, *Fine Texas Horses*, 43, 98.

42 Sketch included in "George A. Feris Family Papers, 1829–1944, undated, bulk 1850–1900," Texas State Archives, Austin; Daniell, *Types of Successful Men of Texas*, 429–32; Chard, "Arabian Horses in Texas Over Eighty Years Ago," 22, 32–33; McLean, *Fine Texas Horses*, 66.

43 Jonnie Lockhart Wallis and Laurance L. Hill, eds., *Sixty Years on the Brazos: The Life and Letters of Dr. John Washington Lockhart* (1930; rpt., Waco: Texian Press, 1967), 48–49, 89–90; Hogan, *The Texas Republic*, 134.

44 *Telegraph and Texas Register* (Houston), July 31, 1839. Also quoted in McLean, *Fine Texas Horses*, 72–73.

45 Muir, ed, *Texas in 1837*, 34; H. P. N. Gammel, comp., "An Act to Suppress Gambling," approved May 26, 1837, in *The Laws of Texas, 1822–1897*, 10 vols. (Austin: Gammel Book Co., 1898), 1:1288–89.

46 Parker, *Trip to the West & Texas*, 154.

47 Original document of the Ables-Sparks race dated June 22, 1839, was filed March 9, 1847, in the District Court, Nacogdoches, Texas; Harriet Smither, ed., "Diary of Adolphus Sterne," *The Southwestern Historical Quarterly*, Vol. 36, No. 3 (January 1933), 217–18; McLean, *Fine Texas Horses*, 70–71.

48 William Physick Zuber, *My Eighty Years in Texas* (Austin, University of Texas Press, 1971), 21–23; McLean, *Fine Texas Horses*, 86.

49 Hogan, *The Texas Republic*, 87.

50 Rogers and Strobel, *A History of Brazoria County Texas*, 54–55; Hogan, *The Texas* Republic, 113; Mooney, *Race Horse Men*, 67.

CHAPTER 3

1 Noah Smithwick, *The Evolution of a State or Recollections of Old Texas Days* (Austin: Gammel Book Co., 1900), 15; Col. Edward Stiff, "Houston, 1839—A Roaring Frontier Town," in Harris County Historical Society, comp., *Houston—A Nation's Capital, 1837–1839* (Houston: D. Armstrong Co., Inc., 1985), 91–92.

2 Hogan, *The Texas Republic*, 219–20, 289.

3 Henson, *Samuel May Williams*, 115; Green, *Recollections and Reflections*, 35–43. In 1850, McKinney hoped he could recover some of the $99,000 owed to McKinney and Williams for financing the Revolution. In 1856, the legislature appropriated $40,729 for the company, but each man only received $8,000. Henson, *McKinney Falls: The Ranch Home of Thomas F. McKinney*, 20–21. See also, Mary H. K. Kerr, "Green, Thomas Jefferson," *NCpedia Online*, accessed March, 22, 2022, https://www.ncpedia.org/biography/green-thomas-jefferson. Green died at Esmeralda Plantation on December 12, 1863.

4 Hogan, *The Texas Republic*, 263.

5 Ibid., 94, 101, 291; McLean, *Fine Texas Horses*, 68; Harriet Smither, ed., "The Diary of Adolphus Sterne," Pt. 9, *Southwestern Historical Quarterly*, Vol. 32, No. 2 (October 1928), 173; Smither, ed., "The Diary of Adolphus Sterne," Pt. 13, *Southwestern Historical Quarterly*, Vol. 33, No. 2 (October 1929), 160; Smither, ed., "The Diary of Adolphus Sterne," Pt. 14, *Southwestern Historical Quarterly*, Vol. 33, No. 3 (January 1930), 231.

6 "An Act Supplementary to an act to Raise Public Revenue by direct Taxation," Gammel, comp., *The Laws of Texas, 1822–1897*, 2:1454–55; *The Morning Star* (Houston), April 17, 1840.

7 Hogan, *The Texas Republic*, 133; Ferdinand Roemer, *Texas with Particular Reference to German Immigration and the Physical Appearance of the Country*, translated by Oswald Mueller (1849; rpt., San Antonio: Standard Printing Co., 1935), 190; Marion Garrett Gibbs, "Bucksnort TX," *Handbook of Texas Online*, accessed March 17, 2025, www.tshaonline.org/handbook/entries/bucksnort-tx. "Site of Bucksnort," The Historical Marker Database, https://www.hmdb.org/m.asp?m=84669 [Accessed February 6, 2022].

8 The following story comes from Luke Lightwood, "A Texas Quarter Race," *Porter's Spirit of the Times* (1857), 149. Pierch was probably named for Baron Johann DeKalb who came to America with the Marquis de Lafayette to fight in the American Revolution, where he died. Pierch may have actually been Pierce, but it is seen as Pierch throughout the article so the author has kept that spelling.

9 Ibid.

10 Ibid.

11 Ibid.

12 Ibid.

13 Ibid.

14 Ibid.

15 Ibid.

16 Roemer, *Texas*, 190.

17 William Bollaert, *William Bollaert's Texas*, edited by W. Eugene Hollon and Ruth Lapham Butler (Norman: University of Oklahoma Press, 1956), 280–82. See also, Don Allon Hinton, "Columbus, TX," *Handbook of Texas Online*, accessed March 18, 2025, https://www.tshaonline.org/handbook/entries/columbus-tx for a description of Robson's castle.

18 Bollaert, *William Bollaert's Texas*, 280–82.

19 Ibid.

20 Rector v. Hudson, 20 *Tex.* 234 (1857). All subsequent court cases come from *Reports of Cases Argued and Decided in the Supreme Court of the State of Texas*. Original volumes accessed at The Portal to Texas History, https://texashistory.unt.edu/.

21 Ibid.

22 Hogan, *The Texas Republic*, 107; *The Northern Standard* (Clarksville), February 23, 1843. Lycurgus stood fifteen and a half hands high and was a deep steel color with black legs, mane, and tail. See also, McLean, *Fine Texas Horses*, 102–103.

23 *The Northern Standard* (Clarksville), December 12, 26, 1844; The December 26 edition spells the name Rackamaroleon; *American Turf Register and Sporting Magazine* (August 1834), 605–607; Hervey, *Racing in America, 1665–1865*, 2:244; McLean, *Fine Texas Horses*, 108–10.

24 *The Northern Standard* (Clarksville), January 23, February 20, March 6, May 18, December 3, 1845; McLean, *Fine Texas Horses*, 109–11, 114–15.

25 *The Northern Standard* (Clarksville), November 6, 1844; May 13, 1845.

26 Wilson v Lorane, 15 *Tex.* 492 (1855); "Thomas A. Moore" in Frank Brown, *Annals of Travis County and the City of Austin (From the Earliest of Times to the Close of 1875)*, typescript. Moore can be found in Volume 6, Chapter 15, p. 33. Accessed at The Portal to Texas History, the entry is located in Volume 6, p. 94 on the web version. See https://texashistory.unt.edu/.

27 Richard F. Selcer, "Hell's Half Acre, Fort Worth," *Handbook of Texas Online*, accessed March 18, 2025, https://www.tshaonline.org/handbook/entries/hells-half-acre-fort-worth; Vivian Elizabeth Smyrl, "Webberville, TX," *Handbook of Texas Online*, accessed March 18, 2025, https://www.tshaonline.org/handbook/entries/webberville-tx; *Rules and Regulations of the Webber's Prairie Jockey Club*, 4, 6.

28 *Rules and Regulations of the Webber's Prairie Jockey Club*, 3–11.

29 Hervey, *Racing in America, 1665–1865*, 2:134; Pedigree Online: Thoroughbred Database, "Rodolph," online database, https://www.pedigreequery.com/rodolph [Accessed August 8, 2021].

30 *Democratic Telegraph and Texas Register* (Houston), August 17, 1848, quoting the *Victoria Advocate*. By 1860, Turner owned real estate valued at $50,000 and a personal estate valued at $20,000 (that included fifteen slaves); *Batchler-Turner Letters*, annotated by H. J. H. Rugeley (Austin: The Steck Company, 1961) vi–vii. See also, United States Eighth Census 1860), Lavaca County, Texas, and Paul C. Boethel, *Colonel Amasa Turner: The Gentleman from Lavaca and Other Captains at San Jacinto* (Austin: Von Boeckmann-Jones, 1963).

31 *The Red-Lander* (San Augustine), March 12, 1846.

32 McLean, *Fine Texas Horses*, 87–88; *Telegraph and Texas Register* (Houston), June 29, 1842. The editor of the *Red-Lander* in San Augustine was quoted in the Houston paper.

33 *Democratic Telegraph and Texas Register* (Houston), September 14, November 16, 1848; *The Red-Lander* (San Augustine), October 30, 1845; McLean, *Fine Texas Horses*, 91.

34 Randolph B. Campbell, *Gone to Texas: A History of the Lone Star State* (New York: Oxford University Press, 2003), 189.

35 John Salmon Ford, *Rip Ford's Texas*, edited by Stephen B. Oates (Austin: University of Texas Press, 1963), 65–66.

36 Letter from Frank H. Stone dated December 9, 1849, in *The Quarter Horse Journal* (April 1959), 16–17.

37 Ibid.

38 Hervey, *Racing in America, 1665–1865*, 2:153–54.

39 Ibid., 156–77; Anderson, *Making the American Thoroughbred*, 208–18; "Jackson, James," *Encyclopedia of Alabama Online*, accessed March 28, 2022, https://encyclopediaofalabama.org/article/james-jackson/.

40 Hervey, *Racing in America, 1665–1865*, 2:170–72; Weeks, *The American Turf*, 35.

41 Hervey, *Racing in America, 1665–1865*, 2:180, 185; *The Times Picayune* (New Orleans), February 27, March 1, 1838. See also, Grace Elizabeth King, *New Orleans: The Place and the People* (1895), http://www.old-new-orleans.com/NO_MetairieRaceCourse.html [Accessed May 21, 2021].

42 Hervey, *Racing in America, 1665–1865*, 2:180, 183–93; *The Times Picayune* (New Orleans), February 27, March 1, 1838. See also, King, *New Orleans: The Place and the People.*

43 Hervey, *Racing in America, 1665–1865*, 2:179, 182 190–97.

44 "Kenner, Duncan Farrar," *Dictionary of Louisiana Biography Online*, accessed January 15, 2024, https://www.lahistory.org/resources/dictionary-louisiana-biography/dictionary-of-louisiana-biography-k/; https://www.nps.gov/nr/travel/louisiana/ash.htm [Accessed September 24, 2021]. See Mooney, *Race Horse Men* for more on Kenner.

45 Hervey, *Racing in America, 1665–1865*, 2:201–202.

CHAPTER 4

1 Mooney, *Race Horse Men*, 91.

2 "Thomas Jefferson Wells," "Montfort Wells," and "James Madison Wells," *Dictionary of Louisiana Biography Online*, accessed January 15, 2024, https://www.lahistory.org/resources/dictionary-louisiana-biography/dictionary-of-louisiana-biography-w/; Hervey, *Racing in America, 1665–1865*, 1:252, 2:198; G. M. G. Stafford, *The Wells Family of Louisiana and Allied Families* (Alexandria, VA: Standard Printing, 1942), 92; Mooney, *Race Horse Men*. 92; Robertson, *A History of Thoroughbred Racing in America*, 74–75; "Section II: The Ante Bellum Period, 1804–1861, Continued," Rapides Parish, Louisiana Genealogy website, http://rapidesgenealogy.org/history/eakin/eakin2b.htm [Accessed September 11, 2021].

3 "The Great Post Stake. Kentucky Victorious!," *Spirit of the Times* (1854), 103.

4 Hervey, *Racing in America, 1665–1865*, 2:286–300; Robertson, *The History of Thoroughbred Racing in America*, 72–76; Weeks, *The American Turf*, 84; Mooney, *Race Horse Men*, 93–98.

5 *Spirit of the Times* (1857), 265; Interview with Lowell (Stretch) Smith Jr. (1933–2021) by the author, August 7, 1982, owner of the Thomas Haley Ranch, Rio Vista, Texas; Haley family information received from Nadine Hodnett of Big Spring, Texas, in 1985.

6 Denhardt, *The Quarter Running Horse*, 135–36; *Spirit of the Times* (1857), 265; Interview with Lowell Smith Jr., August 7, 1982.

7 Interview with Lowell Smith Jr., August 7, 1982; Letters from Mary Alice Christensen (1923–2011) to the author, June 15, September 5, December 15, 1985; March 4, June 5, 1986. She was a great-granddaughter of Charles R. and Alice Haley. Nadine Hodnett was the aunt of Mary Alice Christensen.

8 Interview with Lowell Smith Jr., August 7, 1982; Letters from Mary Alice Christensen to the author, June 15, September 5, December 15, 1985; March 4, June 5, 1986. See also, United States Seventh Census (1850), Johnson County, Texas; United States Eighth Census (1860), Johnson County, Texas; United States Seventh Census (1850) Slave Schedules, Johnson County, Texas.

9 Thomas T. Ewell, *Hood County History* (Granbury, TX: 1895), 63. Ewell's book is reproduced in C. L. Hightower, ed., *Hood County History in Picture and Story 1970* (Fort Worth: Historical Publishers, 1970); Denhardt, *The Quarter Running Horse*, 164–65. Thorp Spring, named for Pleasant Thorp in the 1850s, did not become a community until the 1870s.

10 Kirkland v. Randon, 8 *Tex.* 10 and 8 *Tex.* 94 (1852); Bailes v. Williams, 15 *Tex.* 318 (1855).

11 Pierce v. Randolph, 12 *Tex.* 290 (1854).

12 Ibid.

13 Ibid.

14 Ibid.

15 Ibid. Diogenes was a Greek philosopher who died in 323 B.C.

16 Ibid.

17 Chard, "Arabian Horses in Texas Over Eighty Years Ago," 22, 32–33; Hervey, *Racing in America, 1665–1865*, 2:262–63.

18 Chard, "Arabian Horses in Texas Over Eighty Years Ago," 22, 32–33; Hervey, *Racing in America, 1665–1865*, 2:262–63. Richards went to Arabia in 1853 and 1856.

19 Chard, "Arabian Horses in Texas Over Eighty Years Ago," 22, 32–33; Hervey, *Racing in America, 1665–1865*, 2:262–63.

20 Chard, "Arabian Horses in Texas Over Eighty Years Ago," 22, 32–33; Hervey, *Racing in America, 1665–1865*, 2:262–63.

21 S. D. Bruce, *The American Stud Book* (1868; revised in 2 vols., New York: Sanders D. Bruce, 1873), 1:250; Henson, *McKinney Falls: The Ranch Home of Thomas F. McKinney*, 26. Van Hagen was born in 1814.

22 *The Texas State Times* (Austin), December 16, 23, 1854; July 7, December 8, 1855; May 3, November 15, 1856; November 20, 1858; July 16, 1859; *The Weekly Telegraph* (Austin), November 24, 1858.

23 *The Texas State Times* (Austin), May 12, 1860.

24 Ibid.

25 *Dallas Herald*, May 2, 1860; United States Eighth Census (1860), McLennan County, Texas; United States Eighth Census, Slave Schedule (1860), McLennan County, Texas.

26 *The Texas State Times* (Austin), April 21, 1855; August 25, 1855.

27 John Willingham, "Barnard, George," *Handbook of Texas Online*, accessed March 18, 2025, https://www.tshaonline.org/handbook/entries/barnard-george.

28 Hervey, *Racing in America, 1665–1865*, 2:259–61; Denhardt, *The Quarter Running Horse*, 148–50; Weeks, *The American Turf*, 84–85; Ridley Wills II, *Belle Meade Bloodlines 1816–1904* (Nashville, TN: Ambrose Printing Co., 1990), 2, 12–13.

29 Hervey, *Racing in America, 1665–1865*, 2:262–64.

30 Hervey, *Racing in America, 1665–1865*, 2:254–57; *The Texas Annual* (Austin: Hughes & McLaughlin, 1878), 31. See also, Elizabeth N. Kemp, "Philips, William Copeland," *Handbook of Texas Online*, accessed March 17, 2025, https://www.tshaonline.org/handbook/entries/philips-william-copeland.

31 *Dallas Herald*, November 24, 1858.

32 For Steel Dust and Shiloh there is one "tattered and torn" advertisement for a stallion foaled in 1887, Dan Tucker, that seems to verify the lineage of Steel Dust. Although bred by Samuel Watkins of Petersburg, Illinois, Dan Tucker was sold to Tom Trammel of Sweetwater, one of the most respected of Texas breeders, so there is no reason to question the veracity of the broadsheet. Trammell established one of the first ranches in Nolan County during a time the Comanches and Kiowas still raided the region and registered his brand "9R" around 1866. Although he started by raising short-distance racers, he eventually branched out to Thoroughbreds, many of which later raced in Europe. The advertisement for Dan Tucker gave this information on the pedigree of Steel Dust: "Dan Tucker was sired by Barney Owens. 1st dam, Butt Cut, by Jack Traveller, he by Steel Dust, out of Queen, who was sired by Pilgrim, by Lexington. 2nd dam, June Bug, by Harry Bluff the sire of Steel Dust . . . Jack Traveller was sired by old Steel Dust. Dam, Queen, by Pilgrim, by Lexington. Harry Bluff is Whip and Timoleon stock, and was sired by Short Whip, out of Big Nance, a thoroughbred mare. Barney Owens was sired by Cold Deck, and out of the Overton mare. Cold Deck was by Billy Boy, he by Shiloh, and out of a Steel Dust mare. Cold Deck's dam was Dolly Coker, by Old Rondo." Denhardt, *The Quarter Horse* (1941; rpt., College Station: Texas A&M University Press), 77, advertisement facing page 87; Denhardt, *The Quarter Running Horse*, 248; Robert M. Denhardt, *Foundation Sires of the American Quarter Horse* (Norman: University of Oklahoma Press, 1976), 84, 206–207 Frank S. Hastings, *A Ranchman's Recollections: An Autobiography* (1921; rpt., Big Byte Books, 2014), 111, Kindle edition.

33 The folklore surrounding Steel Dust may or may not be true. Much of what is known of him comes from tales of old-timers who heard them from their parents. The authority on Steel Dust, Wayne Gard (1899–1936), interviewed many of them after he moved to Texas in 1933. Stephen Earl Comer, "Gard, Sanford Wayne," *Handbook of Texas Online*, accessed March 16, 2025, https://www.tshaonline.org/handbook/entries/gard-sanford-wayne. Gard was also the author of the only book about the stud, *Fabulous Quarter Horse: Steel Dust—The Account of the Most Celebrated Texas Stallion* (New York: Duell, Sloan and Pearce, 1958). See also, "Capt. Mid Perry," *Memorial and Biographical History of Dallas County* (Chicago: The Lewis Publishing Co., 1892), 920–21; Gard, *Fabulous Quarter Horse: Steel Dust*, 14.

34 "Jones Green," *Memorial and Biographical History of Dallas County*, 542–43.

35 Gard, *Fabulous Quarter Horse: Steel Dust*, 18–20.

36 Ibid., 19.

37 Artelle Stiff to the author, January 26, 1984; Helen G. Hall to the author, June 3, 1983; United States Seventh Census (1850), Collin County, Texas, and Breckinridge County, Kentucky. Artelle Stiff provided family information and Helen G. Hall provided all

that was known about Harrison Stiff from the Collin County Historical Society, McKinney, Texas.

38 Bob Gray, *Great Horses of the Past* (Houston: Cordovan Corporation, 1967), 97–108; Gard, *Fabulous Quarter Horse: Steel Dust*, 26–28.

39 Gray, *Great Horses of the Past*, 98; Gard, *Fabulous Quarter Horse: Steel Dust*, 27–28.

40 Gray, *Great Horses of the Past*, 100–101.

41 Ibid.

42 "John Batchler," in *A Memorial and Biographical History of Ellis County* (Chicago: The Lewis Publishing Co., 1892), 520–21.

43 Stella Mae Batchler Bass to the author, December 5, 1983; Ollie Joyce Batchler Eaton to the author, February 5, 1995. Stella Mae Batchler Bass was a great-granddaughter of John (Jack) Batchler.

44 Wayne Gard, "Fabulous Steel Dust," *The Cattleman* (September 1948), 165; Denhardt, *The Quarter Running Horse*, 134.

45 The letter appeared in *The Abilene Reporter*, February 26, 1892.

46 Gard, *Fabulous Quarter Horse: Steel Dust*, 29–30.

47 Gard, "Fabulous Steel Dust," 165–66; Wayne Gard, "Hoofbeats of Old Shiloh," *The Cattleman* (September 1953), 39, 66, 70, 72; Gard, "When Texans Shouted for Shiloh" in *The Western Horseman* (August 1949)," 14–15; Letter to the author from Stella May Batchler Bass dated December 5, 1983.

48 *Dallas Herald*, September 29, 1858.

49 Gard, *Fabulous Quarter Horse: Steel Dust*, 37; Gard, "Fabulous Steel Dust," 166–67.

50 Gard, *Fabulous Quarter Horse: Steel Dust*, 34–36; Gard, "Fabulous Steel Dust," 166; Denhardt, *The Quarter Running Horse*, 148.

51 Denhardt, *The Quarter Running Horse*, 150–51, 162–64; Lindeman, *The Quarter Horse Breeder*, 116–17; Denhardt, *Quarter Horses: A Story of Two Centuries*, 29–31; Helen Michaelis, "The Great Little Horse Billy," in Denhardt, *The Quarter Horse*, 96–105.

52 Denhardt, *The Quarter Running Horse*, 162–64; Wikipedia, "Belmont, Texas," last updated August 21, 2024, https://en.wikipedia.org/wiki/Belmont,_Texas [Accessed June 9, 2021]; United States Ninth Census (1870), Guadalupe County, Texas; United Stated Tenth Census (1880), Gonzales County, Texas; United States Twelfth Census (1900), Gonzales County, Texas.

53 Denhardt, *The Quarter Running Horse*, 150–51, 162–64; United States Thirteenth Census (1910), Guadalupe County, Texas; Robert M. Denhardt, *Foundation Dams of the American Quarter Horse* (Norman: University of Oklahoma Press, 1982), 191. Fleming was born November 18, 1830, and died April 30, 1911. He is buried in Matthies Cemetery, Guadalupe County. "W. B. Fleming," Find a Grave website, https://www.findagrave.com/memorial/14749649/w.-b.-fleming [Accessed June 18, 2021]. Texas Historical Marker No. 17932 honors his contribution to the American quarter horse. It is located on Texas state highway 80, just south of where the road crosses the Guadalupe River.

54 *The Northern Standard*, March 15, 1851; March 6, 1852; March 12, 26, 1853.

55 *Dallas Herald*, December 8, 1858; February 23, 1859; October 26, November 2, 1859; October 31, November 2, 7, 14, 1860.

CHAPTER 5

1 Anne J. Bailey, *Texans in the Confederate Cavalry* (1995; rpt., Abilene, TX: McWhiney Foundation Press, 2004), 14.

2 Jack Trammel, "Off and Running: America's Growing Passion for Horse Racing Stayed Strong During the War," *America's Civil War* (July 2018), 32. See also, "Ashland Racecourse," The Ashland Museum website, https://ashlandmuseum.org/businesses-and-organizations/race-course?rq=racecourse [Accessed May 19, 2024].

3 Hervey, *Racing in America, 1665–1865*, 2:353–54.

4 Elias P. Pellet, *History of the 114th Regiment, New York State Volunteers* (Norwich, NY: J. F. Hubbard, 1866), 274; Gene C. Armistead, *Horses and Mules in the Civil War: A Complete History with a Roster of More Than 700 War Horses* (Jefferson, NC: McFarland & Co., Inc., 2013), 90–91.

5 *Governor's Message, November 1, 1861*, 10, Texas Adjutant General, *Report*, November, 1861, 1–2, quoted in Anne J. Bailey, *Between the Enemy and Texas: Parsons's Texas Cavalry in the Civil War* (Fort Worth, Texas Christian University Press, 1989), 8; James A. L. Fremantle, *Three Months in the Southern States: April–June 1863* (New York, John Bradburn,1864), 75; Stephen B. Oates, *Confederate Cavalry West of the River* (Austin: University of Texas Press, 1961), 26–27.

6 Bell Irvin Wiley, *The Life of Johnny Reb: The Common Soldier of the Confederacy* (1943; rpt., Baton Rouge: Louisiana State University Press, 1987), 38.

7 Ibid., 38; David Paul Smith, *Frontier Defense in the Civil War: Texas' Rangers and Rebels* (College Station: Texas A&M University Press, 1992), 21.

8 McCulloch order in Smith, *Frontier Defense in the Civil War*, 179; Trammell, "Off and Running," 34.

9 Perry Obituary, *Dallas Morning News*, February 5, 1892; Mid Perry, Compiled Service Records of Confederate Soldiers who Served in Organizations from the State of Texas, Eighteenth Texas Cavalry (hereinafter cited as Compiled Service Records), National Archives, Washington, DC; "Middleton Perry," Texas, US Muster Rolls Index Cards, 1838–1900, on Ancestry.com [Accessed June 19, 2021]; "Captain Middleton Lee 'Mid' Perry," Find a Grave website, https://www.findagrave.com/memorial/20053178/middleton-lee-perry [Accessed May 1, 2021].

10 There is a Jones Green who enlisted in Capt. John J. Good's Dallas Light Artillery and if this is the same man, he did not remain in the service long. Jones Green, Compiled Service Record; "Jones Green," in *Memorial and Biographical History of Dallas County*, 542–43; "Jones Green," Texas, US Muster Rolls Index Cards, 1838–1900 on Ancestry.com [Accessed June 15, 2021]; "Jones Greene," Find a Grave website, https://www.findagrave.com/memorial/64262631/jones-greene [Accessed June 15, 2021].

11 "John Batchler" in *A Memorial and Biographical History of Ellis County*, 520–21; Wayne Gard, "Hoofbeats of Old Shiloh," 39, 66, 70, 72; Wayne Gard, "When Texans Shouted for Shiloh," 14–15; Gard, *Fabulous Quarter Horse: Steel Dust*, 32.

12 "Wm. Fleming and C. E. Littlefield," Texas, US Muster Rolls Index Cards, 1838–1900, on Ancestry.com [Accessed June 29, 2021]; George S. Burkhardt, *Confederate Rage,*

Yankee Wrath: No Quarter in the Civil War (Carbondale: Southern Illinois University Press, 2007), 222; Chuck Parsons, "Brown, James Madison," *Handbook of Texas Online*, accessed March 17, 2025, https://www.tshaonline.org/handbook/entries/brown-james-madison. Alfred Roman, "Inspection Report of Wheeler's Cavalry Corps in Obedience to Instructions from Headquarters Military Division of the West, Dated December 28, 1864," January 22, 1865, Roman MSS, Library of Congress, Washington, DC.

13 Compiled Service Record of Thomas Haley. See also, Bailey, *Between the Enemy and Texas* for more on Haley's Civil War service.

14 The information on Thomas Franklin Haley comes from the great-granddaughter of Charles R. Haley, Mary Ann Christensen of El Paso, in letters to the author dated June 15, September 5, December 15, 1985; March 4, June 5, 1986. See also, the United States Eighth Census (1860), Johnson County, Texas; Muster Roll of the "Johnson County Slashers," Texas State Archives. Tom Haley was wounded at Yellow Bayou in May 1864 but did not recover. He wrote a will in October 1864 leaving everything to his wife and four sons before dying in February 1865. A copy of the will is in the possession of the author.

15 Henson, *McKinney Falls: The Ranch Home of Thomas F. McKinney*, 29, 35; Margaret S. Henson, "McKinney, Thomas Freeman," *Handbook of Texas Online*, accessed March 16, 2025, https://www.tshaonline.org/handbook/entries/mckinney-thomas-freeman.

16 "Thomas Jefferson Wells," *Dictionary of Louisiana Biography* online; *The Louisiana Democrat* (Alexandria), January 25, 1860. See also, "War Dance (USA)," American Classic Pedigrees website, http://www.americanclassicpedigrees.com/war-dance.html#:~:text=War%20Dance%20was%20bred%20by%20General%20Thomas%20Jefferson,later%20his%20estate%29%20maintained%20ownership%20of%20the%20horse [Accessed July 8, 2021]; Pedigree Online: Thoroughbred Database, "War Dance (USA)," online database, https://www.pedigreequery.com/war+dance [Accessed August 28, 2021]; "Section II: The Ante Bellum Period," [Accessed September 11, 2021].

17 Jeff Wells died in Hempstead, Austin County (now Waller County), July 15, 1863. Six days before his death he wrote a codicil to his Louisiana will in Grimes County which bordered Austin County (now Waller). In it he left his "much beloved adopted daughter Gertrude Wells" all his personal property in her possession. His Louisiana will was in the hands of John K. Elgee, a wealthy Irish-born lawyer in Alexandria, and it was that one that included his race horses. His personal effects with him in Texas he left in the care of his friend L. W. Groce in Hempstead to be given to Gertrude. He also mentioned debts owed to him by John Hark, owner of two racetracks. Codicil signed and dated July 9, 1863, "Probate Minutes, Vol. N, 1860–1865, Texas, US Wills and Probate Records, 1833–1974." For the story of the raid on Kenner's plantation, Ashland see https://www.ancestry.com/imageviewer/collections/2115/images/007574453_00182?usePUB=true&_phsrc=aLI295&phstart=successSource&usePUBJs=true&pId=1983438 [Accessed September 14, 2021].

18 Hervey, *Racing in America, 1665–1865*, 2:352–53; Pedigree Online, "War Dance (USA)," [Accessed February 11, 2021].

19 *The Daily Picayune* (New Orleans), April 18, 19, 1866; April 5, March 8, 9, 1870; "Samuel M. Westmore," *Dictionary of Louisiana Biography* online, https://www.lahistory.org/resources/dictionary-louisiana-biography/dictionary-of-louisiana-biography-w/; Wikipedia, "Reel (horse)," updated September 27, 2024, https://en.wikipedia.org/wiki/Reel_(horse) [Accessed September 11, 2021]. On newspapers.com *The Daily Picayune* is found under *The Times-Picayune*.

20 *The Daily Picayune* (New Orleans), April 18, 19, 1866; April 5, March 8, 9, 1870; *The New Orleans Times*, April 12, 1866. Abe Hawkins died in 1867. Mooney, *Race Horse Men*, 169–70. On newspapers.com *The New Orleans Times* is found under *The Times Democrat*.

21 *The Daily Picayune* (New Orleans), April 18, 19, 1866; April 5, March 8, 9, 1870.

22 Texas had well over 100 numbered or named cavalry organizations, including at least thirty-six numbered regiments, a handful of cavalry regiments without numbers, and several cavalry battalions. See Steward Sifakis, *Compendium of the Confederate Armies: Texas* (New York: Facts on File, Inc., 1995) for a list of all the units.

23 William Andrew Fletcher, *Rebel Private, Front and Rear* (Austin: University of Texas Press, 1954), 91.

24 G. W. Ingram to "My Dear Mat," November 18, 1862, in Henry L. Ingram, comp., *Civil War Letters of George W. and Martha F. Ingram, 1861–1865* (College Station: Texas A&M University Press, 1973), 38; Henry Orr to "Father and Mother," May 30, 1863, Anderson, ed., *Campaigning with Parsons' Texas Cavalry* Brigade, 106. See also, Bailey, *Texans in the Confederate Cavalry*, 29–31.

25 *Democratic Telegraph and Texas Register* (Houston), August 17, 1848, quoting the *Victoria Advocate*; Rugeley, annotator, *Batchler-Turner Letters*, 51–53, 65.

26 McLean, *Fine Texas Horses*, 32–33; E. S. C. Robertson to Mary Robertson, July 5, 1862, E. S. C. Robertson Civil War Letters, copies in possession of the author courtesy of Dr. Malcolm D. McLean.

27 Armistead, *Horses and Mules in the Civil War*, 28, 33.

28 T. J. Stiles, "That Time When Custer Stole a Horse," *Smithsonian Magazine* (November 2015), https://www.smithsonianmag.com/history/when-custer-stole-thoroughbred-180956961/ [Accessed June 22, 2021].

29 Charles H. Lothrop, *A History of the First Regiment Iowa Cavalry, Veteran Volunteers, From its Organization in 1861 to its Muster Out of the United States Service in 1866* (Lyons, IA: Beers & Eaton, Printers, 1890), 237–41.

30 Armistead, *Horses and Mules in the Civil War*, 142.

31 Lothrop, *A History of the First Regiment Iowa Cavalry*. 237–41.

32 Ibid.

33 Ibid.

34 *The Houston Tri-Weekly Telegraph*, March 17, 1865. Singe-cat means a horse that appears of better quality than appearance indicates.

35 *The Houston Tri-Weekly Telegraph*, September 15, 1865.

36 Henson, *McKinney Falls: The Ranch Home of Thomas F. McKinney*, 29, 35.

37 Hervey, *Racing in America, 1665–1865*, 2:353–55; "Metaire Race Track History," *Metairie.com* website, http://www.metairie.com/history/racetrack.htm [Accessed June 25, 2021].

38 Handwritten advertisement, "For Sale," in George A. Feris Family Papers.

39 *The Galveston Daily News*, December 7, 1879; "Contract of J. A. Gibson," in George A. Feris Family Papers; United States Ninth Census (1870), Fort Bend County, Texas.

40 *Tri-Weekly Telegraph* (Houston), March 30, 1866; *Dallas Herald*, November 28, 1868.

41 *Rules and Regulations of the Houston Jockey Club* in George A. Feris Family Papers. Copy in possession of the author; Houston Jockey Club, Texas, *Rules and Regulations*, ca. 1866–1867, in the Texas State Archives. Copy in possession of the author. The rule book in the Feris papers is composed of fifty-three pages unlike one dated around 1866–1867, which was only thirty pages long. See also, Jennifer Caldwell, "Why do Thoroughbreds Share the Same Birth Date of New Year's Day?," Kentucky Derby website, https://www.kentuckyderby.com/horses/news/why-do-thoroughbreds-share-the-same-birth-date-of-new-years-day [Accessed June 26, 2021].

42 Johnson County, United States Eighth Census (1860), Johnson County, Texas; Estate of Thomas Haley, Will Book D, Johnson County, 62–64. The probate lists eighteen horses, valued individually, along with a statement that "some horses still on range not inventoried."

43 *Tri-Weekly Texas State Gazette* (Austin), June 11, 21, 1869.

44 Ibid., June 18, 1869.

45 Ibid., June 21, 1869.

46 Ibid., April 21, 1869.

47 Ibid., March 26, June 4, 1869; United States Ninth Census (1870) Bastrop County, Texas. See also, Henson, *McKinney Falls: The Ranch Home of Thomas F. McKinney*, for Thomas McKinney's last years.

48 Henson, *McKinney Falls: The Ranch Home of Thomas F. McKinney*, 36; *The Austin Weekly Statesman*, October 9, 1873, said that McKinney died at his residence, Thursday morning, at two o'clock.

49 *Dallas Herald*, June 2, 1866; October 31, 1868; October 23, 30, 1869; October 1, 1870; *Memorial and Biographical History of Dallas County, Texas*, 542. In all the stories in the *Dallas Herald* mentioning Jack Batchler in the early 1870s the spelling is Batchelor. Letters to the author from members of the current family spell it Batchler.

50 *Dallas Herald*, August 21, September 4, October 9, December 11, 1869.

CHAPTER 6

1 Campbell, *Gone to Texas*, 290, 304, 306.

2 John D. Young and J. Frank Dobie, *A Vaquero of the Brush Country: The Life and Times of John D. Young* (1929; rpt., Austin: University of Texas Press, 1998), 24; Carl H. Moneyhon, "Reconstruction," *Handbook of Texas Online*, accessed March 16, 2025, https://www.tshaonline.org/handbook/entries/reconstruction.

3 "James Madison Brown," *Handbook of Texas* online; Samuel C. Hildreth and James R. Crowell, *The Spell of the Turf: The Story of American Racing* (Philadelphia: J. B. Lippincott, 1926), 9–10, 18. See also, Bowen, *Masters of the Turf,* 41–82 for more on Hildreth.

4 Hildreth and Crowell, *The Spell of the Turf,* 11, 18–24; Robertson, *The History of Thoroughbred Racing in America*, 203; United States Ninth Census (1870) Nemaha County, Kansas. Forty-six-year-old Vincent Hildreth was seen as Vinson Hildreth in this census.

5 Hildreth and Crowell, *The Spell of the Turf,* 24–25.

6 Ibid., 25.

7 Ibid., 24–27.

8 Young and Dobie, *A Vaquero of the Brush Country*, 77; *The Galveston Daily News*, October 16, 1873; Wayne Gard, "Losin' One's Shirt" in Bob Denhardt, ed., *The Quarter Horse*, 219–20.

9 Wayne Gard, "The Denton Mare," in Gard, *Fabulous Quarter Horse: Steel Dust*, 37–47; Rick Miller, *Sam Bass & Gang* (Austin: State House Press, 1999), 27–37, 39–41; Campbell, *Gone to Texas,* 305. See also, Wayne Gard, *Sam Bass* (Norman: University of Oklahoma Press, 1969) and "Sam Bass: The Texas Bandit from Denton, 1851–1878," Denton Local Wiki website, https://localwiki.org/denton/Sam_Bass [Accessed June 15, 2021].

10 Gard, "The Denton Mare," 47. Other verses can be found when searching for the "Ballad of Sam Bass" in cowboy songs. See Michael Martin Murphy, "Sam Bass," *Cowboy Songs III: Rhymes of the Renegades* (1993), https://genius.com/Michael-martin-murphey-sam-bass-lyrics [Accessed June 15, 2021].

11 Walker v. Armstrong 54 *Tex.* 609 (1881). See also, Armstrong v. Parchman 42 *Tex.* 185 (1874) for a similar case. A brief version of William Armstrong v. Parchman & Walker is found in *The Galveston Daily News*, January 21, 1875.

12 Charles A. Siringo, *A Texas Cowboy or, Fifteen Years on the Hurricane Deck of a Spanish Pony* (1886; rpt., New York: Penguin Books, 2000), 72, 79, 100. Sometimes the horse's name is spelled Whisky-Peat. He died the year after Siringo had to leave him behind at his mother's house when he headed for another cattle drive.

13 S. O. Young, *True Stories of Old Houston and Houstonians* (Galveston: Oscar Springer, publisher, 1913), 242–44. Young served in the Civil War in the Bayou City Guards, which became Company I, Fifth Texas Infantry in John Bell Hood's Texas Brigade.

14 Ibid. See also, United States Ninth Census (1870), Harris County, Texas.

15 Young, *True Stories of Old Houston and Houstonians*, 242–44. For the information on Rush Hutchins, see the United States Ninth Census (1870), Harris County, Texas.

16 *The Houston Daily Age*, April 21, 1874. Copy in George A. Feris Family Papers. See also, United States Ninth Census (1870), Harris County, Texas.

17 *Dallas Herald*, June 11, 18, 1870; *A Memorial and Biographical History of Ellis County*, 521; United States Ninth Census (1870), Dallas County, Texas. Jimmy followed in his father's footsteps and in 1892 was said to own "400 horses and 2,000 head of cattle."

18 *Dallas Herald*, June 18, 1870; *A Memorial and Biographical History of Ellis County*, 521; United States Ninth Census (1870), Ellis County, Texas. Roland Clayton was the son of J. C. Clayton of Waxahachie who gave his occupation as trader in the census.

19 *Dallas Herald*, June 18, July 23, 1870.

20 *Dallas Herald*, July 23, August 20, 1870; *A Memorial and Biographical History of Ellis County*, 521.

21 *Dallas Herald*, July 23, October 1, 28, 1870.

22 Denhardt, *Foundation Sires of the American Quarter Horse*, 172.

23 *The Galveston Daily News*, October 23, 1874.

24 *Dallas Herald*, September 30, 1875. The term "Triple Crown" was not used until the early twentieth century.

25 Ibid.

26 Ibid.; Gard, *Fabulous Quarter Horse: Steel Dust*, 34–36; Gard, "Fabulous Steel Dust," 166; Denhardt, *The Quarter Running Horse*, 148.

27 Hildreth and Crowell, *The Spell of the Turf*, 22; *The Galveston Daily News*, December 20, 1874; Denhardt, *The Quarter Running Horse*, 136. Denhardt identifies the mare stolen as Gray Alice but it could also have been Alice May. The theft was in late 1874 and the race with Alice May was the fall of 1875. Alice May was described as "aged" in the September race. Denhardt also has Brown owning two mares with the name of Gray Alice. See, Denhardt, *Foundation Dams of the American Quarter Horse*, 135. The one in this story is likely the one sired by Steel Dust and bred by Shelby Stanfield of Thorp Spring, although that is not verified.

28 Young and Dobie, *A Vaquero of the Brush Country*, 77–78; *The Galveston Daily News*, February 27, 1878.

29 "James Madison Brown," *Handbook of Texas* online; Hildreth and Crowell, *The Spell of the* Turf, 10; United States Seventh Census (1850), Williamson County, Texas; Eighth Census (1860) San Saba County, Texas; Ninth Census (1870) Washington County, Texas; and Tenth Census (1880) Lee County, Texas. Brown and his wife had five children who lived to adulthood. See Chuck Parsons, *James Madison Brown: Texas Sheriff, Texas Turfman* (Wolfe City, TX: Henington Publishing Co., 1993) for a full biography of Brown.

30 Denhardt, *The Quarter Running Horse*, 160–62, 188.

31 Ibid., 28; Denhardt, *The Quarter Running Horse*, 154; *The Galveston Daily News*, September 9, October 16, 17, 1875; *Weekly Democratic Statesman* (Austin), October 23, 1879.

32 *The Galveston Daily News*, October 17, 1875. Not all names of the horsemen were included at the Gonzales County Fair since some were too blurry to read and there may be errors in transcription of the ones listed.

33 *Fort Worth Daily Democrat*, October 10, 1878.

34 *Weekly Democratic Statesman* (Austin), October 23, 1879; August 12, October 28, 1880. T. A. Gay was probably Thomas A. Gay of Seguin, who in 1870 listed his occupation as stock raiser. The name Eglamore probably comes from an old English verse about Sir Eglamore who slew a dragon. See also, Ninth Census (1870) Guadalupe County, Texas.

35 "William Copeland Philips," *Handbook of Texas* online; *Austin-American Statesman*, July 8, 1873; April 22, 1874; September 18, 1875; October 19, 1875.

36 *Austin-American Statesman*, October 17, 19, November 14, 1875; November 19, 1876; November 18, 1877; August 3, October 10, 19, November 2, 1879; July 14, 1880;

March 19, 1888; Kentucky Kindred Genealogical Research, "The Alexander Family of Woodburn Farm—Woodford County," Kentucky Kindred Genealogy website, last updated May 16, 2020, https://kentuckykindredgenealogy.com/2020/05/16/the-alexander-family-of-woodburn-farm-woodford-county/ [Accessed December 16, 2021]; "Dr. William Copeland Philips," Find a Grave website, https://www.findagrave.com/memorial/14761708/william-copeland-philips [Accessed December 16, 2021].

37 *Austin-American Statesman*, November 2, 1879.

38 Robertson, *History of Thoroughbred Racing in America*, 113–19, 122, 143.

39 Ibid., 148, 157.

40 Mooney, *Race Horse Men*, 160.

41 Jockey Max Hirsch had his start at the Morris Ranch. Weeks, *The American Turf*, 400; Morris Ranch Papers, 1893–1929, Dolph Briscoe Center for American History; Wikipedia, "John Albert Morris," last updated March 13, 2025, https://en.wikipedia.org/wiki/John_Albert_Morris; Wikipedia, "Morris Ranch, Texas" last updated May 20, 2024, https://en.wikipedia.org/wiki/Morris_Ranch,_Texas.

42 Wikipedia, "John Albert Morris;" Robertson, *The History of Thoroughbred Racing in America*, 106–107.

43 *The Sunday Gazetteer* (Denison), May 1, 15, 22, 23; June 5, September 25, October 30, November 6, December 18, 1892.

44 *Brenham Weekly Banner*, January 12, 23, 1880; *The Austin Weekly Statesman*, May 18, 1893; *The Sunday Gazetteer* (Denison), May 1, 15, 22, 23; June 5, September 25, October 30, November 6, December 18, 1892.

45 *The Austin Weekly Statesman*, May 18, 1893; *The Sunday Gazetteer* (Denison), May 1, 15, 22, 23; June 5, September 25, October 30, November 6, December 18, 1892.

CHAPTER 7

1 Robertson, *The History of Thoroughbred Racing in America*, 109.

2 The King Ranch bred many famous quarter horses, including many of the early foundation sires (numbered 1–100) of the American Quarter Horse Association. In Thoroughbreds it is known for Assault, the Triple Crown winner in 1946. In 1950, Middleground won the Kentucky Derby and Belmont Stakes, and High Gun won the Belmont Stakes in 1954. For more information on the quarter horses, see *Combined Stud Book and Registry: Combined Books 1-2-3-4-5, No. 1 thru No. 27,000* (Amarillo: The American Quarter Horse Association, 1961); Robert Kleberg, Jr., "The King Ranch," in Lindeman, *The Quarter Horse Breeder*, 150–54.

3 John Biggs, "Waggoner Estate Quarter Horses," in Lindeman, *The Quarter Horse Breeder*, 156–58; "W. T. Waggoner, Three D's Owner, Stricken," *Daily Racing Form*, May 27, 1933, University of Kentucky Archives, Lexington (The *Daily Racing Form* was a tabloid newspaper founded in 1894 in Chicago.); "Waggoner, William Thomas," *Handbook of Texas Online*, accessed March 18, 2025, https://www.tshaonline.org/handbook/entries/waggoner-william-thomas and David Minor, "Burnett, Samuel Burk," *Handbook of Texas Online*, accessed March 16, 2025, https://www.tshaonline

.org/handbook/entries/burnett-samuel-burk; Obituary of William Thomas Waggoner, *Decatur News*, December 13, 1934. Waggoner and Burnett are buried near each other in Oakwood Cemetery, Fort Worth.

4 *The Dallas Daily Herald*, November 13, 1880; December 2, 1881; Robert A. Calvert and Arnoldo De León, *The History of Texas* (Arlington Heights, IL: Harlan Davidson, 1990), 153.

5 *The Inter Ocean* (Chicago), September 25, 1886; United States Tenth Census (1880), Galveston County, Texas. Also seen as *The Inter-Ocean*.

6 *The Inter Ocean* (Chicago), September 25, 1886.

7 Ibid.

8 *The Galveston Daily News*, July 1, 1880.

9 *The Dallas Daily Herald*, November 13, 1880.

10 Ibid., May 12, 1881; *The Dallas Weekly Herald*, May 26, 1881; October 12, 1882.

11 *The Dallas Daily Herald*, April 1, 1882; *The Dallas Weekly Herald*, October 19, November 15, 1883; *The Galveston Daily News*, October 25, 1882.

12 *Weekly Democratic Statesman* (Austin), October 27, 1881.

13 *The Galveston Daily News*, March 12, 1882.

14 Ibid., February 8, 1871; May 30, November 19, 1882.

15 *The Austin Weekly Statesman*, October 25, 1883; March 27, 1884; *The McKinney Gazette*, June 17, 1886; *Fort Worth Daily Gazette*, October 7, 1886.

16 *Austin Weekly Statesman*, December 18, 1884.

17 *Brenham Daily Banner*, July 31, 1885; *The Galveston Daily News*, September 6, 1885; *Evening Star* (Washington, DC), August 22, 1885; *The Scranton Republican* (Scranton, PA), July 29, 1885; *The Boston Globe*, July 15, 1885; *Liverpool Mercury* (Liverpool, England), June 26, 1885; *The Courier and Argus* (Dundee, Tayside, Scotland), July 3, 1885.

18 The first female jockey to compete in a pari-mutuel race in the United States was more than eighty years after this episode, when, in 1969, Diane Crump started at Hialeah Park. Penny Ann Early received a license in 1968 but jockeys boycotted three races to prevent her participation. *Aberdeen Journal, and General Advertiser* (Aberdeen, Scotland), August 27, 1886; America's Best Racing, "Brilliant Women in U.S. Horse Racing History," online article, https://www.americasbestracing.net/the-sport/2020-brilliant-women-us-horse-racing-history [Accessed September 2, 2021].

19 *The Austin Weekly Statesman*, May 1, 1884. The headline read "FOILED! A DASTARDLY ATTEMPT TO ASSASSINATE THE SHERIFF OF LEE COUNTY." See also, *Weekly Democratic Statesman* (Austin), September 26, 1878. In September 1878 the San Saba County attorney, S. S. Brooks was gunned down. Before he died he stated that "'to the best of my knowledge and belief it was Jim Brown that shot me;' stating also that Brown had called to him on the road, attracting his attention, and then shot him, and that there were two other persons with Brown whom he did not recognize. Mr. Brooks stated further that he, himself, was unarmed and that he ran to the house as soon as fired upon." Although San Saba was turfman Jim Brown's place of birth, it is unknown if this is the same man.

20 The mare Mittie Stephens was named for the sidewheel vessel, the *Mittie Stephens*, that burned near Shreveport on February 12, 1869. Sixty-one people died in the tragedy. Some experts say Rondo was a chestnut foaled in 1880. At the time he was foaled, the Haleys had not moved to Sweetwater. United States Tenth Census (1880), Johnson County, Texas. See also, Denhardt, *Foundation Sires of the American Quarter Horse*, 184, and *Foundation Dams of the American Quarter Horse*, 179; Lindeman, *The Quarter Horse Breeder*, 120. For the tragedy surrounding the vessel, see *The Home Advocate* (Jefferson), February 13, 1869; *Dallas Herald*, February 27, 1869; *Houston Daily Mercury*, September 18, 1873; *Timpson Weekly Times*, December 10, 1934.

21 Estate of Thomas Haley, Will Book D, Johnson County, Texas, 62–64; "Great Quarter Horse Breeders of the Past," *The Quarter Horse Journal* (March 1972), 204–205; Denhardt, *The Quarter Running Horse*, 201–202. Although the story Denhardt recorded involved the Haley brothers, it was Charley who was the one to make a name for himself in later years and probably spoke for his brothers on this occasion.

22 Denhardt, *The Quarter Running Horse*, 201–202. Family information comes from the great-granddaughter of Charles R. Haley, Mary Ann Christensen of El Paso, in letters to the author dated June 15, September 5, December 15, 1985; March 4, June 5, 1986.

23 Denhardt, *The Quarter Running Horse*, 256–57; Denhardt, *Foundation Sires of the American Quarter Horse*, 84, 195. The Haley place still belongs to the Smith family and Lowell Smith Jr. took care of the Haley cemetery until his death in 2021. The Haley home has been gone for many years and a field now covers the track where horses once raced.

24 *The Abilene Reporter*, June 12, 1891; November 4, 18, 1892; August 3, 1900. The paper mistaken identified General Ross' breeder as Dr. T. M. Blakemore on November 4 but corrected it on November 18 to Charley Haley. See also, Denhardt, *Foundation Dams of the American Quarter Horse*, 179, and *Foundation Sires of the American Quarter Horse*, 195; Pedigree Online: Thoroughbred Database, "General Ross," online database, https://www.pedigreequery.com/general+ross3 [Accessed August 28, 2021]; Pedigree Online: Thoroughbred Database, "Silent Friend (USA)," online database, https://www.pedigreequery.com/silent+friend [Accessed August 27, 2021]; "Charles Robert 'Charley' Haley," Find a Grave website, https://www.findagrave.com/memorial/15515102/charles-r-haley [Accessed August 31, 2021].

25 *The Abilene Reporter*, November 25, December 9, 1892; May 5, June 9, 1893; March 30, April 20, May 18, June 1, 1894; February 1, April 12, 1895.

26 Denhardt, *The Quarter Running Horse*, 160–61; United States Ninth Census (1870), Washington County, Texas; United States Tenth Census (1880), Lee County, Texas.

27 *Fort Worth Daily Gazette*, February 11, 1886; Denhardt, *The Quarter Running Horse*, 160–61. Denhardt wrote that quarter horse expert Helen Michaelis (1905–1965) interviewed the Brown children. Since by the time Michaelis was old enough to conduct these interviews Brown and his wife were dead, two of his children were dead (Ed and Annie), one lived alternately in France, Illinois, and Kentucky (Gaylon), Luna was no longer in Texas (she lived in California and was Luna Rose Huff), leaving only William (Billy), living in Fort Worth, who would have been a very small child at the time of the

events having been born around 1878 and was living in the Tarrant County Home when he died in 1949. See also, *Brenham Weekly Banner*, January 19, 1877; February 24, 1881. Luna Rose Brown married first Hugh Testard (1864–1907) who died in San Antonio. Her second marriage was in Fort Worth to William Harrison Rainey (1877–1906). Her third marriage was in Fort Worth to bookkeeper Julius Engelhard (1883–1934); the Engelharts moved to California around 1912. Engelhart is also seen as Englehart. Her final marriage was April 10, 1919, in Los Angeles to Clarence L. Huff (1884–1971). She died February 1, 1953, and is buried in Rosedale Cemetery in Los Angeles. See "Luna Rose *Brown* Huff," Find a Grave website, https://www.findagrave.com/memorial/205549568/luna-rose-huff.

28 The Jockey Club, *The American Stud Book* (New York: The Jockey Club, 1898), 7:614. See also, Pedigree Online: Thoroughbred Database, "Hyder Ali (USA)," online database, https://www.pedigreequery.com/hyder+ali [Accessed September 23, 2021].

29 *Fort Worth Daily Gazette*, February 12, 1886; Richard F. Selcer, "Fort Worth's Wild White Elephant Saloon," https://www.historynet.com/fort-worths-wild-white-elephant-saloon.htm [Accessed July 16, 2021]; Richard F. Selcer, *Hell's Half Acre* (Fort Worth: Texas Christian University Press, 1991), 186–94. Even after Jim Brown's death the family continued to make news. In August 1903 Brown's nephew, stockman James H. Brown of San Saba was gunned down while going home from church in a personal feud regarding some cattle. *The Austin Weekly Statesman*, August 31, 1893.

30 *Fort Worth Daily Democrat*, October 26, 1877; *Fort Worth Daily Gazette*, March 21, 22, 29, November 11, 19, 22, 1883; February 12, 1886. For more on Hell's Half Acres, see Selcer, *Hell's Half Acre*. See also, Fort Worth Chamber of Commerce and Richard Selcer, "Fort Worth History: 'Where the West Begins,'" https://www.fortworthtexas.gov/about/history#:~:text=Meat%20Packing%3A%20Fort%20Worth%E2%80%99s%20First%20Great%20Industry%20As,were%20muddy%2C%20and%20sidewalks%20were%20made%20of%20wood [Accessed July 23, 2021]. For the charter of the Driving Park Association, see "Fort Worth Driving Park Association The Overview," https://www.corporationwiki.com/p/hmsde/fort-worth-driving-park-association-the [Accessed October 28, 2021].

31 *Fort Worth Daily Gazette*, November 11, 19, 1883.

32 Ibid.

33 Ibid., November 22, 1883.

34 Ibid., January 28, 29, May 15, 1885.

35 Nanci Monroe Kimmey and Georgia Kemp Caraway, *North Texas State Fair and Rodeo* (Charleston, SC: Arcadia Publishing, 2016), 7, 13.

36 Ibid., 9, quoting the *Dallas Morning News*; *Fort Worth Daily Gazette*, October 28, 1887.

37 *Fort Worth Daily Gazette*, March 9, 1887.

38 *The Galveston Daily News*, April 6, 10, June 13, 1886; *The Dallas Daily Herald*, December 17, 1886.

39 *The Galveston Daily News*, June 10, 1886.

40 *Fort Worth Daily Gazette*, February 4, 1884.

41 Ibid., September 2, 1883; August 31, 1884.

42 Ibid., August 30, September 26, 1884; United States Tenth Census (1880), Tarrant County, Texas.

43 Nancy Wiley, *The Great State Fair of Texas: An Illustrated History* (Dallas: Taylor Publishing Company, 1985), 1–22. See also, Nancy Wiley, "State Fair of Texas," *Handbook of Texas Online*, accessed March 17, 2025, https://www.tshaonline.org/handbook/entries/state-fair-of-texas; State Fair of Texas, "History," http://bigtex.com/about-us/history/ [Accessed July 22, 2021]. The organization eventually had to sell the site to the city of Dallas, becoming the modern State Fair of Texas. In 1930 tradition says that the track was demolished to provide for the construction of the football stadium that became the Cotton Bowl.

44 *The Dallas Daily Herald*, October 25, 1886.

45 Ibid., October 20, 26, 27, 1886.

46 *Fort Worth Daily Gazette*, November 8, 9, 1886; June 17, 18, 1887; *The Dallas Daily Herald*, August 19, 1887.

47 *The Daily Picayune* (New Orleans), March 10, 12, 1886; *The Brooklyn Daily Eagle* (Brooklyn, NY), May 30, 1886.

48 *Fort Worth Daily Gazette*, November 10, 1886.

49 Ibid.

50 Ibid., October 24, 25, 1887.

51 "Miles Hart" and "Marcus I. Kennard," *A Memorial and Biographical History of Johnson and Hill Counties, Texas* (Chicago: The Lewis Publishing Co., 1892), 619–20, 659–61; Viola Block, *History of Johnson, County and Surrounding Areas* (Waco: Library Binding Co., 1970), 211–23. Kennard (1850–1938) and Hart (1848–1927) are buried in the Kennard Cemetery in Parker, Texas.

52 *Cleburne Chronicle*, April 27, 1895; *Fort Worth Daily Gazette*, November 10, 1886; Denhardt, *Foundation Sires of the American Quarter Horse*, 164, 183; Denhardt, *The Quarter Running Horse*, 202–203, 212–16. The money for the breeding establishment of Kennard and Hart had been made in 1874 when the two men had headed southwest to the Devil's River country near Langtry on the Mexican border to round up cattle they had traded for. It took them almost two years because of trouble with both Indians and outlaws and they had to hire a professional gunfighter to guard the animals while they worked but it had been time well spent. They made enough money to fund their horse business when they returned home.

53 *The Galveston Daily News*, September 8, 1886.

54 *Fort Worth Daily Gazette*, May 25, 1886. Racing resumed in New York state in 1913, but only four tracks had survived: Aqueduct Racetrack, Belmont Park, Jamaica Racetrack, and Saratoga Race Course. See also, Wikipedia, "Brighton Beach Race Course," last updated November 20, 2024, https://en.wikipedia.org/wiki/Brighton_Beach_Race_Course [Accessed July 23, 2021]; Wikipedia, "Hart-Agnew Law," last updated September 15, 2022, https://en.wikipedia.org/wiki/Hart%e2%80%93Agnew_Law [Accessed July 23, 2021].

55 *The Abilene Reporter*, August 9, 1888.

CHAPTER 8

1 *The Galveston Daily News*, November 15, 1894.

2 Weeks, *The American Turf*, 392.

3 Ibid., 78; *Fort Worth Daily Gazette*, October 8, November 3, 1887; November 2, 1890.

4 Mooney, *Race Horse Men*, 4; Hildreth and Crowell, *The Spell of the Turf*, 31–32.

5 *Brenham Weekly Banner*, February 5, 1891; *The Abilene Reporter*, March 6, 1891; Gard, *Fabulous Quarter Horse: Steel Dust*, 36.

6 *The Dallas Daily Herald*, October 29, November 5, 13, 1885; *The Galveston Daily News*, October 29, November 13, 19, 1885; March 11, July 2, 7, 23, 30, 31, August 7, 24, 1886; September 2, 10, 11, 15, 1887; *El Paso Times*, May 30, August 7, 1886; *The New York Times*, August 7, 1886; August 19, 1887; December 14, 1886; *Fort Worth Daily Gazette*, August 18, 1885; October 14, 1886; August 26, 1887; *The Times Picayune*, March 10, 12, 25, 1886; *Brooklyn Daily Eagle*, May 30, 1886.

7 *The Chicago Tribune*, April 23, July 9, 12, 24, 30, August 11, September 5, 11, 27, 29, October 7, 18, 20, 22, November 5, 6, 7, 11, 25, 29, December 11, 28,1891; April 19, May 18, 19, June 28, 29, July 6, 10, 30, October 16, September 2, 1892; *The Inter Ocean* (Chicago), September 7, 1890; August 26, October 1, 1891.

8 *The Inter Ocean* (Chicago), September 7, November 11, 1890.

9 Hildreth and Crowell, *The Spell of the Turf*, 66.

10 Ibid., 66–67.

11 *The Inter Ocean* (Chicago), July 24, 30, 1891.

12 *Brenham Daily Banner*, September 21, 1892; *The Sunday Gazetteer*, September 25, 1892. See also, "Former Lee County Sheriff: Jim Brown Wanted for Murder," September 16, 1892, http://sites.rootsweb.com/~txmdhms/bio_jim_brown.htm for a copy of the Giddings, Texas, *Times & News*, June 24, 1971 [Accessed June 20, 2022].

13 Hildreth and Crowell, *The Spell of the Turf*, 68–72; *The Fort Worth Daily Gazette*, September 7, 11, 1892; *The Austin Weekly Statesman*, September 8, 1892; Robertson, *The History of Thoroughbred Racing in America*, 195; "James Madison Brown," *Handbook of Texas* online. The shoot-out at the Chicago track made headlines across the nation and is mentioned in several books. The quotes come from Hildreth who actually witnessed the event. See also, *The Chicago Tribune*, September 7, 8, 9, 11, 1892; *The Inter Ocean* (Chicago), September 7, 8, 9, 10, 11, 16, 1892; *Evening Messenger* (Marshall), September 7, 1892; *The Galveston News*, September 7, 9, 21, 1892; *Austin Weekly Statesman*, September 8, 1892; *The Temple Times* (Temple), September 8, 1892; *The Daily Hesperian* (Gainesville), September 8, 1892; *Brenham Daily Banner*, September 8, 21, 1892. The killing of two Chicago policemen made the news from coast-to-coast and newspapers are much too numerous to list here. In all cases, the articles described Brown as a Texan, with all the characteristics expected in a man from the frontier state. Northern papers described Brown as a "Texas ruffian."

14 *The Galveston Daily News*, September 7, 1892; *The Temple Times*, September 8, 1892.

15 *Brenham Daily Banner*, September 8, 1892.

16 *The Inter Ocean* (Chicago), September 8, 9, 1892; *The Austin Weekly Statesman*, September 8, 1892; Robertson, *The History of Thoroughbred Racing in America*, 110, 198. Hawthorne is now a suburb of Chicago.

17 Hildreth and Crowell, *Spell of the Turf*, 63–72; *The Fort Worth Gazette*, September 7, 1892; *The Chicago Tribune*, September 7, 8, 11, 1892; *The Inter Ocean* (Chicago), September 10, 16, 1892. Brown is buried in Oakwood Cemetery just north of the Fort Worth courthouse across the Trinity River. His tombstone is of recent origin; no one else in the plot has one. But it is likely the plot contains the remains of his wife Amanda, who died in 1911, son Ed, who died in a train wreck in 1900, and daughter Annie Stouffer, who was murdered in 1905. It is also possible that it is the final resting place of William (Billie) Brown.

18 Weeks, *The American Turf*, 372, 388; Robertson, *The History of Thoroughbred Racing in America*, 168–70; Wikipedia, "Tod Sloan (jockey)," last updated January 26, 2025, https://en.wikipedia.org/wiki/Tod_Sloan_(jockey); Bowen, *Masters of the Turf*, 137.

19 Weeks, *The American Turf*, 392; United States Thirteenth Census (1910), Dallas County, Texas; *Fort Worth Daily Gazette*, October 9, 1890; September 25, 1891; *The Inter Ocean* (Chicago), April 17, 1898; January 22, 1899. The *Fort Worth Star Telegram*, December 22, 1902, announced that Shields was coming home to Dallas and would not ride the following season in Russia.

20 Weeks, *The American Turf*, 400; Wikipedia, "Max Hirsch," last updated April 11, 2025, https://en.wikipedia.org/wiki/Max_Hirsch; Morris Ranch Papers, 1893–1929; Robertson, *The History of Thoroughbred Racing in America*, 313, 382–84; United States Tenth Census (1880), Gillespie County, Texas. Max does not appear in the 1880 census, which was taken June 4–5, 1880, because he was born July 12. See also, Bowen, *Masters of the Turf*, 135–72. Mary eventually gave up training but her husband, racing secretary Charles McLennan, had the second-most important handicap race at Hialeah named for him. The Jockey Club in England had its first female trainer in 1886 when Ellen Chaloner was allowed to retain her husband's license when he died. This was apparently an honor granted to her by The Jockey Club in England in recognition of her husband, who was a famous jockey and trainer. After her retirement in 1894 a woman would not be granted a license in England for many more decades. Wikipedia, "Tom Chaloner," last updated February 1, 2025, https://en.wikipedia.org/wiki/Tom_Chaloner; "Newmarket to Honour Forgotten First Lady of the Turf," BBC website, March 8, 2023, https://www.bbc.com/news/uk-england-suffolk-64878450 [Accessed June 23, 2023]; David Milnes, "Newmarket Honors First Female British Trainer Chaloner," *Blood Horse* magazine website, March 8, 2023, https://www.bloodhorse.com/horse-racing/articles/267076/newmarket-honors-first-female-british-trainer-chaloner [Accessed June 6, 2023].

21 Wharton, *Wharton's History of Fort Bend County*, 157; "John Huggins Dead in Texas," *Daily Racing Form*, May 11, 1917; Wikipedia, "John Huggins (racehorse trainer)," last updated February 24, 2025, https://en.wikipedia.org/wiki/John_Huggins_(racehorse_trainer).

22 *The Inter Ocean* (Chicago), September 7, November 11, 1890.

23 *Chicago Tribune*, September 10, November 28, 1892; *The Inter Ocean* (Chicago), September 9, 1892.

24 *The Inter Ocean* (Chicago), September 7, 1892.

25 Ibid., December 8, 1898; June 14, 1904; *Fort Worth Telegram*, May 3, 1905; *Jefferson Jimplecute* (Jefferson), May 6, 1905; *The Lexington Herald* (Lexington, KY), March 2, 1925; March 27, 1926; February 23, June 17, June 26, 1928; November 11, 1929. See also, Kentucky Bureau of Vital Statistics, Department of Health, City of Covington, Kentucky, Certificate of Death, "Ed Brown," and "John Gaylon Brown," in the Illinois, US, Deaths and Stillbirths Index, 1916–1947. For Gaylon Brown, see the *Lexington Leader* (Lexington, KY), May 13, 1938. Gaylon Brown and his wife Norma are in the Lexington Cemetery. Shandon Farm, founded in 1891, still exists. See "Shandon Farm," Facebook, https://www.facebook.com/shandonfarm [Accessed January 18, 2022]. The Harlem track opened in 1894. See Jill Wagner, "The Harlem Race Track," Forest Park Review website, October 27, 2021, https://www.forestparkreview.com/2021/10/27/the-harlem-race-track/ [Accessed January 18, 2022]. See also, US Passport Applications, 1795–1925 and New York, US Arriving Passenger and Crew Lists, 1820–1957, both sources found on ancestry.com. It was November 1906 when Jim Brown's estate was finally settled. It had been going from one probate court to higher court in Illinois since 1892 and the heirs finally won in 1906. The estate amounted to $30,000 divided among the surviving children and grandchildren. *Fort Worth Star Telegram*, November 7, 8, 1906.

26 *The Galveston Daily News*, November 12, 1893; *Brenham Daily Banner*, November 12, December 3, 1893; *The Waco Evening News*, November 10, 1893; *The Austin Weekly Statesman*, November 16, 23, 1893; *Brenham Daily Banner*, December 3, 1893. The Austin paper reported in November under the headline "JIM BROWN'S DAUGHTER" that "Mr. and Mrs. Hugh A. Testard, whose sensational domestic troubles have been noticed extensively in the newspaper of the country, and in which their little daughter figured prominently, appear to have become thoroughly reconciled and are living together in Dallas and may make this their permanent home. . . . Mr. Testard has withdrawn all the reflections made upon his wife and now declares them without foundation." The marriage did not last. By December Luna had filed for divorce.

27 *The Cleburne Chronicle*, October 17, 24, 1890.

28 Ibid., June 27, October 17, 1890; August 21, 1891. There were city races described in the paper on April 5, 1889, and also at Frank F. Adams's race course on August 23, 1889. Races were still publicized in the paper on September 2, 1893.

29 "Texas Racing Circuit," undated newspaper clipping in George A. Feris Family Papers. Since Feris was born in 1817 and is described as being in his seventies the probable date would be the mid-to-late 1890s. See also, "Explore the History of Houston," Greater Houston Partnership website, https://www.houston.org/timeline [Accessed June 2, 2021].

30 *The Galveston Daily News*, March 23, 1893.

31 "Texas Racing Circuit."

32 *Fort Worth Daily Gazette*, October 3, 1894.

33 Ibid., October 24, 27, 30, 31, November 1, 2, 1894; *The Galveston Daily News*, October 25, 31,1894; The Jockey Club, *The American Stud Book*, 7:611.

See also, Pedigree Online: Thoroughbred Database website (*pedigreequery.com*) and Pedigree Online: All Breeds Database website (*allbreedpedigree.com*) [Accessed June 1, 2022].

[34] *The Galveston Daily News*, October 31, 1894; *Fort Worth Daily Gazette*, October 31, 1894.

[35] *Fort Worth Daily Gazette*, May 18, 24, September 26, October 24, 27, 30, 31, November 1, 2, 1894; *The Galveston Daily News*, August 31, September 29, October 23, 25, 31, 1894.

[36] *The Galveston Daily News*, November 23, 25, 26, December 2, 1894; *Fort Worth Daily Gazette*, November 25, 1894; March 26, 27, August 9, October 4, 23, 1985.

[37] *Fort Worth Daily Gazette*, September 16, 1894.

[38] *The Abilene Reporter*, March 6, 1891; March 11, 1892.

[39] W. S. Vosburgh, *Racing in America, 1866–1921* (New York: Privately Printed, The Jockey Club, 1922), 43–48; Robertson, *The History of Thoroughbred Racing in America*, 174–76; "History of The Jockey Club," The Jockey Club website, http://www.jockeyclub.com/Default.asp?section=About&area=0 [Accessed June 2, 2021].

[40] *The Inter Ocean* (Chicago), October 17, 1893; March 9, 1896. See also, Wikipedia, "Starting gate," last updated October 9, 2023, https://en.wikipedia.org/wiki/Starting_gate.

[41] "Lillian Russell to Maintain a Stable," *Daily Racing Form*, August 14, 1906; "'Diamond' Jim Brady Dead," *Daily Racing Form*, April 14, 1917.

[42] Hervey, *Racing in America, 1665–1865*, 2:352; Vosburgh, *Racing in America, 1866–1921*, 162–63; Robertson, *The History of Thoroughbred Racing in America*, 152–56; Hollingsworth, *The Kentucky Thoroughbred*, 55–73; Wikipedia, "Domino (horse)," last updated August 31, 2024, https://en.wikipedia.org/wiki/Domino_(horse); "War Dance (USA)," American Classic Pedigrees website, last updated June 15, 2022, http://www.americanclassicpedigrees.com/war-dance.html [Accessed July 13, 2021]; "Domino," Pedigree Online: All Breed Database website, https://www.allbreedpedigree.com/domino [Accessed July 13, 2021].

[43] *Fort Worth Gazette*, October 3, 1894; *Southern Mercury* (Dallas), November 8, 1894; October 3, 1895; *Cleburne Chronicle*. October 11, 1895.

[44] Hollingsworth, *The Kentucky Thoroughbred*, 56; Denhardt, *Quarter Horses: A Story of Two Centuries*, 42–44; Denhardt, *The Quarter Running Horse*. 206–207.

[45] "Prohibiting the Buying and Selling of on Horse Races," H. B. 196, in H. P. N. Gammel, comp., *The Laws of Texas, 1903–1905* (Austin: Gammel's Book Store, 1906), 68–69, 398–99.

The law read:
Section I: If any person shall engage or assist in pool selling, book making, taking or accepting any bet on any horse race, he shall be punished by a fine of not less than two hundred nor more than five hundred dollars, and imprisonment in the county jail for not less than thirty nor more than ninety days.

Section II: If any person shall buy, pool or otherwise wager anything of value on any horse race at any time or place, he shall be punished by a fine of not less than twenty-five dollars nor more than one hundred dollars.

Section III: If any owner or lessee of any property in this State shall permit the same to be used as a place for the sale of pools, book making or wagering on any horse race to be had in this or any other State he shall be punished by a fine of not less than two hundred nor more than five hundred dollars, and imprisonment in the county jail for not less than thirty days nor more than ninety days, and each and every day that the provisions of this article are violated shall constitute a separate offense. It being the intention in the foregoing Article to prohibit. . . . Wagering anything of value on horseracing.

46 *The Southern Mercury* (Dallas), November 19, 1903.

47 Ibid., July 30, August 6, 1903.

48 Hildreth and Crowell, *The Spell of the Turf*, 72; *The Inter Ocean* (Chicago), September 7, 1892.

49 *Cleburne Daily Enterprise*, July 29, 1902. This is the only instance the author encountered where the death of a race horse made the front page of a newspaper in Texas.

EPILOGUE

1 Gammel, comp., "Prohibiting the Buying and Selling of on Horse Races," *The Houston Daily Post*, January 2, 1903; *The Southern Mercury* (Dallas), January 8, 1903.

2 *The Southern Mercury* (Dallas), February 5, 1903; *The Houston Daily Post*, February 20, 1903; *The Brand* (Hereford), March 27, 1903.

3 Ockerman, *Hidden History of Horse Racing in Kentucky*, 46–47.

4 "State Fair of Texas," *Handbook of Texas* online.

5 *Fort Worth Star Telegram*, September 10, 14, 17, October 3, November 6, 7, 8, 13, 19, 24, 1929; February 11, 1983; March 16, 1997. This is just a sampling of the articles that appeared before the track's opening in 1929.

6 Gary West, "A day at the races: Back in the 1930s Arlington was the place to go to bet on ponies," *Fort Worth Star Telegram*, December 25, 1987; *The Galveston Daily News*, November 2, 1933; Wikipedia, "Arlington Downs," last updated November 20, 2024, https://en.wikipedia.org/wiki/Arlington_Downs [Accessed June 30, 2021].

7 *Galveston Daily News,* November 20, 23, 24, December 1, 9, 13, 29, 1933; James E. Fisher, "Epsom Downs," *Handbook of Texas Online*, https://www.tshaonline.org/handbook/entries/epsom-downs [accessed March 15, 2025]; Wikipedia, "Arlington Downs"; Houstorian Tracy, "Epsom Downs and Arrowhead Park," Houston Past website, https://houstorian.wordpress.com/2008/07/25/epsom-downs-and-arrowhead-park/ [Accessed June 30, 2021].

8 *Galveston Daily News,* December 3, 5, 7, 13, 17, 20, 24, 27, 28, 29, 30, 31, 1933. This is just a sampling of numerous articles about the track.

9 *Fort Worth Star Telegram*, April 23, 1934; Paula Allen, "In '30s, Alamo Downs had a short run," MySA website, July 3, 2011, https://www.mysanantonio.com/news/article/Paula-Allen-In-30s-Alamo-Downs-had-a-short-run-1447995.php [Accessed September 10, 2022]. Allen writes that construction price was $200,000.

10 Wiley, *The Great State Fair of Texas*, 112; *Fort Worth Star Telegram*, April 3, 22, 25, 26, 27, 28, 29, 1934.

11 The Texas Racing Commissions was created in 1933 (House Bill 12, 43rd Texas Legislature, 1st Called Session) to create and enforce rules and regulations, restrictions, and conditions applying to all horse races and exhibitions of riding horses. See also, *Annual Report of the Texas Racing Commission to the Governor of Texas* (1934), original in possession of the author.

12 Ibid.

13 Ibid.

14 Ibid.

15 Ibid.

16 Ibid.

17 Ibid.

18 *Rules of Racing adopted by the Texas Racing Commission*, also entitled *Texas Law and Rules Governing Horse Racing* (Austin, 1934), 84–85, original in possession of the author.

19 Ibid., 11–14, 40, 46, 58, 60–61.

20 *Fort Worth Star Telegram*, March 26, 27, 30, June 5, 6, 17, 18, 20, 26, 1937; *The Granbury News*, September 3, 1937; West, "A day at the races"; Alan Bogan, "Parimutuel Betting: Off to the Races?" *D Magazine* (October 1987) at https://www.dmagazine.com/publications/d-magazine/1987/october/parimutuel-betting-off-to-the-races/ [Accessed June 15, 2021]; Wikipedia, "Epsom Downs Racecourse," last updated March 10, 2025, https://en.wikipedia.org/wiki/Epsom_Downs_Racecourse; Wikipedia, "Arlington Downs Racetrack."

21 Hedspeth, *They Rode Good Horses*, 1–5; Denhardt, Bob, "Anson Talks about Quarter Horses," *The Cattleman*, Vol. 37, No. 4, 55, 138–40; American Quarter Horse Association, "William Anson," AQHA website, https://www.aqha.com/-/william-anson [Accessed July 7, 2021]; American Quarter Horse Association, "Robert M. Denhardt," AQHA website, https://www.aqha.com/-/robert-m-denhardt [Accessed July 7, 2021].

22 For a detailed look at the differences, see Hedspeth, "The Bulldog Men: The 1940s," 1–22.

23 Ibid., 3, 5, 9.

24 Rodeo became the official sport of Texas in 1997. Mary Lou LeCompte, "The First American Rodeo Never Happened," *Journal of Sport History*, Vol. 9, No. 2 (Summer 1982): 89–96; Mary Lou LeCompte, "Wild West Frontier Days. Roundups and Stampedes: Rodeo Before There Was Rodeo," *Canadian Journal of History of Sport*, Vol. 16, No. 2 (December 1985): 54–67.

Select Bibliography

MANUSCRIPT COLLECTIONS

Dolph Briscoe Center for American History, University of Texas at Austin

Morris Ranch Papers, 1893–1929.

Ashbel Smith Papers, 1823–1926.

Samuel May Williams Papers, 1830–1891.

Thomas Freeman McKinney Papers, 1828–1873.

Private Collections: Anne J. Bailey

Annual Report of the Texas Racing Commission to the Governor of Texas. 1934.

Stella Mae Batchler Bass correspondence.

Mary Ann Christensen correspondence.

Nadine Hodnett correspondence.

Elijah Sterling Clack Robertson Correspondence, 1862–1863. Photocopies courtesy of Malcolm D. McLean.

Lowell Smith Jr. correspondence.

The Texas Racing Commission. *Rules of Racing adopted by the Texas Racing Commission,* also entitled *Texas Law and Rules Governing Horse Racing.* Austin: 1934.

Southern Historical Collection, University of North Carolina Library, Chapel Hill

Thomas Jefferson Green Papers.

Southwest Collection, Special Collection Library, Texas Tech University, Lubbock.

Donald Emmet Worcester Papers.

Texas State Archives, Austin

George A. Feris Family Papers.

Rules and Regulations of the Houston Jockey Club.

Rules and Regulations of the Metairie Jockey Club. Published for the Club, 1860.

Rules and Regulations of the Webber's Prairie Jockey Club. Austin: William H. Cushnew, printer, 1849.

NEWSPAPERS AND PERIODICALS

Aberdeen Journal, and General Advertiser (Aberdeen, Scotland).
The Abilene Reporter (Abilene).
American Turf Register and Sporting Magazine (New York, NY).
Austin City Gazette (Austin).
The Austin Weekly Statesman (Austin).
The Boston Globe (Boston, MA).
The Brand (Hereford).
Brazos Courier (Brazoria).
Brenham Daily Banner (Brenham).
Brenham Weekly Banner (Brenham).
The Brooklyn Daily Eagle (Brooklyn, NY).
The Cattleman (Fort Worth).
Chicago Examiner (Chicago, IL).
Chicago Tribune (Chicago, IL).
Cleburne Chronicle (Cleburne).
Cleburne Daily Enterprise (Cleburne).
Cleburne Examiner (Cleburne).
The Daily Hesperian (Gainesville).
The Daily Picayune (New Orleans, LA).
Daily Racing Form (Chicago, IL).
The Dallas Daily Herald (Dallas).
Dallas Herald (Dallas).
Dallas Morning News (Dallas).
The Dallas Weekly Herald (Dallas).
Decatur News (Decatur).
Democratic Telegraph and Texas Register (Houston).
El Paso Times (El Paso).
Evening Star (Washington, DC).
Fort Worth Daily Democrat (Fort Worth).
Fort Worth Daily Gazette (Fort Worth).
Fort Worth Gazette (Fort Worth).
The Galveston Daily News (Galveston).
The Granbury News (Granbury).
The Home Advocate (Jefferson).
The Houston Daily Age (Houston).
Houston Daily Mercury (Houston).
The Houston Tri-Weekly Telegraph (Houston).
The Inter-Ocean (Chicago, IL).

Jefferson Jimplecute (Jefferson).
Journal and Advertiser (San Augustine).
Lexington Herald-Leader (Lexington, KY).
Liverpool Mercury (Liverpool, England).
The McKinney Gazette (McKinney).
The Morning Star (Houston).
The New Orleans Times (New Orleans, LA).
The New York Times (New York, NY).
The Northern Standard (Clarksville).
The Quarter Horse Journal (Amarillo).
The Red-Lander (San Augustine).
The Scranton Republican (Scranton, PA).
Spirit of the Times/Porter's Spirit of the Times (New York, NY).
The Southern Mercury (Dallas).
The Standard (Clarksville).
The Sunday Gazetteer (Denison).
Telegraph and Texas Register (Houston).
The Temple Times (Temple).
The Texas Gazette (San Felipe de Austin).
The Texas State Times (Austin).
The Texian Democrat (Houston).
The Times Democrat (New Orleans, LA).
The Times Picayune (New Orleans, LA).
Timpson Weekly Times (Timpson).
Tri-Weekly Telegraph (Houston).
Tri-Weekly Texas State Gazette (Austin).
The Waco Evening News (Waco).
The Weekly Citizen (Houston).
Weekly Democratic Statesman (Austin).
Victoria Advocate (Victoria).

PRIMARY SOURCES

Anderson, John Q., ed. *Campaigning with Parsons' Brigade, CSA: The War Journals and Letters of the Four Orr Brothers, 12th Texas Cavalry Regiment.* Hillsboro: Hill Junior College Press, 1967.

Bolleart, William. *William Bolleart's Texas.* Edited by W. Eugene Hollon and Ruth Lapham Butler. Norman: University of Oklahoma Press, 1956.

Bruce, S. D. *The American Stud Book.* 1868; revised in 2 vols. New York: Sanders D. Bruce, 1873.

Bryan, James Perry, ed. *Mary Austin Holley: The Texas Diary, 1835–1838.* Austin: University of Texas Press, 1965.

Carroll, B. H., ed. *Standard History of Houston, Texas from a Study of the Original Sources.* Knoxville: H. W. Crew & Co., 1912.

Combined Stud Book and Registry: Combined Books 1-2-3-4-5, No. 1 thru No. 27,000. Amarillo: The American Quarter Horse Association, 1961.

"Concerning Philip Nolan." *The Quarterly of the Texas State Historical Association,* Vol. 7, No. 4 (April 1904).

Crocket, George L. *Two Centuries in East Texas.* Dallas: Southwest Press, 1932.

Duval, John C. *Early Times in Texas.* Dallas: H. P. N. Gammel & Co., 1892.

Fithian, Philip Vickers. *Philip Vickers Fithian: Journal and Letters, 1767–1774.* Edited by John Rogers Williams. Princeton, NJ: The University Library, 1900.

Fletcher, William Andrew. *Rebel Private, Front and Rear.* Austin: University of Texas Press, 1954.

Ford, John Salmon. *Rip Ford's Texas.* Edited by Stephen B. Oates. Austin: University of Texas Press, 1963.

Fremantle, James A. L. *Three Months in the Southern States April–June 1863.* 1864; rpt., Alexandria, VA: Time-Life Books, Inc., 1984.

Freund, Max, ed. *Gustav Dresel's Houston Journal: Adventures in North American and Texas, 1837–1841.* Austin: University of Texas Press, 1954.

Gammel, H. P. N., comp. *The Laws of Texas, 1822–1897.* 10 vols. Austin: Gammel Book Co., 1898.

______. *The Laws of Texas, 1903–1905.* Vol. 12. Austin: Von Boeckmann-Jones Co., 1906.

Green, Wharton J. *Recollections and Reflections: An Auto of Half a Century and More.* N.P.: Edwards and Broughton Printing Co., 1906.

Hastings, Frank S. *A Ranchman's Recollections: An Autobiography.* 1921; rpt., Big Byte Books, 2014.

Hatcher, Mattie Austin, ed. *Letters of an Early American Traveller, Mary Austin Holley: Her Life and Her Works, 1784–1846.* Dallas: Southwest Press, 1933.

Harris County Historical Society, comp. *Houston—A Nation's Capital, 1837–1839.* Houston: D. Armstrong Co., Inc., 1985.

Herbert, Henry William. *Frank Forrester's Horse and Horsemanship of the United States.* 2 vols. New York: Stringer & Townsend, 1857.

Hildreth, Samuel C. and James R. Crowell. *The Spell of the Turf: The Story of American Racing.* Philadelphia: J. B. Lippincott, 1926.

Houston, Matilda Charlotte. *Texas and the Gulf of Mexico; or Yachting in the New World.* 2nd ed. Philadelphia: G. B. Zieber & Co, 1845.

Ingram, Henry, comp. *Civil War Letters of George W. and Martha F. Ingram, 1861–1865.* College Station: Texas A&M University Press, 1973.

The Jockey Club. *The American Stud Book.* New York: The Jockey Club, 1898.

King, Grace Elizabeth. *New Orleans: The Place and the People.* 1895.

Lale, Max S., ed. "The Boy-Bugler in the Third Texas Cavalry: The A. B. Blocker Narrative," Part 3. *Military History of Texas and the Southwest.* 1978.

Lothrop, Charles H. *A History of the First Regiment Iowa Cavalry, Veteran Volunteers, From its Organization in 1861 to its Muster Out of the United States Service in 1866.* Lyons, IA: Beers & Eaton, Printers, 1890.

Lowe, Richard, ed. *A Texas Cavalry Officer's Civil War: The Diary and Letters James C. Bates.* Baton Rouge: Louisiana State University Press, 1999.

McLean, Malcolm D., ed. *Papers Concerning Robertson's Colony in Texas: Those Eleven League Grants, December 6, 1831, through October, 1833.* Arlington: University of Texas at Arlington Press, 1980.

______. *Papers Concerning Robertson's Colony in Texas: Robertson's Colony, November, 1833, through September, 1834.* Arlington: University of Texas at Arlington Press, 1981.

Muir, Andrew Forest, ed. "Diary of a Young Man in Houston, 1838." *The Southwestern Historical Quarterly*, Vol. 53, No. 3 (January 1950).

______. *Texas in 1837: An Anonymous, Contemporary Narrative.* Austin: University of Texas Press, 1958.

O'Connor, John L., comp. *Notes on the Thoroughbred from Kentucky Newspapers.* Lexington: Transylvania Printing Company, c. 1927.

Ockerman, Foster Jr. *Hidden History of Horse Racing in Kentucky.* Charleston, SC: The History Press, 2019.

Parker, A. A. *Trip to the West & Texas.* 1836; rpt., Prabhat Prakashan, 2017.

Pellet, Elias P. *History of the 114th Regiment, New York State Volunteers.* Norwich, NY: Telegraph & Chronicle Power Press Print, 1866.

Pratt, Willis W., ed. *Galveston Island: Or a Few Months Off the Coast of Texas: The Journal of Francis C. Sheridan, 1839–1840.* Austin: University of Texas Press, 1954.

Ray, Johnette Highsmith, ed. "Civil War Letters from Parsons' Texas Cavalry Brigade." *The Southwestern Historical Quarterly*, Vol. 69, No. 2 (October 1965).

"Reminiscences of Mrs. Dilue Harris," Pt. 3. *The Quarterly of the Texas State Historical Association*, Vol. 7, No. 3 (January 1904).

Reports of Cases Argued and Decided in the Supreme Court of the State of Texas.

Roemer, Ferdinand. *Texas with Particular Reference to German Immigration and the Physical Appearance of the Country.* Translated by Oswald Mueller. 1849; rpt., San Antonio: Standard Printing Co., 1935.

Rous, John Henry. *On the Laws and Practice of Horse Racing.* London: A. H. Baily & Company, 1866.

Rugeley, H. J. H. *Batchelor-Turner Letters, 1861–1865.* Austin: The Steck Company, 1961.

Siringo, Charles A. *A Texas Cowboy or, Fifteen Years on the Hurricane Deck of a Spanish Pony.* 1886; rpt., New York: Penguin Books, 2000.

Smither, Harriet, ed. "The Diary of Adolphus Sterne," Pt. 9. *Southwestern Historical Quarterly*, Vol. 32, No. 2 (October 1928).

______. "The Diary of Adolphus Sterne," Pt. 13. *Southwestern Historical Quarterly*, Vol. 33, No. 2 (October 1929).

______. "The Diary of Adolphus Sterne," Pt. 14. *Southwestern Historical Quarterly*, Vol. 33, No. 3 (January 1930).

_____. "Diary of Adolphus Sterne," Pt. 26. *The Southwestern Historical Quarterly*, Vol. 36, No. 3 (January 1933).

Smithwick, Noah. *The Evolution of a State*. Austin: Gammel Book Co., 1900.

Smyth, John Ferdinand Dalziel. *A Tour of the United States of America*. London: G. Robinson, J. Robson, and J. Sewell, 1784.

Stone, Frank H. Letter. December 9, 1849. *The Quarter Horse Journal* (April 1959).

The Texas Annual. Austin: Hughes & McLaughlin, 1878.

Twaites, Reuben Gold, ed. *Early Western Travels, 1748–1846*. 32 vols. Cleveland, OH: Arthur H. Clark Company, 1904.

Wallis, Jonnie Lockhart and Laurance L. Hill, eds. *Sixty Years on the Brazos: The Life and Letters of Dr. John Washington Lockhart*. 1930; rpt., Waco: Texian Press, 1967.

White, Gifford. *The 1840 Census of the Republic of Texas*. Austin: Pemberton Press, 1966.

Young, John D. and J. Frank Dobie. *A Vaquero of the Brush Country: The Life and Times of John D. Young*, 1929; rpt., Austin: University of Texas Press, 1998.

Zuber, William Physick. *My Eighty Years in Texas*. Austin: University of Texas Press, 1971.

SECONDARY SOURCES

A Memorial and Biographical History of Ellis County. Chicago: The Lewis Publishing Co., 1892.

A Memorial and Biographical History of Johnson and Hill Counties, Texas. Chicago: The Lewis Publishing Co., 1892.

Anderson, James Douglas. *Making the American Thoroughbred*. Norwood, MA: The Plimpton Press, 1916.

Armistead, Gene C. *Horses and Mules in the Civil War: A Complete History with a Roster of More Than 700 War Horses*. Jefferson, NC: McFarland & Co., Inc., 2013.

Bailey, Anne. "The Steel Dust Legacy." *Western Horse Tales*. Edited by Don Worcester. Plano: Republic of Texas Press, 1994, 105–12.

Bailey, Anne J. *Between the Enemy and Texas: Parsons's Texas Cavalry in the Civil War*. Fort Worth, Texas Christian University Press, 1989.

_____. *In the Saddle with the Texans: Day-by-Day with Parsons's Cavalry Brigade, 1862–1865*. Abilene, TX: McWhiney Foundation Press, 2004.

_____. *Texans in the Confederate Cavalry*. 1995; rpt., Abilene, TX: McWhiney Foundation Press, 2004.

Bailey, Georgianne. "Texas Turf: The Men and their Horses to the Civil War." M.A. thesis, Texas Christian University, 1984.

Baker, D. W. C. *A Texas Scrapbook*. New York, Chicago, and New Orleans: A. S. Barnes and Company, 1875.

Bertleth, Rosa Groce. "Jared Ellison Groce." *The Southwestern Historical Quarterly*, Vol. 20 No. 4 (April 1917).

Block, Viola. *History of Johnson, County and Surrounding Area*. Waco: Library Binding Co., 1970.

Boethel, Paul C. *Colonel Amasa Turner: The Gentleman from Lavaca and Other Captains at San Jacinto*. Austin: Von Broeckmann-Jones, 1963.

Blanchard, Elizabeth Ann Cameron and Manly Wade Wellman. *The Life and Times of Sir Archy*. Chapel Hill: University of North Carolina Press, 1958.

Brazoria County Centennial Club. *Velasco in Texas History*. 1936; rpt., Velasco United Methodist Church Historical Museum, April 1992.

Brown, Frank. *Annals of Travis County and the City of Austin (From the Earliest of Times to the Close of 1875)*. Typescript, no date. The Portal to Texas History website. https://texashistory.unt.edu/search/?q=Annals+of+Travis+county&t=fulltext&sort=&fq= [Accessed July, 2, 2022].

Burkhardt, George S. *Confederate Rage, Yankee Wrath: No Quarter in the Civil War*. Carbondale: Southern Illinois University Press, 2007.

Calvert, Robert A. and Arnoldo De León. *The History of Texas*. Arlington Heights, IL: Harlan Davidson, 1990.

Campbell, Randolph B. *Gone to Texas: A History of the Lone Star State*. New York: Oxford University Press, 2003.

Carroll, B. H., ed. *Standard History of Houston: Texas from a Study of the Original Sources*. Knoxville: H. W. Crew & Co., 1912.

Chard, Thornton. "Arabian Horses in Texas Over Eighty Years Ago: Dr. George A. Feris' Stud at Fort Bend and Richmond." *The Cattleman* (September 1944).

Daniell, L. E. *Types of Successful Men in Texas*. Austin: Eugene Von Boeckmann, 1890.

Denhardt, Robert Moorman. *Foundation Dams of the American Quarter Horse*. Norman: University of Oklahoma Press, 1982.

______. *Foundation Sires of the American Quarter Horse*. Norman: University of Oklahoma Press, 1976.

______. *The Horse of the Americas*. 1947; rpt., Norman: University of Oklahoma Press, 1975.

______. *The Quarter Horse: A Story of Two Centuries*. 1967; rpt., Norman: University of Oklahoma Press, 1980.

______. *The Quarter Horse*. 1941; rpt., College Station: Texas A&M University Press, 1982.

______. *The Quarter Running Horse: America's Oldest Breed*. Norman: University of Oklahoma Press, 1979.

Dictionary of Louisiana Biography. Website. Louisiana Historical Association. https://www.lahistory.org/resources/dictionary-louisiana-biography/

Dobie, J. Frank, Mody C. Boatright, Harry H. Ransom, eds. *Mustangs and Cow Horses*. 1940; rpt., Denton: University of North Texas Press, 2000.

Encyclopedia of Alabama. Website. Alabama Humanities Alliance. https://encyclopediaofalabama.org/

Encyclopedia of North Carolina. NCpedia website. https://www.ncpedia.org/

Ewell, Thomas T. *Hood County History*. Granbury, Texas, 1895. Reproduced in Hightower, C. L., ed., *Hood County History in Picture and Story 1970*. Fort Worth: Historical Publishers, 1970.

Fehrenbach, T. R. *Comanches: The Destruction of a People*. 1974; rpt., New York: Da Capo Press, 1994.

Gard, Wayne. *Fabulous Quarter Horse: Steel Dust—The Account of the Most Celebrated Texas Stallion*. New York: Duell, Sloan and Pearce, 1958.

______. "Fabulous Steel Dust." *The Cattleman* (September 1948).

______. "Hoofbeats of Old Shiloh." *The Cattleman* (September 1953).

______. *Sam Bass.* Norman: University of Oklahoma Press, 1969.

______. "When Texans Shouted for Shiloh." *The Western Horseman* (August 1949).

Gray, Bob. *Great Horses of the Past.* Houston: Cordovan Corporation, 1967.

Handbook of Texas. Website. Texas State Historical Association. https://www.tshaonline.org/handbook

Harrison, Fairfax. *Early American Turf Stock, 1730–1830.* 2 vols. Richmond, VA: The Old Dominion Press, 1934–1935.

Hayes, Charles W. *History of the Island and the City of Galveston: From the Discovery of the Island in 1526, from the Founding of the City in 1837, Down to the Year 1879.* 1879; rpt., Austin: Jenkins Garrett Press, 1974.

Hedgpeth, Don. *They Rode Good Horses: The First Fifty Years of the American Quarter Horse Association.* Amarillo: American Quarter Horse Association, 1990.

Henson, Margaret Swett. *McKinney Falls: The Ranch Home of Thomas F. McKinney, Pioneer Texas Entrepreneur.* Austin: Texas State Historical Association, 1999.

______. *Samuel May Williams: Early Texas Entrepreneur.* College Station: Texas A&M University Press, 1976.

Hervey, John Hervey. *Racing in America, 1665–1865.* 2 vols. New York: Privately Printed, The Jockey Club, 1944.

History of Brazoria County. Brazoria County Federation of Women's Clubs, 1940.

Hogan, William Ransom. *The Texas Republic: A Social and Economic History.* 1946; rpt., Austin: University of Texas Press, 1969.

Hollingsworth, Kent. *The Kentucky Thoroughbred.* Lexington: University Press of Kentucky, 1976.

Kimmey, Nanci Monroe and Georgia Kemp Caraway. *North Texas State Fair and Rodeo.* Charleston, SC: Arcadia Publishing, 2016.

LeCompte, Mary Lou. "The First American Rodeo Never Happened." *Journal of Sport History,* Vol. 9, No. 2 (Summer 1982): 89–96.

______. "Wild West Frontier Days. Roundups and Stampedes: Rodeo Before There Was Rodeo." *Canadian Journal of History of Sport*, Vol. 16, No. 2 (December 1985): 54–67.

Lewis, Preston. *Betting on Horses: Racing as an Economic Development Tool in Frontier West Texas, 1886–1896.* San Angelo: Bariso Press, 2024.

Lindeman, M. H. *The Quarter Horse Breeder.* Wichita Falls, TX: Humphrey Printing Co., 1959.

Mason, Richard. *The Gentleman's New Pocket Farrier.* Philadelphia: Grigg & Elliott, 1841.

McBee, May Wilson. *The Life and Times of David Smith, Patriot, Pioneer and Indian Fighter.* Kansas City, MO: E. L. Mendenhall, Inc., 1959.

McLean, Malcolm D. *Fine Texas Horses: Their Pedigrees and Performance, 1830–1845.* Fort Worth: Texas Christian University Press, 1966.

McWhiney, Grady. *Cracker Culture: Celtic Ways in the Old South.* Tuscaloosa: University of Alabama Press, 1988.

Memorial and Biographical History of Dallas County. Chicago: The Lewis Publishing Co., 1892.

Michaelis, Helen. "The Sons of Janus." *The Quarter Horse Journal* (July 1971).
Miller, Rick. *Sam Bass & Gang.* Austin: State House Press, 1999.
Mooney, Katherine C. *Race Horse Men: How Slavery and Freedom were made at the Racetrack.* Cambridge: Harvard University Press, 2014.
Oates, Stephen B. *Confederate Cavalry West of the River.* Austin: University of Texas Press, 1961.
Ockerman, Foster Jr. *Hidden History of Horse Racing in Kentucky.* Charleston, SC: The History Press, 2019.
Osborne, Walter. "Mighty Janus." *The Quarter Horse Journal* (November 1967).
Parsons, Chuck. *James Madison Brown: Texas Sheriff, Texas Turfman.* Wolfe City, TX: Henington Publishing Co., 1993.
Robertson, William H. P. *The History of Thoroughbred Racing in America.* New York: Bonanza Books, 1964.
Rogers, Mary Nixon Rogers and Abner J. Strobel. *A History of Brazoria County Texas: The Old Plantations and their Owners of Brazoria County, Texas, Texas: Steamboats on the Brazos.* 1958; rpt., Literary Licensing, LLC, 2012.
Schmitz, Joseph William. *Thus They Lived: Social Life in the Republic of Texas.* San Antonio: The Naylor Company, 1936.
Schoen, Harold. "The Free Negro in the Republic of Texas," Pt. 2. *The Southwestern Historical Quarterly*, Vol. 40, No. 1 (July 1936).
Selcer, Richard F. *Hell's Half Acre.* Fort Worth: Texas Christian University Press, 1991.
Sifakis, Steward. *Compendium of the Confederate Armies: Texas.* New York: Facts on File, Inc., 1995.
Smith, David Paul. *Frontier Defense in the Civil War: Texas' Rangers and Rebels.* College Station: Texas A&M University Press, 1992.
Sowell, A. J. *History of Fort Bend County.* Houston: W. H. Coyle & Co., 1904.
Stafford, G. M. G. *The Wells Family of Louisiana and Allied Families.* Alexandria, VA: Standard Printing, 1942.
Strobel, Abner J. *The Old Plantations and their Owners of Brazoria County Texas.* Houston: The Union National Bank, 1930.
Thomas, Keith. *Man and the Natural World: A History of the Modern Sensibility.* New York: Pantheon Books, 1983.
Tolbert, Frank X. *The Day of San Jacinto.* New York: McGraw-Hill Book Company, 1959.
Trammel, Jack. "Off and Running: America's Growing Passion for Horse Racing Stayed Strong During the War." *America's Civil War* (July 2018).
Velasco in Texas History. Prepared by the Brazoria County Centennial Club. 1936; rpt., Velasco United Methodist Church Historical Museum, 1992.
Vosburgh, W. S. *Racing in America, 1866–1921.* New York: Private Printed, The Jockey Club, 1922.
Wallace, John Hankins. *The Horse of America in his Derivation, History, and Development.* New York: Published by the author, 1897.
Weeks, Lyman Horace. *The American Turf: An Historical Account of Racing in the United States with Biographical Sketches of Turf Celebrities.* New York: The Historical Company, 1898.

Wharton, Clarence R. *Wharton's History of Fort Bend County.* Houston: The Anson Jones Press, 1939.

Wiley, Bell Irvin. *The Life of Johnny Reb: The Common Soldier of the Confederacy.* 1943; rpt., Baton Rouge: Louisiana State University Press, 1987.

Wiley, Nancy. *The Great State Fair of Texas: An Illustrated History.* Dallas: Taylor Publishing Company, 1985.

Wills, Ridley II. *Belle Meade Bloodlines 1816–1904.* Nashville, TN: Ambrose Printing Co., 1990.

Wilson, Maurine T. and Jack Jackson. *Philip Nolan and Texas Expeditions to the Unknown Land, 1791–1801.* Waco: Texian Press, 1988.

Worcester, Don, ed. *Western Horse Tales.* Plano: Wordware Publishing, Inc., 1994.

Young, S. O. *True Stories of Old Houston and Houstonians.* Galveston: Oscar Springer, publisher, 1913.

Index

O

P

Q

R

Y

Z

www.ingramcontent.com/pod-product-compliance
Lightning Source LLC
Chambersburg PA
CBHW061757060925
31996CB00001BA/1
* 9 7 8 1 6 4 9 6 7 0 2 6 7 *